ANALYSING THE TRUST–TRANSPARENCY NEXUS

Civil Society and Social Change

Series Editors: **Ian Rees Jones** and
Paul Chaney, Cardiff University,
Mike Woods, Aberystwyth University

This series provides interdisciplinary and comparative
perspectives on the rapidly changing nature of civil society
at local, regional, national and global scales.

Also in the series:

Local Civil Society
By **Robin Mann, David Dallimore, Howard Davis,
Graham Day** and **Marta Eichsteller**

City Regions and Devolution in the UK
By **David Beel, Martin Jones** and **Ian Rees Jones**

Civil Society and the Family
By **Esther Muddiman, Sally Power** and **Chris Taylor**

Civil Society through the Lifecourse
Edited by **Sally Power**

The Foundational Economy and Citizenship
Edited by **Filippo Barbera** and **Ian Rees Jones**

Putting Civil Society in Its Place
By **Bob Jessop**

Published with the Wales Institute of Social and
Economic Research and Data

Find out more at
**policy.bristoluniversitypress.co.uk/
civil-society-and-social-change**

ANALYSING THE TRUST–TRANSPARENCY NEXUS: MULTI-LEVEL GOVERNANCE IN THE UK, FRANCE AND GERMANY

Ian Stafford, Alistair Cole and Dominic Heinz

First published in Great Britain in 2022 by

Policy Press, an imprint of
Bristol University Press
University of Bristol
1-9 Old Park Hill
Bristol
BS2 8BB
UK
t: +44 (0)117 954 5940
e: bup-info@bristol.ac.uk

Details of international sales and distribution partners are available at
policy.bristoluniversitypress.co.uk

© Bristol University Press 2022

British Library Cataloguing in Publication Data
A catalogue record for this book is available from the British Library

ISBN 978-1-4473-5521-2 hardcover
ISBN 978-1-4473-5524-3 ePub
ISBN 978-1-4473-5523-6 ePdf

Cover design: Clifford Hayes
Front cover image: Freepik.com
Bristol University Press and Policy Press use environmentally responsible
print partners.
Printed and bound in Great Britain by CPI Group (UK) Ltd,
Croydon, CR0 4YY

FSC
www.fsc.org
MIX
Paper from
responsible sources
FSC® C013604

To Ben and Phoebe – for only occasionally invading when I have been teaching online or writing! (IS)

To Caroline – for enduring patience (AC)

Contents

List of figures and tables

Figures

Tables

List of abbreviations

AfD	Alternative für Deutschland
AGMA	Association of Greater Manchester Authorities
CCGs	Clinical Commissioning Groups
CDU/CSU	Christian Democratic Union of Germany
CEVIPOF	Centre de Recherches Politiques de Sciences Po
COVID-19	Coronavirus Disease 2019
CSU	Christlich Soziale Union
EELV	Europe Écologie les Verts
EPCI	Etablissements publics de coopération intercommunale
ESS	European Social Survey
FDP	Free Democratic Party
FN	Front National
FOI	Freedom of Information
FRG	Federal Republic of Germany
GDR	German Democratic Republic
GfK	Gesellschaft für Konsumforschung
GMCA	Greater Manchester Combined Authority
GMCR	Greater Manchester City Region
GMHSCP	Greater Manchester Health and Social Care Partnership
GNP	Gross national product
GRECO	Group of States against Corruption
LCR	Liverpool City Region
LCRCA	Liverpool City Region Combined Authority
LEP	Local Enterprise Partnership
MLG	Multi-level governance
MoU	Memorandum of understanding
OECD	Organisation for Economic Co-operation and Development
OURdata Index	Open, Useful and Reusable Government Data Index
PDS	Party of Democratic Socialism
PPE	Personal protective equipment
RAI	Regional Authority Index
RDA	Regional Development Agency
RN	Rassemblement National
SED	Sozialistische Einheitspartei Deutschlands
SPD	Social Democratic Party of Germany

UN	United Nations
VCSE	Voluntary, community and social enterprise sector
VSNW	Voluntary Sector North West
WDI	World Development Indicators
WJP	World Justice Project

About the authors

Ian Stafford is Senior Lecturer in Politics at the Department of Politics and International Relations, School of Law and Politics, Cardiff University.

Alistair Cole is Professor in Politics and Head of the Department of Government and International Studies at Hong Kong Baptist University.

Dominic Heinz is Lecturer for the German Academic Exchange Service (DAAD) at the Türk-Alman Üniversitesi / Türkisch Deutsche Universität in Istanbul.

Acknowledgements

This book is the product of a three-year research project, 'Building trust? Institutions and interactions of multi-level governance in the UK, Germany and France', that was part of the Wales Institute of Social and Economic Research and Data (WISERD) Civil Society Research Centre (ESRC Award No: ES/S012435/1). However, in many senses it explores recurring themes that have been highlighted in the fieldwork of a variety of research projects carried out across Western Europe over the past two decades. During this period the authors have had an opportunity to discuss a wide range of questions related to policy-making and territorial politics with people from different sectors, including government officials and civil servants, politicians at all levels of government, interest groups and third-sector organisations. The research in this book and previous publications was entirely reliant on these people finding the time to speak to us about their experiences and their understanding of the world around them. We are extremely grateful to all of them for giving us part of their time, but in particular we would like to thank the participants in this most recent project, who provided such valuable insights and reflections about trust and their relationships.

Any research project is not carried out in a vacuum, and therefore the list of colleagues and collaborators that we could thank for their input into our research or that have provided inspiration through their own work is lengthy, and if we tried to name everyone, we would inevitably miss someone out. However, we were incredibly fortunate to have carried out our research project within the WISERD Civil Society research centre, and in particular, the Individuals, Institutions and Governance thematic area led by Paul Chaney. We would like to thank Paul, and the Civil Society Centre Director, Ian Rees Jones, for their support during the project. In addition, the comments and suggestions provided by WISERD colleagues, either at Away Days or WISERD Conferences have proved invaluable. In particular, many thanks to Stuart Fox, Elin Royles, Rhys Jones, Chris Taylor, Gareth Rees, Daniel Wincott, Christala Sophocleous, Martin Jones, David Beel, Sally Power, Jesse Heley, Michael Woods, Bettina Petersohn, Dion Curry and Matthew Wall.

The research outlined in this book has also benefited from discussions at numerous international conferences, including the Political Studies Association Annual Conference, the Council for European Studies International Conference of Europeanists and European Consortium for Political Research (ECPR) General Conference.

The project gained immensely from the participation and involvement of colleagues in France, especially Romain Pasquier, CNRS Research Professor at the Institute of Political Studies in Rennes, and Jeanne Chauvel, the post-doctoral research assistant who carried out interviews in Bretagne and with whom it was a pleasure to interact. Interim findings were discussed at a specially organised conference in Lyon, France, in May 2018. We are very grateful to the Institute of Political Studies in Lyon, France, to current and former directors Renaud Payre and Gilles Pollet and to the director of the TRIANGLE Research laboratory, Claude Gautier, for making this possible and for providing a conducive atmosphere for the Auvergne-Rhône-Alpes fieldwork. Particular thanks go to Christophe Parnet, who undertook a number of interviews on our behalf and helped to organise the conference. The French YouGov survey was funded by PALSE-Idex-ANR [grant number ANR-11-IDEX-0007] and by the Territorial Chair of Sciences Po Rennes, while the Scientific Committee of Sciences Po Lyon provided additional funding. We sincerely thank these funders for their support.

We would also like to thank the team at Policy Press, particularly Laura Vickers-Rendall and Caroline Astley, who have been a pleasure to work with throughout the project. And we thank the anonymous reviewer whose feedback undoubtedly helped us strengthen the manuscript.

Finally, the writing of this book coincided with the COVID-19 pandemic and therefore has fought for our attention alongside what feels like endless hours of online meetings, the challenges of teaching and researching entirely remotely, and adapting to life during a global pandemic. The authors have been spread across three different time zones, and therefore have faced different challenges, from home-schooling to lockdown. However, a common factor is that we have only managed to get to this point with the help of our incredibly supportive and understanding families – this book is dedicated to them.

Introduction

The decline of trust has become a dominant narrative within both the contemporary academic literature and the media. Onora O'Neill (2002: 8), as part of her 2002 BBC Reith Lectures, observed that sociologists and journalists have reported that 'mistrust and suspicion have spread across all areas of life' and therefore 'loss of trust has become a cliché of our times.' In a September 2018 address to the United Nations (UN) General Assembly, the UN Secretary General, Antonio Guterres, diagnosed that the world was suffering from a 'bad case of Trust Deficit Disorder' and that people's trust in institutions at both the national and international level was at 'breaking point' (UN Secretary General, 2018, cited in Jennings et al, 2019). Evidence for the perceived crisis in trust is frequently provided by national and international surveys: for example, the 2020 Edelman Trust Barometer (2020) reported a 'trust paradox' where strong economic performance was accompanied by a stagnation of trust in key institutions, such as government and the media. Furthermore, the coronavirus pandemic which swept over the world from early 2020 refocused attention on trust –in terms of both the impact of the presence or absence of trust for governmental policy responses and the impact of the pandemic on existing levels of trust (Devine et al, 2021). Indeed, many policy responses to the pandemic were framed within the context of trust. For example, part of the rationale for the Welsh Government using a locally organised 'Test and Trace' service rather than the centralised service set up by the United Kingdom (UK) Government was the assumption that people living in Wales were more likely to follow the advice of someone who sounded as if they were familiar with their community.

Even putting the coronavirus pandemic to one side, in European politics a set of unprecedented events have disrupted existing equilibria. In the UK a long-lasting debate about membership of the European Union (EU) finally resulted in Britain's exit from the EU at the end of January 2020. In France public riots around the yellow vests ('gilets jaunes') shattered the calm of Macron's second year in office. In Germany the right-wing party Alternative für Deutschland (AfD) has been elected in almost every state parliament in the country, enduringly establishing a party to the right of the Christian Democrats (CDU/CSU) in the political landscape. Further afield, the international context has been one of electoral successes of right-wing parties and individuals, such as Trump in the United States of America and Bolsonaro in Brazil. At the same time, trust in political institutions has steadily declined. Surveys including the Edelman Trust Index, the Eurobarometer, the Gesellschaft für Konsumforschung (GfK) trust index and the Centre de Recherches Politiques de Sciences Po's (CEVIPOF) trust barometer all show declining levels of trust.

The decline of trust has been identified within the conventional literature as a fundamental threat to democracy, driven by events such as the 2007–8 financial crisis and leading to the rise of populism across the world (Hosking, 2019). A range of potential remedies have been offered to counter this malaise in trust. The Edelman Trust Barometer (2020: 8), for example, emphasised the importance of competence and ethical behaviour – 'being honest, having a vision, being purpose-driven and being fair' – in rebuilding trust. The latter emphasis on 'being honest' is linked to the wider concept of transparency explored in this book. As O'Neill (2002: 44) observes, transparency has been portrayed as acting 'like great draughts of Heineken, reaching parts that supposedly less developed forms of accountability did not reach.' However, the dominant narrative around the decline of trust, its consequences for democracy and potential remedies has not gone unchallenged. Norris and colleagues (2019: 14) challenge the conventional concerns regarding low or declining trust, noting that 'deep cynicism can be dysfunctional for society and for democracy, but equally there are dangers arising at the opposite extreme among credulous citizens who support dishonest, incompetent, and corrupt leaders blindly irrespective of their performance in serving the public interest in office.' Similarly, Möllering and Sydow (2019: 144) note that the 'dark side of trust' has been identified within the academic literature, notably the 'notion that one should not trust too much, because a "surfeit" of trust or "excessive trust" can make it "too much of a good thing" in interpersonal as well as inter-organizational relationships.' Therefore, important questions remain regarding how we can understand the perceived decline in trust, whether trust is a prerequisite for good democratic government, the potential solutions to reverse this trend and "build" trust, and perhaps most fundamentally how we can actually conceptualise trust and trustworthiness in the contemporary context (van Deth et al, 1991; Lenard, 2005; Fisher et al, 2010).

Across the social sciences trust has long been identified as an essential component of social, economic and political life. Since the 1990s, as Newton (2007: 342) notes, there has been an 'explosion of interest' in the concept driven by its perceived decline and re-engagement with concepts of social capital (Putnam, 1993, 2000; Fukuyama, 1995; Seligman, 1997; Braithwaite and Levi, 1998; Warren, 1999a; Hardin, 2002, 2006; Uslaner, 2002; Zmerli and Hooghe, 2011). In reviewing the social science literature Barbalet (2019: 13) observes that 'while different theorists draw upon distinctive vocabularies there is arguably a convergence of ideas which suggest that in late modernity trust becomes important for the maintenance of social order by preserving the viability of social relationships.' Therefore, a crisis of trust logically entails a crisis of the existing social order and of democracy. The wider literature has identified a range of potential factors underpinning trust, such as citizen satisfaction with policy, economic performance, the prevalence of political scandals and corruption, and the influence of social capital. Parker and colleagues (2014: 87) sum up the underlying assumption in much of the literature that 'the public is more trusting when they are satisfied with policy outcomes, the economy is booming, citizens are pleased with incumbents and institutions, political scandals are non-existent, crime is low, a war is popular, the country is threatened, and social capital is high.' However, as will be explored in Chapter 1, trust performs a key role not just in the relationship between the individual citizen and the state, but also within the context of civil society and the increasingly complex relationships that characterise contemporary multi-level governance (Edelenbos and Eshuis, 2012).

The picture painted by much of the contemporary literature on trust suggests that it is diminishing and frequently linked to the rise of mistrust, though the latter phenomenon also has its own distinct literature (Fraser, 1970; Davis, 1976; Sztompka, 2006; Avery, 2009). Problems of democratic deficit, of the misfit between politics and policy, of political corruption, apparently undermine trust in politicians and underpin the emergence in most EU polities of forms of national populist party responses (Schmidt, 2006). There is a strong and growing demand for more diverse and effective forms of citizen engagement to increase levels of trust and engage an increasingly diverse, busy and complex urban population (Fledderus, 2015).

Therefore, the general context for this book and the research project upon which it draws was one of the decline in trust in Western democracies, evidenced by cross-national studies such as the World Values Survey (Balme et al, 2003; Dalton, 2004, 2013; Dogan, 2005; Boy and Chiche, 2010; Cautrès, 2017; Grossman and Sauger, 2017). There are powerful causal narratives around the loss of trust in democratic politics. Much research has focused on Western democracies (Anderson et al, 2006; Schwadel and Stout, 2012; Clark, 2014; Dalton and Welzel, 2014). Three types of explanation are typically provided. Is the loss of trust a consequence of poor performance (after a decade of sluggish economic growth and inability to recover from the financial crisis of 2008–9)? Or the result of a democratic disconnect and distance between government and citizens, with the former unable to accommodate the preferences of the latter (Warren, 1999b; Hardin, 2002; Uslaner, 2002; Schmidt, 2006; Fisher et al, 2010; Fledderus et al, 2014)? Or does it result from a common belief that politicians in general are corrupt and self-serving? On each of these three dimensions, transparency is lauded by 'optimists' for having a trust-enhancing effect. Transparency is celebrated as the remedy to restore financial performance; to enhance democratic efficiency and performance; and to increase accountability mechanisms, ensuring openness and honesty. However, the potential benefits of transparency remain contested. For example, in some instances it may undermine trust, disrupting the tight policy communities identified by Marsh and Rhodes (1992) over two decades ago or depriving decision-making of the confidentiality that is sometimes required.

These high-profile debates provide the starting points for this book. We draw on an empirical research project framed by the core observation that issues of trust and transparency have developed across multiple scales, from the international to the local level. The assumptions underpinning the research project and the arguments developed in this book draw on the contention that social science analysis needs to move beyond 'methodological nationalism' and explore the more complex multi-levelled form of political organisation that characterises many contemporary European states (Jeffery and Wincott, 2010; Jeffery, 2014). Therefore, the overarching aim of this research is to explore the dynamics of trust and transparency – or what is termed the trust–transparency nexus – within a multi-level context, comparing these processes both within and between contemporary states. The horizontal and the vertical dimensions of multi-level governance raise overarching questions: firstly, how trust can be built and maintained in the context of increasingly complex forms of networked governance (Klijn and Koppenjan, 2016); and secondly, the extent to which different layers of governance have varied in their capacity to retain or build trust. Specifically, the research focuses on the subnational governance of our cases, exploring the interplay between local and regional levels of governance and civil society actors. In exploring the trust–transparency nexus within this context, we are guided, in general terms, by several interlocking questions:

- How is it possible to build or restore trust in political systems within the context of complex forms of governance?
- Do current political systems operate under preconditions (like political trust) that they cannot produce themselves?
- To what extent can transparency facilitate the building of trust?
- Is transparency a necessary condition to build and restore citizen and civil society trust in a post-democratic epoch?

Research design: comparing the trust–transparency nexus

The research adopts a comparative case study research design to explore the research questions outlined. We agree with Bennett and George (2005: 6) that case studies have a comparative advantage compared to statistical methods under certain conditions and offer the opportunity to explore complex variables. In this book, we undertake some quantitative analysis (especially in France) in order to examine the wider picture of trust, but most of our comparative analysis is centred on comparing the key factors shaping the trust–transparency nexus across our three countries and six subnational territories. Comparative case study analysis provides scope to identify new variables in an inductive manner and refine new hypotheses (that might be tested later by the team or by other researchers). In the formulation of Muno (2009), our case studies lie between theory-generating (the core challenge, using inductively generated causal mechanisms) and theory-testing (insofar as the cases confront an existing body of the trust, transparency and trust–transparency literatures). Finally, the comparative case study approach is best suited to formulating contingent generalisations or typological theories, such as in the case of the trust–transparency matrix elaborated in Chapter 2. Such theories are best understood as middle-range trade-offs between the depth of individual case studies and the breadth required for meaningful understanding and further conceptualisation.

Comparisons across space: from state traditions to multi-level governance

In general terms, a comparative analysis involves the identification of 'a spatially delimited phenomenon (a unit)' (Gerring, 2007: 19). For Landman (2000), who adopts a broad definition of comparative political science, a case more often than not means a country. If this spatial definition of a case is assumed, then there are three types of comparison: first, a comparison of many countries; second, a comparison of few countries; and third, a case study with an investigation of a single country. However, this approach appears too imprecise and overly simplistic. As noted earlier, this assumes a 'methodological nationalism' which ignores the increased regional differentiation that has characterised many contemporary European states but also ignores the temporal dimension (Jeffery, 2014). In terms of the latter, simply put, a single country or unit can be investigated at different points in time. In the same way that Rose (1993) noted that policy lessons could be drawn across both space and time, comparisons of different times and territorial levels mean that the objects to be investigated increase with so-called synchronic comparisons in one country. However, we can explore multiple cases within a single country. This can be illustrated if we consider Putnam's (1993) *Making Democracy Work: Civic Traditions in Modern Italy*, which investigates the ways of working across different governments in Italy. In one sense, the study could be identified as a single-country qualitative study focused on Italy ($n = 1$), but it also provides a quantitative analysis of Italian regions ($n = 20$).

In a similar exercise, this book provides country-level comparisons of three European states (France, Germany and the UK), drawing largely on secondary quantitative data and more fine-grained, primarily qualitative analyses of six subnational territories (Bretagne, Auvergne-Rhône-Alpes, Hesse, Saxony-Anhalt, North West England, Wales). These cases cover a range of different administrative contexts at the state level: a federal state (Germany); a predominantly unitary state modified by forms of asymmetrical devolution (UK); and a decentralised but still unitary state (France). The research design used to explore the trust–transparency nexus across these cases draws on the approach developed by John and Cole (2000), combining national, regional or subnational and sectional comparisons. The sectional-level comparisons are based on semi-structured interviews with civil society actors within the six subnational territories. Combining levels of analysis facilitates an in-depth understanding of the production and consumption of trust.

National trust–transparency profiles

Our first level of comparison explores the potential variation between three major European states: France, Germany and the UK. For each state we draw on secondary quantitative data to produce a National Trust–Transparency Profile. It is designed to elicit basic national variation in attitudes towards trust and transparency, exploring where possible the distinct levels of inter-personal relations (individual level), trust in institutions (aggregate level), and social trust (ideally, an interactive process). As Levi and Stoker (2000: 476–77) note, the combination of questions and indicators that are used to judge trust evolved from a range of influential early studies by authors such as Stokes (1962), Easton (1965) and Gamson (1968). This mainstream approach to measuring trust, often using single-item survey measures, is not without its problems (Bauer and Freitag, 2017). Seyd (2016: 3), for example, argues that these types of measures have four key weaknesses: (i) they only weakly tap the background concept; (ii) they trigger variations in understanding among survey respondents; (iii) they fail to capture ambivalence in attitudes among respondents; and (iv) they fail to provide a generalised, as opposed to an incumbent-driven, assessment of the political system. However, for the purpose of our National Trust–Transparency Profiles, they provide robust longitudinal data collected across our cases. The profiles draw on two main datasets, the Eurobarometer and the European Social Survey (ESS), and are supplemented by a small number of nation-specific secondary data, for example, in the UK case, the British Election Survey and Committee on Standards in Public Life surveys. The secondary data focused on transparency has grown steadily in recent years but is still very much in its infancy as an area of research. The National Trust–Transparency Profiles also encompass some existing comparable measures, specifically the World Justice Project (WJP) Open Government Index and the Organisation for Economic Co-operation and Development's (OECD) Open, Useful and Reusable Government Data index (OURdata index). It is important to note that both measures provide fairly narrow conceptions of transparency around the accessibility of data and therefore they provide only a partial picture at best.

Regional trust–transparency profiles

Of particular interest in our research design is the role, if any, of territorial identity markers as intermediaries between trust and transparency. Hence the focus on Regional Trust–Transparency Profiles. How do these vary within states? In each country, we select one 'strong identity' region or territory (Wales, Bretagne, Saxony-Anhalt) and one 'instrumental' region or territory (North West England, Auvergne-Rhône-Alpes, Hesse); this comparative mix allows for varying identities, institutional configurations and resource profiles to be captured. Our regions are also drawn from across the spectrum of the Regional Authority Index developed by Hooghe and colleagues (2010). In addition to their latent economic fragility, Saxony-Anhalt, Wales and Bretagne all have pronounced historical identities. North West England allows us to capture processes of meso-level convergence and divergence in a context where no formal regional political institutions exist; Auvergne-Rhône-Alpes and Hesse are regions with less marked historical identities, but more powerful economic and institutional resources. In each case, the selection of one strong identity, yet economically dependent region, and another more powerful instrumental region allows for within-case comparisons to occur. In the three larger regions or territories, there is a metropolitan dimension; the existence of powerful cities – Frankfurt, Lyon, Manchester/Liverpool – raises broader questions of the agglomeration effects of city-regions and of interactions between city and regional scales. The comparative case sample, which includes coordinative- and communicative-style polities, is designed to control for systemic variation in these issues of trust and transparency. The originality of the project is to admit the possibility that these trust and transparency mixes might vary as much *within* as across European states, and that they are variable according to policy sector.

A key challenge in formulating the Regional Trust–Transparency Profiles to complement the National Trust–Transparency Profiles is the relatively paucity of secondary data. Attempts to measure or evaluate levels of political trust have generally been applied to the national level or, within the European context, the EU level (Citrin and Muste, 1999; Kaase, 1999; van de Walle et al, 2008; van der Meer, 2010; Muñoz et al, 2011; van der Meer and Dekker, 2011; van der Meer and Hakhverdian, 2017). Rahn and Rudolph (2005: 531) observe that attempts to evaluate trust in local or subnational government 'have long been hampered by a dearth of suitable data'. Therefore, the Regional Trust–Transparency Profiles rely on a relatively limited range of secondary data and proxy measures.

Blurring distinctions: complexity, multi-level governance and civil society

The debates over levels or scales of government are complicated by the reality across Europe of variable forms of multi-level governance (MLG), understood here across its two principal dimensions: multiple levels of delivery and regulation of public services (from local to European), and multiple interactions, especially beyond the state, often involving the private delivery of public goods and assuming the role of lobbies and interests in policy formulation (Piatonni, 2010). Public services are usually delivered as part of a broader pattern of multi-level governance, the parameters of which are shaped differentially in distinct state traditions. It is difficult, though not impossible, to capture the multi-level dimension as it feeds into debates over trust and transparency. Our three states provide a useful fit, which encompass Hooghe and Marks (2001) type 1 and type 2 forms of MLG. The classic formulation of MLG (type 1) 'conceives of dispersion of authority to multi-task, territorially mutually exclusive jurisdictions in a relatively stable system with limited jurisdictional levels and a limited number of units'. In contrast, type 2 MLG 'pictures specialized, territorially overlapping jurisdictions in a relatively flexible, non-tiered system with a large number of jurisdictions' (Hooghe and Marks, 2001: 1). The German model fits best the classic type 1 description, while – borrowing a metaphor from the federalism literature – the French model of MLG is more akin to a marble cake (random and fruity), rather than a well-ordered layer cake, with neatly distributed competencies between levels (Entwistle et al, 2014). In the case of the UK, territorial asymmetry makes any overall framing much more difficult. This categorisation is important insofar as it allows the project as a whole to contribute to debates about the territorial dimensions of trust and transparency.

The book also situates questions of trust and transparency in the context of broader debates about styles of democratic governance and, specifically, the role of civil society. The primary data used to analyse the trust–transparency nexus within this context is a series of interviews carried out with civil society actors in each subnational territory using a semi-structured interview schedule that links trust and transparency to scalar preferences, institutional configurations, identity mixes, and perceptions of social and cultural capital and output legitimacy. This fieldwork was carried out between 2016 and 2019, with over 100 interviews taking place in the six identified subnational territories (about 20 per region). The interviewees were drawn from functionally equivalent panels, determined via purposive sampling. In each territory, the sample was recruited from three core groups: a political group, a policy interest group and a wider civil society group. In identifying interview subjects, the authors made efforts to ensure party balance, territorial spread, position, tenure and gender. The focus on civil society actors enables the analysis to explore the interplay between interpersonal and organisational forms of trust, notably highlighted by Nooteboom (2002) (explored in Chapter 1).

In the interests of the transparency of the research process, we encountered a range of issues and obstacles in carrying out the fieldwork. Firstly, the period of the fieldwork coincided with a period of significant changes in governance arrangements in two of our subnational cases: the 2016 reorganisation of French regions, which led to the amalgamation of the Auvergne and Rhône-Alpes regions, and the devolution of power to the Greater Manchester Combined Authority (GMCA) and Liverpool City Region Combined Authority (LCRCA) in North West England, agreed in November 2014 and November 2015 respectively. On the one hand, this provided an opportunity to explore the building of trust within the context of new institutions and governance arrangements, but on the other, the fieldwork coincided with a distinct phase in the development of these subnational territories. Second, in terms of the specific cases, the team encountered some difficulty in recruiting to the political panels in the German subnational cases, and in general in talking to public officials, taking refuge behind the shield of confidentiality. The overarching political situation in Hesse and Saxony-Anhalt was a contributory factor in rendering access more difficult. In the case of Wales, traditionally considered to be one of the most open and transparent research terrains, the team also encountered some resistance from the political group, but high levels of buy-in from the policy interest groups and wider civil society organisations. The Welsh case contrasted with the Greater Manchester City Region (GMCR) and Liverpool City Region (LCR), where the launching of a new process of devolution encouraged key actors across the whole panel to participate willingly in the research process. Finally, there were no clear obstacles reported in either of the French regions, Bretagne and Auvergne-Rhône-Alpes.

The organisation of the book

The book is organised into two main sections. The first, slightly shorter section explores contemporary debates around the concepts of trust and transparency, and the conceptual framework, the trust–transparency matrix, that will be used to explore our empirical cases. In this section, Chapter 1 frames the project and engages in an extensive literature review of contemporary debates on trust. It reviews the way in which trust has been conceptualised and operationalised across the academic literature and provides the foundations for our own research. Chapter 2 introduces transparency and its relationship with the different forms of trust introduced in the previous chapter. Finally, this chapter provides an overview of the conceptual framework that is operationalised in order to carry out cross-national multi-level comparisons of trust and transparency, the trust–transparency matrix. An important point which is stressed within the chapter is that the matrix is operationalised as a heuristic tool to facilitate the comparative analysis of the case studies by establishing ideal types in relation to trust–transparency dynamics, rather than an explanatory device designed to measure the causal relationship between the two concepts.

The second section of the book is centred on the empirical fieldwork which lies at the heart of the research. Chapter 3 explores in greater depth the rationale for the comparative design of the research and introduces the three country-level cases and the six subnational territories that form our empirical work. Chapters 4, 5 and 6 provide detailed empirical analyses of these cases, applying the trust–transparency matrix to explore the trust–transparency nexus within each setting. The final concluding chapter brings together the findings of the six subnational case studies set across the three states to reflect on the nature of trust and transparency within the restructuring of contemporary states within Western Europe. Furthermore, it identifies the key factors which shape processes of building and maintaining trust within increasingly complex forms of MLG. In doing so, it identifies approaches to generating trust within and between civil society actors but also evaluates the potential role of civil society as a mechanism for strengthening trust and transparency within contemporary democracies. In addition, it reflects on the trust–transparency matrix and the comparative case study method operationalised within the research.

1

Building trust in an age of transparency

Trust is perhaps one of the most contested and nebulous concepts within contemporary academic research. Grimmelikhuijsen and colleagues (2013: 577) note that 'across and even within disciplines, a myriad of definitions, concepts, and operationalizations are being used in research' and therefore providing clarity in terms of what we mean and understand when discussing trust is itself challenging. Levi (1998: 79, quoted in Newton 2007: 343), for example, noted that trust 'is not one thing and it does not have one source; it has a variety of forms and causes'. Any academic journal article, monograph or edited volume which directly or indirectly engages with questions of trust is relatively incomplete without a section or chapter devoted to what we mean by trust. Rousseau and colleagues (1998: 394), for example, tackled this challenge head-on in their attempt to develop a multidisciplinary view of trust which provides 'clear boundaries to usefully inform research and theory'. They settle on a definition where trust is characterised as 'a psychological state comprising the intention to accept vulnerability based upon positive expectations of the intentions or behaviour of another' (Rousseau et al, 1998: 395). While this parsimonious definition provides a useful starting point for a cross-disciplinary discussion of trust, it does not go very far in terms of understanding the dynamics of building trust and of different dimensions of trust which characterise contemporary governance, such as interpersonal, institutional and interorganisational dynamics (Nooteboom, 1996; Edelenbos and Klijn, 2007; Klijn et al, 2010; Edelenbos and Eshuis, 2012; Fuglsang and Jagd, 2015).

This chapter explores approaches to contemporary debates on the concept of trust. It takes as a starting point that trust can be understood as a complex, multidimensional concept and that context is potentially key (Zmerli and Hooghe, 2011; Grimmelikhuijsen et al, 2013; Meijer, 2013). The chapter is divided into four sections. The first examines contemporary approaches to defining and conceptualising trust. The second explores core assumptions about how trust can be utilised within the context of our multi-level cases. The third section explores how we can understand the dynamics between interpersonal and interorganisational trust. And the fourth engages in a discussion of trust and closely related concepts.

Defining trust: levels of analysis

Trust needs to be understood as a generic term to describe dynamics taking place at different levels of analysis: interpersonal, social and collective. Literature from political science, especially relating to the three levels of trust of Hooghe and Zmerli (2011), allows a fairly precise operationalisation. Social science relies on theorising at three main levels of analysis: individual, intermediate and institutional. Each type of analysis carries a distinctive contribution and the stakes of each are high; psychological well-being, civil society and trust in government. In terms of comprehension, trust does not necessarily gain from moving between these levels of analysis in an indiscriminate manner, but substantive distinctions are important.

'Trust' is defined first as an analysis of the *relationship* between a subject (the one who trusts) and an object (the one who is trusted). Putnam (1995) draws a distinction between generalised and interpersonal trust. Newton (2001) also distinguishes between social (interpersonal) and political (institutional) trust, arguing that they are distinct traits that should not be assumed to represent a generalised tendency to trust anyone/anything in one's social environment. Zmerli and Newton (2011: 69) further delineate three forms of trust: 'particular social trust', which involves those known to us personally, such as family, friends or work colleagues; 'general social trust', which is that placed in 'unknown others'; and finally 'political trust', defined as 'either trust in particular politicians or trust in the main institutions of government and public life'. Likewise, the European Social Survey and World Values Study divide trust into social (interpersonal) and political (institutional) dimensions.

Interpersonal trust: Rousseau and colleagues (1998: 395) define trust as 'a psychological state comprising the intention to accept vulnerability based upon positive expectations of the intentions or behaviour of another'. It involves an interpersonal relationship, with at least two players, as in a clinician–patient relationship. In another close formulation, 'particular social trust' involves those known to us personally, such as family, friends or work colleagues. A breakdown of trust shatters this psychological equilibrium. Cross-national evidence from lockdowns and confinements illuminates the challenged state of psychological well-being of individuals, especially in terms of their primary networks (friends, family) and practices (as a result of social distancing). Even within these tight personal networks, evidence from scholars working on psychological indicators points to an increase in indicators of social tension, such as divorce, gender violence and isolation as a result of the COVID-19 crisis, for example (Boserup et al, 2020).

One rich strand of literature on interpersonal trust comes from business and management studies and analyses trust in terms of exchange relationships. Vanneste and colleagues (2014) build on Ring and van de Ven's (1994) premise that trust increases over time in relationships, and they find that there is a correlation between trust and relationship duration. They also contend that the development of trust is affected (that is, it increases, remains constant or decreases) by four different mechanisms: initial bias correction; change in relationship value; identification; and trust-based selection. They base their arguments on the hypothetical relationship between a trustor, who must decide whether or not to establish a relationship, and a trustee of unknown trustworthiness.

Trustworthiness represents the active dimension of interpersonal relationships and gives rise to a set of mechanisms. The first of these is initial bias correction: a trustor may be pessimistic, unbiased or optimistic about the partner's trustworthiness. The initial bias of the trustor affects the evolution of trust within a relationship once it is established. When the trustor engages in a relationship then they receive first-hand evidence which influences the trustor's estimate of the partner's trustworthiness. Depending on the initial bias of the trustor (optimism or pessimism), the trust will be increased or reduced during the duration of the relationship. In the second mechanism (exogenous change in relationship), the importance of the context is highlighted. A party might be trusted in one context but not in another. If a trustor and trustee interact in different contexts over time, then trust can change even when perceived trustworthiness in the relationship remains constant. The third mechanism (identification) is about the repetition of interactions. As X and Y interact with each other repeatedly, X begins to care about good and bad outcomes for Y and considers them as also being good and bad for themself. Also, as X begins to care about Y receiving good outcomes, X becomes more trustworthy from Y's perspective. The final one (trust-based selection) considers the possibility of exit from a relationship. Given the possibility of exit, a trustor will continue to interact only with partners that are trusted. A trustor's long-lived relationships will then be primarily with trustworthy partners because untrustworthy ones are deselected over time. Therefore, trust should be high in long-lived relationships.

Social or collective trust: 'General social trust' is that placed in 'unknown others'. This form of trust performs a key function in modern societies, as Newton (2007: 349) notes, because 'much social interaction is between people who neither know one another nor share a common social background'. Generalised social trust or 'thin trust' is centred on more general information about social groups and situations. The ability to empathise with members of an imagined community (region, nation, even continent) is a core element of community integration.

Another study (Colquitt et al, 2012) about exchange and trust centres on social exchange theory which argues that trust is vital to the development and deepening of social exchange relationships. Unspecified favours are exchanged over an indefinite time horizon because this reduces uncertainty about a partner's reciprocation while fostering a sense of obligation. When trust is present, exchange partners are more likely to discharge their obligations, in part because they believe that such efforts will be reciprocated in the future. In the classic formulation by Blau (1964: 93–94),

> social exchange involves favors that create diffuse future obligations, not precisely specified ones, and the nature of the return cannot be bargained about but must be left to the discretion of the one who makes it … Since there is no way to assure an appropriate return for a favor, social exchange requires trusting others to discharge their obligations.

Community trust represents a different form of social relationship. In his study of risk management and trust in civic emergency planning agencies, Paton (2013) hypothesises that levels of trust are influenced by community characteristics. Trust influences perception of others' motives, their competence and the credibility of the information they provide. Building on Earle (2004), Paton examines the relationship between community characteristics and levels of social trust. He recognises that people's perception of risk is influenced by social context and proposes that trust will be influenced by community characteristics that influence people's capacity to confront the uncertainty associated with complex, infrequently occurring natural hazards.

Discussion about community trust has also occurred in the context of municipal government, notably by Wollebæk and colleagues (2012). They consider community trust as a distinct form of trust. They argue that the most widely used dichotomy in the literature (between generalised and particularised trust) needs to be supplemented by a third trust form: community trust. It is a distinct category which is bounded in space rather than personal interactions. As such, it is neither fully particularised nor fully generalised, but a qualitatively different category. It is much more directly connected to communal problem-solving in neighbourhoods and municipalities than generalised or particularised trust. Community trust is partially a product of personal experiences with the people with whom the space is shared, and partially based on socially formed perceptions of that shared, lived space as context. It can be thought of as a form of localised collective memory, where actual lived experience is mixed with impressions gained from local folklore, stories told by others in the community and reports in the media. The ethnic or social composition of the community (municipality or neighbourhood), the speed of the changes therein, the individual experiences within the community, the extension of the residential tenure and the size of the community are some of the determinants of the level of community trust (Wollebæk et al, 2012: 322–25).

Trust in government provides our third dimension. High levels of political trust have been identified as key factors in well-functioning democracies, for example, associated with higher levels of engagement in civic affairs (Putnam 1993; Paxton and Ressler, 2018). Furthermore, higher levels of political trust are associated with certain types of behaviours, such as cooperation with legal authorities or tax compliance (Bradford et al, 2018; Chan et al, 2018). A common theme in research during the COVID-19 pandemic was the influence of political trust on compliance with restrictive measures such as social distancing and lockdown rules (Fancourt et al, 2020; Newton, 2020; Woelfert and Kunst, 2020; Cairney and Wellstead, 2021). Bish and Michie (2010: 813) argue that trust in government is a key variable affecting individual behaviour during a pandemic because 'a lack of trust in authorities is likely to affect how people process and interpret health messages and risk communication advice', potentially leading to an erosion of compliance. Hooghe and Zmerli (2011: 3) define political trust as a 'very thin form of trust' characterised by a 'kind of general expectation that on the whole, political leaders will act according to the rules of the game as they are agreed upon in a democratic regime'. Most of the empirical data in the book concerns this broad category of political trust, which is further developed in our discussion of thick and thin forms of trust.

Exploring core assumptions

A range of core assumptions can be identified as underpinning many contemporary approaches or conceptions of trust. Lane (1998: 3) argues that most concepts of personal trust share three common elements: (i) a degree of interdependence between the trustor and trustee; (ii) trust provides a way to cope with risk or uncertainty in exchange relationships; and (iii) the vulnerability resulting from the acceptance of risk will not be taken advantage of by the other party in the relationship. Similarly, Edelenbos and Klijn (2007) also trace three broad characteristics of trust within the literature: (i) an assumption of vulnerability; (ii) the presence of risk; and (iii) the role of expectations. Both of these attempts to identify core elements or characteristics of trust are reflected in the previously noted broad multidisciplinary definition of trust developed by Rousseau and colleagues (1998), but there are sharp contrasts within the literature regarding the basis for these trust relations. Hardin (2006: 16–17), for example, identifies three distinct approaches: (i) the encapsulated interest account 'grounded in an assumption that the potentially trusted person has an interest in maintaining a relationship with the truster'; (ii) trust as a matter of moral commitment; and (iii) trust as a matter of character or disposition. Lenard (2005: 365) simplifies this distinction into two broad approaches to thinking about trust. The first of these encompasses Hardin's encapsulated interest account, emphasising 'the strategic risk-taking elements of trust' and draws on rational choice theory to assume that 'both the truster and the trusted will act, in general, to maximise their own interests'. The second, Lenard argues, suggests that 'we ought to think of it (trust) as a generalised attitude towards others, rather than a feature of one-shot (or even repeated) interactions between specific individuals, in which they act solely to maximize their own self-interest' (Lenard 2005: 365). This encompasses trust as a moral commitment or social-psychological predisposition and is highlighted in Uslaner's (2002) conception of 'moralistic trust'.

In addition to encapsulated interest and moralistic accounts of trust, Lane (1998: 10) identifies 'cognition-or-expectations-based trust' as a concept operationalised in a variety of research designs, including social exchange theory (Blau, 1964; Simmel, 1978), ethnomethodology (Garfinkel, 1967), phenomenology (Zucker, 1986), systems theory (Luhmann, 1979) and structuration theory (Giddens, 1984). These different approaches provide the basis for 'institutional trust' or 'system trust', which shifts the focus away from a focus on interpersonal sources of trust, such as familiarity and a common history, to 'formal, socially produced and legitimated structures which guarantee trust' (Lane, 1998: 15). Zucker (1986, cited in Fuglsang and Jagd, 2015: 26), for example, identified three different sources of trust: characteristic-based trust, process-based trust and institutional-based trust.

Characteristic-based trust is underpinned by social similarities, such as ethnicity or gender. Zucker (1986: 63) affirms that 'the greater the number of social similarities, the more interactants assume that common background expectations do exist, hence trust can be relied upon'. Process-based trust is centred on past experiences or exchanges, characterised by Lane (1998: 11) as entailing 'the incremental process of building trust through the gradual accumulation of either direct or indirect knowledge about the other'. Finally, institutional trust provides a more impersonal form of trust where common characteristics or a shared history of interaction or exchange may be absent. Zucker (1986: 11) characterises this form of trust as being underpinned by 'institutionalization: the process of redefining acts as exterior when intersubjective understanding causes them to be seen as part of the external world and objective when they are repeatable by others without changing the common understanding of the acts'. Importantly for Zucker (1986: 63), this form of trust can be produced, for example, through the creation of rules and formal structures, and therefore extended from a small number of exchanges to the 'external world known in common'. Fisher and colleagues (2010: 167) develop a similar concept, deliberative trust, which focuses on 'the presence of mechanisms to protect the truster from betrayal by the trustee'. Many of the assumptions which underpin approaches to building trust explored in the next section, such as the key roles played by knowledge and information, appear to fit more neatly with ideas of 'institutional' or 'deliberative' trust, and to a lesser extent 'strategic' trust, rather than the 'moralistic' conception.

The differing bases for trust are reflected in the distinction within the literature related to different forms of trust or levels of analysis, perhaps most notably between types of social and political trust. Khodyakov (2007: 123) notes that the language varies by academic discipline: for example, political scientists refer to 'political trust', whereas sociologists refer to 'system trust' in discussing more impersonal forms of trust. 'Particular social trust' or 'thick trust' is characterised as being interpersonal, described by Putnam (2000: 136) as 'embedded in personal relations that are strong, frequent and nested in wider networks'. However, this form of trust is inherently limited because outsiders or strangers are likely to be distrusted, echoing the advantages and disadvantages of 'bonding social capital'. In contrast, generalised social trust or 'thin trust' is centred on more general information about social groups and situations. This form of trust performs a key function in modern societies, as Newton (2007: 349) notes, because 'much social interaction is between people who neither know one another nor share a common social background'. These two forms of interpersonal trust contrast with the characterisations of political trust. As previously noted, Hooghe and Zmerli (2011: 3) draw on Easton's (1965) idea of diffused support to describe political trust as a 'very thin form of trust' characterised by an expectation around the behaviour of political elites. Therefore, whether this expectation is experience-based does not make a significant difference. Khodyakov (2007) helpfully reframes these three forms of trust as thick and thin forms of interpersonal trust together with institutional trust.

The distinction between different forms of trust and levels of analysis are key to understanding contemporary research on the dynamics of interpersonal and institutional trust, and processes of building trust within the context of governance. Khodyakov (2007: 118) challenges the assumption that he identifies in Fukuyama's work (1995, 1999) that 'if there is no interpersonal trust, institutional trust is impossible' and instead argues that the relationship between different forms of trust flows in both directions. Institutional forms of trust may be explained as much by the effective performance of institutions as the overall level of thick (particular social trust) or thin (general social trust) forms of trust. Therefore, institutional trust may be as much a question of confidence as trust. Seligman (1997: 148) draws on the work of Giddens (1990) and Luhmann (1979) to identify 'the public realm with the phenomenon of confidence in systematically enforced expectations and the private with those of trust, individual agency, and a space for the negotiation of role expectations'. However, importantly, this is not an absolute distinction but rather a continuum whereby 'the more negotiation, agency, and trust existing in an interaction, the more it can usefully be conceived as being of private nature and the more confidence in systematically mandated (and sanctioned) forms of interaction, the more public its nature' (Seligman, 1997: 148–49). He provides the example of the interaction between a parent and child in different social settings, but we may similarly identify the interactions of different individuals and organisations within the complex decision- and policy-making processes that characterise contemporary governance.

Building trust in the context of multi-level governance: from individual to organisational

The literature focused on the 'crisis of trust', as Muñoz and colleagues (2011) note, has traditionally adopted an explicitly 'state-centred perspective' and frequently has concentrated on survey-based analyses of public attitudes to formal political institutions at the nation state level. The focus and design of these studies raises at least two key methodological and conceptual problems. First, by focusing narrowly on the nation-state level and traditional political institutions, the literature ignores the dramatic processes of state rescaling and restructuring that have taken place across many democratic countries, highlighted by influential concepts such as multi-level governance (Marks et al, 1996; Keating, 1998; Hooghe and Marks, 2003; Rodriguez-Pose and Gill, 2003; Brenner, 2004, 2009; MacLeod and Jones, 2007; Jessop et al, 2008; Hooghe et al, 2010; Piattoni, 2010). For example, Passey and Tonkiss (2000: 50) note that the traditional characterisation of civil society as being differentiated from the state and the economy has broken down through the increased role of civil society organisations in delivering public services and as a 'crucial arena for state legitimacy'. Second, as a consequence of these developments, trust has been identified as a key factor in enabling collaboration and partnership within these complex governance settings. Edelenbos and Eshuis (2012: 195) observe that if 'horizontal, voluntary relations in modern societies are increasing in importance, trust becomes an important coordination mechanism since uncertainties can no longer be managed through hierarchical power, direct surveillance or detailed contracts'. In order to examine the role of trust within the context of these increasingly complex forms of governance it is necessary to consider the potential benefits that trust delivers, how the different forms of trust discussed in the previous section relate to decision and policy-making processes and, finally, perspectives on processes of building or maintaining trust.

Trust has been identified as a key factor in the wide-ranging literature that explores collaboration and interorganisational relations within the context of increasingly complex decision-making networks and governance (Ring and van de Ven, 1994; Lane and Bachmann, 1998; Sullivan and Skelcher, 2002; Huxham and Vangen, 2005; Edelenbos and Klijn, 2007; Edelenbos and Eshuis, 2012; Klijn and Koppenjan, 2016). Huxham and Vangen (2005: 66), for example, note that the 'common wisdom' suggests that trust is 'a precondition for successful collaboration' but the 'common practice' appears to be that mutual suspicion is often the starting point. Therefore, they argue, it is evident that trust needs to be carefully built and maintained for successful collaboration to be achieved. Similarly, Edelenbos and Klijn's (2007: 30) survey of the literature focused on trust and complex interorganisational cooperation identified three main benefits of trust: (i) facilitating cooperation; (ii) solidifying cooperation; and (iii) enhancing the performance of cooperation. In terms of improving the performance of cooperation or collaboration, Klijn and Koppenjan (2016: 116) argue that 'a high degree of trust decreases transaction costs between cooperating actors, enhances the probability that actors will exchange information even when the results are uncertain, and encourages learning and innovation'. However, too much trust might lead to sub-optimal outcomes (Möllering and Sydow, 2019). For example, Edelenbos and Klijn (2007: 34) argue that too much trust can lead to 'a network of people and organizations that all think alike' whereby groupthink and parties developing 'blind trust' may be almost as counterproductive as weak levels of trust. Despite the relative consensus regarding the important role performed by trust in facilitating cooperation, a key issue remains as to whether we are envisaging trust on the interpersonal or micro level, the interorganisational or macro level, or both.

One of the central dilemmas in discussing trust within the context of the interorganisational networks that characterise contemporary governance is whether the form of trust that is unlocking the perceived benefits identified in the previous paragraph is driven by interpersonal interaction or some form of institutional or organisation factors – or both. Zaheer and colleagues (1998: 141) observe that 'not clearly specifying how trust translates from the individual to the organisation level leads to theoretical confusion'; for example, we may identify an interorganisational basis for trust when it is actually underpinned by interpersonal interaction. The dynamics between interorganisational and individual trust are illustrated by Vanneste (2014: 7). He notes that we may identify the presence of interorganisational trust between two organisations, A and B, and this in turn implies that individuals from both organisations trust each other. However, Vanneste raises the question 'if Alice (a member of Organisation A) trusts Bob (a member of Organisation B), why should it follow that Amy (another member of A) trusts Brad (another member of B)?' Alternatively, and more broadly framed, 'how does interpersonal trust (i.e. trust between individuals) lead to interorganisational trust (i.e. trust between groups of individuals)?' A common factor identified within the contemporary literature, for example, has been the role performed by boundary spanners in terms of building and maintaining trust (Williams 2012).

The discussion of the relationship between interpersonal and interorganisational trust brings us back to the forms of trust introduced in the previous section and specifically to the distinction made within the literature between micro and macro levels of trust (Bachmann, 2001). Micro-level trust is characterised by interpersonal face-to-face contacts; it is often time-consuming to build and personnel change may lead to a breakdown in relations (Nooteboom, 1996). In contrast, the macro level is defined by institutional trust, which, as Bachmann and Inkpen (2011: 282) note, enables both parties to 'refer to institutional safeguards in their decisions and actions and can thus develop trust without having any prior personal experience in dealing with one another'. This is not to say that micro and macro forms of trust are mutually exclusive. A range of authors have explored the importance of social interaction and sense-making within the context of institutionally based trust (Zaheer et al, 1998; Sydow, 2006; Fuglsang and Jagd, 2015). Zaheer and colleagues (1998: 144), for example, argue that institutionalising processes provide the link between interpersonal and interorganisational trust – individual actors, such as boundary spanners, are socialised into the norms of the 'mini-society' which are 'internalized and recreated in boundary spanners' interpersonal trust orientations toward each other in the process of conducting exchange'. However, they note that at the same time, 'interpersonal trust becomes reinstitutionalized and boundary spanners' trust orientation in turn influences the orientation of other organizational members toward the partner organization' (Zaheer et al, 1998: 144). Therefore, in analysing the building and maintaining of trust in collaborative and interorganisational settings, we must be aware of the dynamics between micro and macro levels.

The recognition of the dynamics between interpersonal and institutional forms of trust is useful in terms of informing how trust can be built and maintained but it perhaps tells us somewhat less regarding what we mean by trust in this context. To put it more simply, what exactly are we trying to build and how can we go about building it? Mayer and colleagues (1995: 717–20) put forward an influential account of variation in trust centred on how a trustor perceives the trustworthiness of a trustee, encompassing three key elements:

(i) Ability – 'that group of skills, competencies, and characteristics that enable a party to have influence within some specific domain. The domain of the ability is specific because the trustee may be highly competent in some technical area, affording that person trust on tasks related to that area'.

(ii) Benevolence – 'the extent to which a trustee is believed to want to do good to the trustor, aside from an egocentric profit motive. Benevolence suggests that the trustee has some specific attachment to the trustor'.

(iii) Integrity – 'involves the trustor's perception that the trustee adheres to a set of principles that the trustor finds acceptable ... Such issues as the consistency of the party's past actions, credible communications about the trustee from other parties, belief that the trustee has a strong sense of justice, and the extent to which the party's actions are congruent with his or her words all affect the degree to which the party is judged to have integrity'.

Mayer and colleagues' model was originally developed to focus on the micro or interpersonal level, but Svare and colleagues (2020: 588–89) argue that this framework can be adapted to analyse trust dynamics at the macro or interorganisational level. They put forward an adapted version of Mayer and colleagues' three core elements to reflect the interorganisational context:

(i) Interorganisational-level ability – 'the group of skills, competencies and characteristics that enable an organisation to exert influence within some specific domain. Moreover, we posit that the way in which an organisation perceives another organisation's ability will influence the trust it places in it, in cases where such ability is relevant'.

(ii) Interorganisational-level benevolence – '[A] benevolent organisation is an organisation which has not only its own interests in mind but is able to align this interest with an intention to do well to other organisations. Alternatively, we may define organisational benevolence indirectly, through the concept of opportunism. High levels of opportunism correspond to low levels of benevolence, with a subsequent negative impact on the trust received, in cases where such benevolence is relevant.'

(iii) Interorganisational-level integrity – 'An organisation is perceived to have integrity when it honours previously established agreements by acting in accordance with them and acts according to established norms of justice.'

This adapted version of Mayer and colleagues' model provides a potentially useful tool to analyse the process of trust-building between organisations and has also been operationalised by recent attempts to analyse the role of transparency in fostering trust. Although this framework may give us a greater sense of what the focus of trust-building exercises should be, it says relatively little about the process of building it.

In the existing academic literature there is a wide range of strategies for building trust within both interpersonal and interorganisational contexts. Zand's (1972: 231) influential analysis focuses on the micro level and identifies three core factors in building trust:

(i) Information – 'disclose more accurate, relevant, and complete data about the problem, one's thoughts and one's feeling'.

(ii) Influence – 'accept more influence from others in selection of goals, choice of methods, evaluation of progress'.

(iii) Control – 'accept more interdependence with others. Impose less procedure to control others. Greater confidence others will do what they agree to. Greater commitment to do what one agreed to'.

By enhancing these behavioural aspects, he argued that trust was strengthened and the result was 'less socially generated uncertainty and problems are solved more effectively' (Zand, 1972: 238). From a more macro-level perspective, Bachmann and Inkpen (2011: 289) identify four 'concrete mechanisms through which institutions can specifically reduce risk and foster trust building processes in inter-organizational relationships': (i) legal regulation; (ii) reputation; (iii) certification of exchange partners; and (iv) community norms, structures and procedures. Focusing on building trust in business relationships, they argue that the more formal institutions (legal regulations and certification) tend to influence what they describe as 'the behavioural antecedents of relationships', whereas the more informal institutions (reputation and norms) target the processes that are instrumental in building trust-based relationships (Bachmann and Inkpen, 2011: 292–93). In terms of both the micro/interpersonal and macro/interorganisational dimensions of building trust, we can see that the establishment of institutional trust plays a fundamental role in terms of establishing clear expectations and norms of behaviour. However, it is important to recognise trust as process-based which, as Edelenbos and Klijn (2007: 33) observe, 'does not appear at a snap of a finger, but must be built up in the interaction among actors'. Indeed, Huxham and Vangen (2005: 68) introduce the concept of a 'trust building loop', designed to build trust through small, initially modest steps but that deliver successful outcomes which in turn reinforce trusting attitudes and provide the foundations for more ambitious collaboration.

Linking trust and related concepts

Trust is defined as much by its linkage with other concepts as by its own inherent properties: notably, trust and vulnerability; trust and confidence; and trust and transparency. The close linkage between trust and transparency in particular provides a distinctive angle to linking levels of analysis in our study. Transparency refers to 'the characteristic of being easy to see through' (Cambridge Dictionary, 2018). It underpins a diverse set of literatures, ranging from participatory democracy, ethics and fair processes, to policy instruments and new public management (based on transparent procedures and indicators, and clear incentives) (Grimmelikhuijsen, 2012; Heald, 2018; Hood, 2007). With respect to political trust, one hypothesis postulates that transparency improves the relationship between citizens and administration in a context of public deficit, loss of trust and corruption (Pasquier and Villeneuve, 2007). In terms of policy relationships, as noted previously, transparency is potentially disruptive to the tight policy communities identified by Marsh and Rhodes (1992). This central relationship is developed further in the next chapter.

Closely related and pertinent in the field of public services is the model of trust and confidence. In their 'Trust, Confidence and Cooperation' model, Earle and Siegrist (2008) distinguish between trust and confidence. Trust is defined as the willingness to make oneself vulnerable to another based on a judgement of similarity of intentions or values. It involves an interpersonal relationship, with at least two players, as in a clinician–patient relationship. Confidence is defined as the belief based on past experience or evidence that certain events will occur as expected. Both trust and confidence influence people's willingness to cooperate. In terms of trust and confidence, the individual level is key, because individual perceptions of risk are germane to the adoption of preventive measures (Khosravi, 2020). While trust can involve belief, confidence is based on expectations of behaviour based on prior performance or reputation.

The recent COVID-19 pandemic illustrated these dynamics. Citing studies of various countries, Siegrist and Zingg (2013: 25) had already suggested that 'trust had a positive impact on adopting precautionary behavior during a pandemic'. This finding was backed by van der Weerd and colleagues (2011) in their study of the H1N1 flu pandemic in the Netherlands: most of the respondents wanted the information about infection prevention to come from the municipal health services, health care providers and the media, rather than central government. During pandemics, most people are not in a position to evaluate the information about the risks and benefits associated with vaccination. Therefore, they rely on experts, especially those experts they trust, who are once removed from government. Cross-national surveys all pointed in the same direction: that health professionals were trusted far more than governments, which responded logically by associating experts with their decisions and allowing medical experts to make public policy declarations.

Similarly, a growing body of the literature suggests that public trust or distrust is one of the most important factors in predicting the public acceptability of energy technologies (including smart grids), policies and projects (Perlaviciute et al, 2018). Citizens' trust/confidence in government, experts, institutions and markets is critical in the energy transition context because many decisions on energy choices must be made on the basis of incomplete information and technological risks (Loorbach and Verbong, 2012).

The COVID-19 pandemic revealed how administrative complexity can be an independent factor of mistrust. Who does what is a vital question in terms of basic transparency, and competition between bureaus can have a debilitating effect in terms of access to public services, especially during a period of pandemic. In the case of France, for example, obtaining masks, gloves, sprays, or simply taking a test involved intense inter-agency (Regional Health Agency, prefectures) and intergovernmental (state against the regions) competition. Similar stories emerged elsewhere, not least between the central government and the devolved administrations in the UK. This issue is not a simple one of distinction between types of polity – for example, federal versus unitary systems. While the US and Brazilian federations descended into partisan-based rivalries between states, federal Germany demonstrated one of the most joined-up responses to the pandemic.

Conclusion

Whether we conceptualise trust in terms of levels, properties or relationships; or whether we link it with related concepts (such as transparency) will have a major impact in terms of how we study the phenomenon. One angle is to distinguish between thick and thinner forms of trust. Thick trust implies understanding it as an interpersonal relationship, based on vulnerability, reciprocity and 'positive expectations of the intentions or behaviour of another' (Rousseau et al, 1998: 395). Trust in government, on the other hand, has been characterised as a 'very thin form of trust' (Hooghe and Zmerli, 2011: 3). It is closer to confidence, defined by Earle and Siegrist (2008: 20) as 'the belief, based on experience or evidence (e.g. past performance) that certain future events will occur as expected', than to interpersonal or even social trust. Thus framed, questions around trust arguably require a mixed-methods approach; as such, an approach promises the potential to capture both thin and thick forms of interaction. Political trust is commonly understood as a form of thin trust: it is classically measured by surveys. Thicker forms of interpersonal or social trust are more difficult to observe or capture with purely quantitative instruments of the survey type. We can best approach this dimension via trust in policy communities. Collective interviews (focus groups) provide one means of interactive data collection; such methods lie outside the scope of this inquiry. For logistical reasons, we adopted an approach based on cognate purposive samples of actors situated at the level of two regions in each country.

2

The trust–transparency nexus

In the previous chapter, trust was defined as much by its linkage with other concepts as by its own inherent properties. This is especially the case with trust and transparency, the core relationship we explore in this book. Rather than straightforward explanations in terms of independent, intermediary and dependent variables, we present trust as a contextually and institutionally contingent phenomenon based on the perceived competence and, to a lesser extent, benevolence and honesty of government and other actors within governance networks. What we label as the trust–transparency matrix presents a general heuristic, which facilitates carrying out cross-national multi-level comparisons of trust and transparency. The chapter is divided into four sections. The first examines contemporary approaches to defining and conceptualising transparency. The second explores the range of existing approaches to studying transparency within contemporary research. The third section examines the trust–transparency nexus, and existing studies designed to explore the link between increased transparency and levels of trust. The final extended section introduces the trust–transparency matrix, drawing on the debates explored in the current and previous chapters, which will be operationalised in the second section of the book.

Conceptualising transparency

Transparency, as Hood (2006: 3) notes, has 'attained a quasi-religious significance' over recent decades and this is reflected in the increasingly wide-ranging literature examining this concept, its rise to prominence and its potential consequences (Oliver, 2004; Hood and Heald, 2006; Fung et al, 2007; Bowles et al, 2014; Han, 2015; Schudson, 2015; Taylor and Kelsey, 2016; Fenster, 2017; Alloa and Thomä, 2018; Pozen and Schudson, 2018). Although the broader concept of transparency predates the late twentieth century, much like the concept of trust explored earlier in the book, transparency in the contemporary context is a multifaceted and contested concept that has risen to prominence in the past two decades (Heald, 2006; Mabillard and Pasquier, 2016). Cucciniello and colleagues' (2017) review of the transparency literature notes that it has been defined and operationalised in a variety of different ways. Similarly, Alloa (2018: 29–30) identifies ten different aspirations attributed to transparency in different contexts:

1. 'Transparency as accessibility: Ensuring informational access to all citizens and implementing a "right to know."'
2. 'Transparency as procedural fairness: Safeguarding due process to all parties involved.'
3. 'Transparency as accountability: By making decisions available to the public, stakeholders are meant to develop a sharpened sense of responsibility and improved accountability.'
4. 'Transparency as asymmetry reduction: Against practices of secrecy, which give certain actors an excessive power over certain sectors, disclosure generally is held to re-establish a certain balance of power.'
5. 'Transparency as a public good: When actions are placed under public scrutiny, reducing (if not removing altogether) actions driven by self-interest.'
6. 'Transparency as rationalization: Forcing actors to give reasons for their actions leads to pervasive bettering of rational behavioral standards.'
7. 'Transparency as truth-making: By compelling individuals to speak out, deceit, falseness and duplicity are dispelled.'
8. 'Transparency as moralization: Where everything is under permanent exposure, individuals are forced to act virtuously.'
9. 'Transparency as (self-)knowledge: Only a subject that knows about herself knows what she can rely on and what she can account for.'
10. 'Transparency as authenticity: Only where nothing is withheld can things be genuine and subjects true to themselves.'

The breadth of these different aspirations highlights the wide range of ways in which transparency has been conceptualised and brought to bear on contrasting phenomena. Indeed, Hood (2006: 19) notes that perhaps much of the attraction of transparency may 'lie in its potential to appeal to those with very different, indeed contradictory, attitudes and worldviews'. It is clear that the potential promise of transparency, particularly in terms of strengthening governance and addressing some of the contemporary challenges facing democracy, has led to an increased interest in the concept in recent years.

The increased interest in transparency was reflected in the OECD's (2017) report 'Trust and Public Policy: How Better Governance Can Help Rebuild Public Trust', which identified the significant growth of legislation on access to information across OECD states over the past 50 years, from five countries in the 1961–70 period to 34 in the 2001–16 period. Similarly, Cucciniello and colleagues' (2017: 36) review of transparency-related research also highlights a major increase in publications since 2010. Grimmelikhuijsen and colleagues (2013: 575) note that transparency has increasingly become a 'goal in itself' and can 'help prevent corruption, contribute to legitimacy, enhance government performance by increasing efficiency, and promote principles of good governance'. Furthermore, they argue that 'transparency is now proposed as the solution to one of the most intangible problems of democratic governance: citizens' increasing mistrust of government'. Thus, the potential positive impact of transparency on trust has been one of the core foci of contemporary research. However, before engaging with the trust–transparency nexus, it is essential to first identify what is meant by transparency and how it can be analysed.

Defining transparency has perhaps not generated the same weight of academic debate as concepts such as trust, but there remain nuances in the way that it has been defined and utilised by authors. Hood (2001: 701, cited in Hood, 2006: 5) states that transparency 'denotes government according to fixed and published rules, on the basis of information and procedures that are accessible to the public'. Furthermore, government transparency is seen by some authors such as Birkinshaw (2006) and Birkinshaw and Varney (2019) as a goal in itself in the sense of a 'right to know'; it is a core moral claim, and the right for citizens to access government information is generally accepted in democratic societies (Pasquier and Villeneuve, 2007). The increasing importance of transparency implies the end of the political culture of secrecy, and a certain level of surveillance to allow citizens access to information about government. External individuals or groups have a legal and moral right to monitor the activities and performance of public organisations.

Grimmelikhuijsen (2012: 53) provides a slightly broader but similarly straightforward definition: transparency is 'the availability of information about an organisation or actor which allows external actors to monitor the internal workings or performance of that organisation or actor'. Taylor and Kelsey (2016: 65) extend their definition to encompass a sense of fairness: 'the transparency of any organisation, authority or decision-making process is the degree to which someone affected by it can evidence whether or not it is treating them fairly'. They argue that this definition has important consequences, notably – somewhat echoing O'Neill (2002) – increasing access to information does not automatically increase transparency because the quality of information is more important than the sheer quantity, and complete transparency, or providing 'enough information to definitively evidence whether someone's treatment is fair or not', is unachievable (Taylor and Kelsey, 2016: 72). Although the general concept of transparency is fairly well-established, it is a multidimensional concept that is more complex than these initial definitions suggest. Heald (2006: 27–28), for example, notes that transparency can move in as many as four different directions:

1. Transparency upwards – 'means that the hierarchical superior/principal can observe the conduct, behaviour, and/or "results" of the hierarchical subordinate/agent'.

2. Transparency downwards – 'is when the "ruled" can observe the conduct, behaviour, and/or "results" of their "rulers"'.
3. Transparency outwards – 'occurs when the hierarchical subordinate or agent can observe what is happening "outside" the organization'.
4. Transparency inwards – 'is when those outside can observe what is going on inside the organization and has the connotation of surveillance and being watched by peers'.

Importantly for Heald, these four directions of transparency are not mutually exclusive but can occur simultaneously. For example, local government may be transparent 'upwards' to central government in terms of monitoring the implementation of policy decided at the centre but also 'downwards' to actors who may be responsible for the delivery of policy and ultimately citizens/voters.

The literature on transparency has also explored the form or focus that transparency takes. Heald (2006: 29), for example, argues that three dichotomies can be used to identify different varieties of transparency with distinct characteristics and consequences. The first dichotomy – event versus process transparency – focuses on the different subject matter of transparency. Heald (2006: 29–30) argues that 'event transparency' focuses on inputs, outputs and outcomes within an organisation; and in contrast 'process transparency' centres on the procedural and operational aspects within an organisation which link these events. On the one hand, the 'events' are relatively straightforward to measure – for example, the growth of league tables to measure outputs – but on the other hand, measuring or analysing processes is difficult. Furthermore, Heald (2006: 31) argues that process transparency may actually have negative consequences in terms of efficiency and effectiveness because 'it directly consumes resources and because it induces defensive behaviour in the face of what is perceived as oppressive surveillance'.

The second dichotomy identified by Heald focuses on the timing of transparency and whether it takes place in retrospect or in real time. Heald (2006: 33) characterises the contrast as being between a reporting cycle and continuous surveillance. In the former, there is a 'reporting lag' between the operating period and the 'accountability window' within which an organisation is able to prepare its 'account' before releasing this information. This effectively affords a degree of management of transparency as an organisation moves from one reporting cycle to the next. In sharp contrast, the 'accountability window' is always open in the case of continuous surveillance and once again potentially increases the costs of transparency.

The final dichotomy identified by Heald (2006: 34) centres on nominal versus effective transparency and engages with what he describes as the 'transparency illusion'. The key point that Heald (2006: 35) makes is that simply increasing the amount of transparency is not an end in itself; for it to be effective 'there must be receptors capable of processing, digesting, and using the information'. Furthermore, information overload may actually undermine and damage transparency. Simply put, in terms of transparency quality is often better than quantity.

The three dichotomies identified by Heald provide a useful starting point for examining the dynamics of transparency, but they are by no means exhaustive. Mabillard and Pasquier (2016: 73) identify two forms of transparency: active release, where disclosure is on 'a proactive and voluntary basis' – for example, the publication of performance indicators; and passive release, where applications are submitted by citizens or external actors, such as freedom of information (FOI) requests. Both of these forms of transparency are intentional but Mabillard and Pasquier (2016) note that they can be supplemented by a further form of unintentional or 'forced' kind of transparency via leaking or whistleblowing. Further, Heald (2006: 35) adds a fourth issue to his discussion of transparency: the role of timing distinct from the earlier discussion of retrospective and real-time transparency. He points out that, on the one hand, 'sudden and unforeseen moves to transparency may disrupt expectations' while, on the other, if a policy actor is perceived as orchestrating the timing too carefully this could lead to 'suspicions of malevolence'.

Therefore, it is not just the quality of transparency that is important but also the way in which it is delivered. If information is overly controlled or perhaps only accessible via a hard-fought FOI request, the potential benefits of transparency may be undermined. For example, in the wake of the Grenfell Tower fire on 14 June 2017 a story published in May 2017 in the trade magazine *Inside Housing* received national attention. The story, based on a FOI request, noted that a 2016 London Fire Brigade report on a previous fire in a Shepherd's Bush tower block indicated that external cladding was 'likely to have assisted the fire spreading up the outside of the building' and therefore the existing policy of advising residents to 'stay put' in their homes was potentially catastrophic (Inside Housing, 2017). Given the circumstances of the Grenfell fire, this passive form of transparency fed into concerns regarding the governance arrangements around fire safety and also demonstrated a further point highlighted by Heald (2006: 36) that unless it is seen to make a difference, 'introducing or increasing transparency may have damaging rather than beneficial effects'. In this case, the passive system of transparency appeared to work and to an extent was effectively used by the receptor (Inside Housing) but for a variety of reasons failed to lead to policy change.

The subject matter encompassed in transparency has also been a key dimension of the existing literature. Cuccinello and colleagues (2017) identified two overarching approaches to classifying forms of transparency: the first by sets of activities undertaken by government and the second by the area of government that it elucidates. The first approach can be highlighted in Heald's (2006) initial distinction between events and process identified earlier. Grimmelikhuijsen and Welch (2012: 563) refine Heald's analysis and identify three aspects within 'events and processes' that can be the subject of transparency:

1. Transparency of decision-making process – 'the degree of openness about the steps taken to reach a decision and the rationale behind the decision'.
2. Transparency of policy content – 'the information disclosed by government about policies: what the adopted measures are, how they are supposed to solve a problem, how they will be implemented, and what implications they will have for citizens and other affected groups'.
3. Transparency of policy outcomes or effects – 'captures the provision and timeliness of information about the effects of policies'.

This distinction enables the analysis of transparency to focus on a specific stage or aspect of policy- or decision-making – for example, de Fine Licht's (2011) experiment on the allocation of health-care resources raised question marks regarding the role of transparency for delivering perceived legitimacy of decision-making.

The second approach to classifying does not focus on a specific activity or stage of policy-making but on a set of activities related to an object. Cucciniello and colleagues (2017: 34) identify two variations of this approach: Cucciniello and Nasi's (2014) threefold distinction between financial/budget, administrative and political transparency and Meijer and colleagues' (2018) distinction between political and administrative transparency. The latter draws on the existing literature to identify potential criteria to evaluate transparency within political and administrative settings. Political transparency encompasses three dimensions: the democratic perspective – 'whether transparency arrangements strengthen the (information) position of citizens'; the constitutional perspective – 'whether transparency strengthens or undermines institutional checks and balances'; and the social learning perspective – 'whether transparency strengthens the quality of public debate and collective problem-solving capacity' (Meijer et al, 2018: 506). Administrative transparency is also made up of three elements: the economy/efficiency perspective – 'whether transparency contributes to the achievement of policy objectives and whether it promotes the search for the most efficient ways of realizing these'; the integrity perspective – 'whether transparency induces officials to use their mandates and the resources at their disposal to implement the public will and not for the advancement their own interests or those of particular others'; and the resilience perspective – 'whether transparency enhances the robustness and adaptive capacity of administrative systems in the face of ongoing and episodic, even spasmodic, changes, risks, and threats' (Meijer et al, 2018: 514). Meijer and colleagues (2018) utilise this distinction to develop an interpretative assessment framework to evaluate the introduction of FOI legislation in the UK. Importantly, transparency within this context is not simply a proxy for either the participation of stakeholders in policy-making or a general commitment to openness. Rather, as Meijer (2013) and Heald (2006) note, transparency can take on a variety of forms including institutional relations, information exchange, performance and the workings of government. Therefore, measures such as the OECD's Open, Useful and Reusable Government Data index, which provides a benchmark of the design and implementation of open data policies, only provide a partial picture of transparency (OECD, 2020).

Exploring transparency research

The empirical analysis of transparency has grown steadily in recent years but is still in relative infancy as an area of research. However, what is notable from Cucciniello and colleagues' (2017) review of the literature is the variety of research methodologies and approaches used to measure or evaluate transparency. Unlike many areas of public administration or public policy, neither qualitative nor quantitative approaches have come to dominate and a small but influential strand of experimental studies has emerged. Attempts to measure transparency or the effects of transparency have focused on a wide range of areas, including computer-mediated transparency (Meijer, 2009; Grimmelikhuijsen and Welch, 2012), analysis of website content (Grimmelikhuijsen and Welch, 2012; Ferreira da Cruz et al, 2016), citizen-focused experiments (de Fine Licht, 2011, 2014; Grimmelikhuijsen and Meijer, 2014), data dissemination (Hollyer et al, 2014), public perceptions of transparency (Park and Blenkinsopp, 2011; Piotrowski et al, 2017; Porumbescu et al, 2017) and experiments featuring requests for information (Worthy et al, 2017; Grimmelikhuijsen et al, 2019). Grimmelikhuijsen and colleagues (2017) review much of this literature and argue that although non-experimental studies had provided 'valuable insights', there were some concerns regarding the nature of the research methodologies being utilised. They note that studies which identify the role of external pressures for driving transparency may be prone to 'reverse causality'; for example, stronger external pressure groups may be the product of an already transparent government, rather than a causal factor. However, a key conclusion of their review was a recognition of the 'contingency of transparency effects', and there was thus a need to explore different policies and forms of transparency in a more systematic way. Although not utilising an experimental research design, the potentially highly contingent nature of both transparency and trust provides a core rationale for the research explored in this book.

The range of studies on transparency have varied in their precise research designs: for example, some have explicitly attempted to develop objective measures of transparency whereas others have focused on subjective assessments. In terms of objective measures, Hollyer and colleagues (2014) construct a measure using 240 items drawn from the World Bank's World Development Indicators (WDI) data series, which treats transparency as a latent predictor of the reporting or non-reporting of data. Meijer and colleagues (2018: 19) reject this type of analysis, arguing that the study of transparency 'can never be reduced to simple metrics and box-ticking exercises as it requires explicit incorporation and comparison of distinct political and administrative value sets'. In contrast, they put forward an instrument aimed at engaging stakeholders in a structured but discursive debate around the performance of transparency mechanisms (see Table 2.1). They argue that systematically engaging research subjects with the value sets outlined in Table 2.1 offers 'a conceptually rich yet methodically parsimonious way of identifying areas of consensus and disagreement in the way stakeholders judge the performance of existing and new transparency mechanisms in and around government' (Meijer et al, 2018: 519). From this perspective, transparent procedures, results and policies are more likely to enhance trust in the overall political system. The presupposition that transparency produces better outcomes underpins much contemporary

Table 2.1: Assessing government transparency: synthetic propositions

Realm	Perspective	Golden mean	
Politics	Democracy	Transparency strengthens **civic competence** ◄────►	Transparency creates **inequality** between groups of citizens
	Constitutional state	Transparency strengthens **checks and balances** ◄────►	Transparency generates **risk avoidance** and **goal displacement**
	Learning	Transparency feeds **public debates** with open information ◄────►	Transparency generates **public confusion**
Administration	Economy/ efficiency	Transparency produces **policy error reduction** ◄────►	Transparency generates **administrative burdens**
	Integrity	Transparency prevents **corruption** ◄────►	Transparency inflicts upon the **individual space to think**
	Resilience	Transparency facilitates **risk management** ◄────►	Transparency **amplifies risk** (perceptions)

Source: Meijer et al. (2018: 520).

policy: the register of interests in the EU Commission and European and national parliaments, the diffusion of FOI legislation, the publication of performance data all testify to this. However, Meijer and colleagues' (2018) framework offers the potential flexibility to explore the point that the introduction of transparency-based measures may not produce better outcomes, and indeed may lead to sub-optimal or unintended outcomes.

The trust–transparency nexus

Parallel to the growth of the transparency literature identified in the previous chapter, studies exploring the link between enhanced transparency and levels of trust have become an increasingly prominent feature of the wider literature. There is a relatively small but growing literature focused on analysing the relationship between trust and transparency (Worthy, 2010, 2013; de Fine Licht, 2011, 2014; Grimmelikhuijsen, 2011, 2012; Grimmelikhuijsen and Welch, 2012; Grimmelikhuijsen et al, 2013; Mason et al, 2013; de Fine Licht et al, 2014; Grimmelikhuijsen and Meijer, 2014; Grimmelikhuijsen and Klijn, 2015; Porumbescu, 2015a, 2015b; Douglas and Meijer, 2016; Mabillard and Pasquier, 2016; Piotrowski et al, 2017; Worthy et al, 2017; Heald, 2018; Meijer et al, 2018). This literature has explored a wide range of settings but has generally tended to be citizen-focused and often centred on computer-mediated transparency. For example, Porumbescu (2015b) examines the relationship between increased exposure to computer-mediated transparency and citizen perceptions of government performance utilising an online survey in Seoul. The studies draw on a range of research designs, including experiments, but the number of comparative studies is fairly limited (Grimmelikhuijsen et al, 2013; Mabillard and Pasquier, 2016). They also tend to focus on national or local levels of government and therefore the more complex picture presented by multi-level governance is somewhat absent. The starting point for much of this research, as noted by Porumbescu (2015a: 520), is the belief put forward by its supporters that 'greater transparency fosters greater trust in government', which is 'premised upon an assumption that the more objective information citizens have about their government, the more positively they will perceive their government'. The core focus for the majority of contemporary studies has been to evaluate these starting assumptions and explore the dynamic between transparency and trust.

Transparency is seen for many as essential for democracy as citizens are asked to vote and to make informed decisions. In the theory of rationality, free access to information gives citizens the ability to make rational and conscious decisions. From this perspective, transparent procedures, results and policies are more likely to enhance trust within the overall political system. Grimmelikhuijsen (2012) illustrated in an experiment that the effect of transparency on trust is also partly due to an emotional factor related to the act of transparency as such (as opposed to a cognitive one), the fact that a government appears to be transparent is potentially in itself a factor of the perceived competence dimension of trust. For many, transparency is supposed to foster trust because it leads to a culture of openness, which generates trust, and helps people to become more familiar with government, which creates understanding. Citizens' positive assessments of government performance towards more transparency can serve as a key variable that affects public trust in government (Kim and Lee, 2012).

Much of the academic literature exploring the trust–transparency nexus can be divided, as Grimmelikhuijsen and Meijer (2014: 137–38) note, between 'transparency optimists' who emphasise the positive benefits that providing increased information to citizens will have for trust in government and 'transparency pessimists' who are sceptical of the relationship and argue it may lead to greater cynicism and distrust. For 'transparency optimists', the introduction of measures such as FOI legislation fosters a 'culture of openness' within organisations and institutions, which in turn has a positive effect on trust. Worthy and Grimmelikhuijsen (2012: 5) argue that this core assumption is built upon the argument that 'transparency helps people become more familiar with government and brings them closer together and creates understanding'. However, in stark contrast, 'transparency pessimists' not only question whether such measures have a trust-building function, but argue that in practice they may actually erode trust. Etzioni (2014), for example, argues that transparency is 'vastly oversold' due to a naïve assumption that voters are deeply engaged with government policy and performance. Similarly, O'Neill (2002: 81) argues that transparency 'mandates disclosure or dissemination, but does not require effective communication with any audience' and therefore, somewhat unsurprisingly, individuals unable to understand the information communicated are unlikely to have any reasons to trust more. However, she takes this argument one step further by noting that 'transparency certainly destroys secrecy: but it may not limit the deception and deliberate misinformation that undermine relations of trust' (O'Neill, 2002: 70). Furthermore, she goes on to argue that transparency mechanisms may actually 'encourage people to be less honest, so increasing deception and reducing reasons for trust: those who know that everything they say or write is to be made public may massage the truth' (O'Neill, 2002: 73).

Not everybody shares the optimistic stance on transparency. The dynamics of transparency are subject to misunderstandings. These relate in part to difficulties in pinning down the object of analysis. In the definitional morass briefly considered in this chapter, transparency is a challengingly plural object, depending on interpretations (positive and negative); dynamics (upwards, downwards, horizontally outwards, horizontally inwards), underlying timescapes (real time versus retrospective), objects of analysis (events versus process) and multiple levels of analysis.

The extent to which transparency has a positive effect on trust is key to understanding both whether the 'optimists' or 'pessimists' are accurate in their assumptions, and whether transparency-oriented tools and procedures can be reliably built into trust-building processes. In general, the findings of studies exploring these dynamics present at best a mixed picture. Grimmelikhuijsen and Klijn's (2015) analysis of judicial transparency and public trust, for example, concluded that there appears to be an overall positive effect on trust in judges but de Fine Licht's (2011) analysis of decision-making procedures in health care suggested that transparency may actually weaken trust. Mabillard and Pasquier (2016: 76) provide a useful assessment, noting that the absence of a clear empirical evidence base for a linear relationship between trust and transparency suggests that the reasonable interpretation may be that the 'effects of transparency on trust in government should not be overestimated', particularly when other variables are factored into the analysis. Indeed, perhaps one of the most interesting themes highlighted within the contemporary trust–transparency literature has been the identification of variables which complicate the link between the two, notably the ways in which transparency is delivered, the characteristics of individuals engaging with the information disclosed and the wider institutional setting and political culture within which these processes take place.

The starting assumptions of the positive effects of transparency, and sometimes the negative effects as well, are often framed in relatively abstract terms. Worthy and Grimmelikhuijsen (2012: 1) argue that such an approach is fundamentally flawed because the trust–transparency nexus 'does not exist in isolation' but 'is shaped by a range of external influences in the political environment and subjective factors based on the individual interacting with the mechanisms'. They provide a useful distinction between two broad categories of influences (Worthy and Grimmelikhuijsen, 2012: 6):

1. External or Macro Influences – the wider political environment in which transparency reforms take place, including the political system, media relations and pre-existing public attitudes.
2. Internal or Micro Influence – factors related to the individual use of information, including individual users' knowledge, pre-existing attitudes and predispositions towards government.

The key implication of this argument is that any analysis of the trust––transparency nexus needs to be cognisant of the potential influence of a wide range of factors and variables which mediate or shape this relationship. In other words, not only may the same transparency initiative differ in its impact from one to locality to another; the diverse individual actors within these localities, whether they are citizens or organisations, are also likely to respond differently. It is worthwhile exploring the dynamics of external/macro and internal/micro influences that have been highlighted in contemporary studies.

A variety of studies have identified factors influencing the trust–transparency nexus which may broadly be categorised within Worthy and Grimmelikhuijsen's (2012) characterisation of external and internal influences. Piotrowski and colleagues (2017: 2), for example, argue that the majority of studies evaluating the impact of transparency have focused on the availability of information rather than how that information is presented, and this misses a key part of the process because 'transparency is not achieved through a binary choice of simply disclosing information or not, but rather how information is disclosed'. They identify two potential strategies which may shape the outcome of transparency: an informational strategy centred on providing the 'facts and figures' and a transformational strategy which relates the factual information to an individual's personal experiences. Their analysis concludes that the framing of information or the 'message strategy' matters, but notably it is also interpreted differently due to the types of factors identified in 'micro influences', in this case the level of citizen engagement.

Therefore, it is almost inevitable that the trust–transparency nexus will be shaped by a combination of external/macro and internal/micro influences – which may interact as part of this process. A further illustration can be found in the question of 'how' information is conveyed, which can be as important as 'who' is delivering this information. Porumbescu (2015a), for example, notes that existing analysis suggests the information disseminated by credible civil society or professional organisations is more likely to build trust than if the same information were to be released by government organisations. At the other end of the scale, transparency measures, such as FOI legislation, can be weaponised by the media where there are pre-existing tensions (Worthy, 2013). More broadly, a range of studies identify the importance of institutional, historical and political factors which shape the nature of the relationship between trust and transparency (Grimmelikhuijsen et al, 2013; de Fine Licht, 2014; Mabillard and Pasquier, 2016). The recent COVID-19 pandemic illustrated these complex dynamics. Citing studies of various countries, Siegrist and Zingg (2013: 25) had already suggested that 'trust had a positive impact on adopting precautionary behavior during a pandemic'. This finding was backed by van der Weerd and colleagues (2011) in their study of the H1N1 flu pandemic in the Netherlands: most respondents wanted the information about infection prevention to come from the municipal health services, health-care providers and the media, rather than central government. During pandemics, most people are not in a position to independently evaluate the information about the risks and benefits associated with vaccination. Therefore, they rely on experts, especially those experts they trust, who are once removed from government. Cross-national surveys all pointed in the same direction: that health professionals were trusted far more than governments, which responded logically by associating experts with their decisions and allowing medical experts to make public policy declarations.

Building the trust–transparency matrix

The existing trust–transparency studies, as noted in the previous section, tend to focus on the national or local levels and therefore the potential role of the regional or subnational level is largely absent. Although there is recognition of the importance of contextual factors in shaping trust–transparency dynamics, in many ways they reflect the methodological nationalism that can be identified in wider comparative politics research (Jeffery and Wincott, 2010; Jeffery, 2014). Jeffery (2014: 4) notes that over the past few decades regional decision-making authorities in advanced democracies have exercised an increasingly wide range of policy responsibilities and therefore 'regions now matter much more directly to voters, parties and interest groups'. Therefore, in considering questions around the state of trust and transparency in these advanced democracies, the subnational or regional level potentially performs an increasingly important role. For example, Denters (2002) notes in his comparison of local and national levels in Netherlands, Norway and the UK that trust in local officeholders was generally higher and at times considerably higher than trust in national office-holders. Furthermore, Grimmelikhuijsen and colleagues (2013: 584) note that 'national cultural values play a significant role in how people perceive and appreciate government transparency' but that this 'may even count for subcultures within countries or between regions and needs further investigation'. Therefore, exploring the potential variations within and between states in terms of trust and transparency is a key objective for the research.

In order to carry out cross-national multi-level comparisons of trust and transparency we put forward a heuristic tool, the trust–transparency matrix (Table 2.2). Drawing on the arguments put forward by Meijer and colleagues (2018: 19), the matrix is not designed to provide a simple metric of the trust–transparency nexus or to provide a calculative tool for the formal measurement of the causal relationship between the two variables. Instead, much like Meijer and colleagues' (2018) framework outlined in the previous section, the matrix is designed to provide a heuristic device to guide the collection of data and enable the systematic comparative analysis of the cases considered within the second half of this book.

Table 2.2 is deliberately parsimonious in outlining ideal types of the trust–transparency nexus and provides the logical states of trust and transparency

Table 2.2: Trust–transparency matrix

Trust	Transparency	
	High	Low
High	Synergy	Blind faith
Low	Negligible or counterproductive effects	Dual dysfunctionality

that we might find in our cases. Again, the matrix is not designed to provide a calculative tool but to enable a comparison of the relationship between trust and transparency within and between our cases. However, in order to operationalise the matrix and explore the relationship between trust and transparency, we must understand what we are focusing on in relation to both concepts, and this takes us back to the reviews of trust and transparency outlined in Chapter 1 and this chapter respectively.

The substantive dimensions of the proposed trust–transparency matrix combine configurations and properties of trust and types of transparency. The preferred properties of trust are adapted from those articulated by of Mayer and colleagues (1995), Grimmelikhuijsen (2012) and Svare and colleagues (2020) as set out in Chapter 1:

- Perceived competence/ability: the extent to which an individual or organisation perceives an organisation, an individual or a relationship to be capable, effective, skilful and professional in a specific domain.
- Perceived benevolence: the extent to which an individual or organisation perceives an organisation, an individual or a relationship to act not only with its own interests in mind but also to align this interest with an intention to do good to other individuals, organisations or the public.
- Perceived integrity: the extent to which an individual or organisation perceives an organisation, an individual or a relationship to be sincere, to tell the truth and to honour previously established agreements.

It is important to note that these three dimensions are by no means exhaustive, but they are operationalised in our research as they capture the bedrock of trust that defines relationships – whether that be on an individual or organisational level. Taken together, they are consistent with the varied understandings of trust explored in Chapter 2, such as encapsulated interest, moralistic accounts or strategic gaming. We recognise that further dimensions could be built into this framework, for example, 'perceived competence' acts as something of a proxy for confidence, but it could be argued that dimensions such as vulnerability and risk are down-played.

In relation to transparency, we select distinct dimensions of this concept adopted in the literature. These are intended to capture both the individual and organisational levels of analysis: for example, the term 'grouping' is adopted because at times multiple individuals or organisations may be working in partnership and be the subject of transparency. These elements draw directly on Grimmelikhuijsen and Welch's (2012) refinement of Heald's (2006) identification of different subjects of transparency:

- Transparency of decision-making process: the degree of openness about the steps taken by an individual, organisation or grouping to reach a decision and the rationale behind the decision.
- Transparency of policy content: the information disclosed by an individual, organisation or grouping about policies – what the adopted measures are, how they are supposed to solve a problem, how they will be implemented, and what implications they will have for individuals, organisations and other affected groups or citizens.
- Transparency of policy outcomes or effects: the information disclosed by an individual, organisation or grouping about performance – captures the provision and timeliness of information about the effects of policies or decisions.

Once again, it is important to note that these subjects are not intended to be exhaustive, but they provide a useful reference point for our research, particularly for our analysis of the experiences and perceptions of civil society actors within our cases. Furthermore, these elements of trust and transparency may be stronger or weaker; for example, an individual or organisation may be perceived to be honest and benevolent but not necessarily competent, or an individual or organisation may be perceived as transparent in relation to the decision-making process and policy content, but not in relation to policy outcomes. However, these sets of dimensions explore the properties of trust and transparency, and in operationalising the trust–transparency matrix we have to bring these dimensions together to explore the relationship or interplay between the two.

The 'High Trust, High Transparency' ideal type outlined in the matrix refers to what might be seen as the optimal scenario characterised by high levels of both trust and transparency. The interplay between the different dimensions of trust and transparency effectively binds individuals, organisations and relationships, creating a trust–transparency synergy, a 'virtuous circle' reminiscent of Huxham and Vangen's (2005) trust-building loop identified in Chapter 1. If we explore the different subjects of transparency outlined earlier, this provides a clear picture of how high levels of trust might shape the transparency of decision-making, policy content and policy outcomes. In terms of decision-making, we might expect to find that open and deliberative decision-making processes underpin the positive perceptions of an individual, an organisation or a relationship as being competent, benevolent and honest.

Similarly, in terms of policy content, this ideal type assumes that the disclosure of policy-relevant information underpins the positive perception of an individual, organisation or relationship as competent, benevolent and honest. Finally, in terms of policy outcomes, this ideal type would characterise the provision of timely and useful information on the effects or outcomes of policies as underpinning the positive perception of an organisation, individual or relationship as competent, benevolent and honest. It is worth noting that the information may not necessarily be positive and this may have an impact on the different dimensions of trust – for example, a government which releases information relating to a failed policy or initiative in a timely and accessible way may enhance its reputation as an honest actor, but undermine perceptions of its competence. However, the expectation within this ideal type is that perceptions of competence would remain high.

The second ideal type presented in the matrix is characterised by high levels of trust but relatively low levels of transparency. We characterise this form of trust–transparency relations as 'blind faith' – despite low levels of transparency an individual or organisation has high levels of trust in individuals, organisations and relationships. Therefore, transparency (or more specifically the absence of transparency) has limited impact on levels of different forms of trust. In relation to decision-making, this ideal type would be characterised by a closed decision-making process, but an individual or organisation continuing to be perceived as being competent, benevolent and honest. In terms of policy content and policy outcomes, the absence or limited level of public information on policy measures and the failure to provide timely information about a policy's outcome or effects does not damage the positive perception of an individual or organisation as competent, benevolent and honest. An important sub-category which sits somewhere between these initial ideal types is confidential trust, whereby relationships require absolute confidentiality and are liable to be disrupted in the event of formal transparency. This highlights the discursive nature of these judgements; for example, an individual or organisation might inspire broad public trust by high levels of transparency but at times building effective, high-trust relationships may require limited transparency and a degree of confidentiality. Therefore, trust and transparency may lie in the eye of the beholder depending upon their relationship with a specific individual or organisation.

The third ideal type is characterised by a dynamic whereby high levels of transparency either cause or at least fail to address the negative perceptions of an individual or organisation as being low in competence or incompetent, uncaring and dishonest. Therefore, we characterise this essentially negative-sum ideal type as being defined by 'negligible or counterproductive effects' – rather than strengthen levels of trust, high levels of transparency actually erode or at best have minimal effects. In many senses, this reflects established lines of enquiry within academic research. Hibbing and Theiss-Morse (2001) argue that the more members of the public know about the US Congress, the less they tend to trust it. As an illustration of the potentially negative effect of transparency on trust, surveys show that public trust in government has not increased due to the introduction of FOI laws in Anglo-American democracies. As with the first and second ideal types within the matrix, we can provide outlines of how we might characterise processes of decision-making, policy content and policy outcomes. In terms of decision-making, the process may be open and deliberative but this either contributes to or fails to reverse negative perceptions of an individual or organisation as incompetent, uncaring or dishonest. For example, if individuals or organisations have high levels of distrust in relations, it is possible that continuous interaction may actually exacerbate these problems and lead to a 'spiral of distrust' (Sydow, 1998: 38). Similarly, in this third ideal type high levels of transparency in terms of policy content and outcomes either exacerbates or fails to address negative perceptions of an individual or organisation. Once again, there are discursive factors that may be at play in these dimensions: the information provided in relation to policy outcomes may be negative, for example, painting a picture of programmatic policy failure (McConnell, 2010; Bovens and t'Hart, 2016), or individuals or organisations may be suffering from information overload.

The final ideal type provides a broadly negative picture, where both trust and transparency are characterised as being at low levels, depicted in the matrix as 'dual dysfunctionality'. In terms of decision-making, this ideal type is defined by closed decision-making processes that are at least partly responsible for negative perceptions of an individual or organisation as incompetent, uncaring and dishonest. In relation to policy content and policy outcomes there is a similar picture – the absence of information on policy measures and the failure to provide timely information about the effects of policies either contributes to or fails to remedy the negative perception of individuals or organisations. In many senses, this ideal type leaves hope for the transparency optimists identified by Grimmelikhuijsen and Meijer (2014), because there is still the potential that enhanced transparency may help build trust and deliver the virtuous circle that characterises the 'synergy' ideal type. In contrast, for transparency pessimists this ideal type is also just one step away from the negative-sum setting of the 'negligible or counterproductive effects' ideal type.

Drawing on this and the last chapter's discussion of how trust and transparency have been conceptualised and analysed, the starting point for this research in terms of how the trust–transparency matrix will be applied in our cases is that perceptions of both phenomena are contingent upon what Worthy and Grimmelikhuijsen (2012: 6) characterise as 'external' (the wider political environment) and 'internal' (individual-based factors) factors. In addition, institutionalising processes of sense-making and social interaction play a key role in the interplay between interpersonal and interorganisational levels of trust (Zaheer et al, 1998). These starting assumptions are reflected in the interpretive design of the heuristic framework, which has been used to initially frame and then analyse the semi-structured interviews carried out as part of our comparative analysis. The external or macro influences within the context of our qualitative fieldwork relate to the political context of our subnational territories, notably in terms of the institutional configurations, identity mixes, and perceptions of social and cultural capital. The internal or micro influences relate to the specific experiences and perceptions of our interviewees, such as their past interactions with and predispositions towards other individuals and organisations. These internal and external influences enable a clearer understanding of the context-specific configurations that are inherent in the idea of a trust–transparency matrix, and therefore allow us to identify and recognise variations across our case studies. It is likely that a specific case may demonstrate elements from different parts of the matrix: for example, different policy areas may be more open or closed in relation to decision-making within a specific territory (de Fine Licht et al, 2014).

Conclusion

The book thus far has identified the contested and multidimensional nature of the concepts of trust and transparency. Any attempt to analyse the trust–transparency nexus needs to recognise that defining both concepts is difficult and that exploring contemporary debates, such as approaches to building trust and the potential role of transparency in these processes, unlocks greater complexity. However, the recognition of these complex dynamics, such as the interplay of interpersonal and institutional trust, or the role of external and influences on transparency, provides a useful focus for the comparative analysis developed within this book. In particular, the recognition that context matters in terms of building and retaining trust, and the relative impact of transparency, underpins the rationale for the comparative analysis operationalised in the second part of the book, and specifically the hypothesis that trust–transparency dynamics may differ as much within states as between them. Furthermore, there is a real gap in relation to trust–transparency dynamics at the subnational level. This gap is particularly problematic given the argument developed within the existing literature that both trust and transparency are deeply embedded in the wider web of social, economic and political features of society (Newton, 2007; Grimmelikhuijsen et al, 2013) and that they potentially vary between levels of governance (Worthy and Grimmelikhuijsen, 2012). In the second part of the book, we turn to our detailed case studies of trust and transparency in France, Germany and the UK.

3

Comparing cases

The research project that provides the source for this book is first and foremost a comparative one. According to Swanson (1971: 145), 'thinking without comparison is unthinkable. And, in the absence of comparison, so is all scientific thought and scientific research'. Ragin (1987: 6) contends that comparison allows identification of the similarities and differences between political phenomena. Furthermore, 'this knowledge provides the key to understanding, explaining, and interpreting diverse historical outcomes and processes and their significance for current institutional arrangements'. The next three chapters exploring our cases are designed to fulfil the aims identified by Ragin, and the final chapter brings together our findings. This chapter provides the foundations for this comparative analysis. The first section will position the approach adopted in the second half of the book within the context of comparative social research. The second section will begin to introduce our three cases, providing an overview of their wider context. The final section features introductions to the multi-level government contexts within each of the three country cases and specifically the six territorial cases that are the primary focus of our research.

Our comparative approach

The debates around the strengths and weaknesses of the variety of types and forms of comparative analysis are well rehearsed in the academic literature. Peters (2013: 6), for example, argues that despite contrasting approaches to comparative politics that can be found within the academic literature, they all 'confront a fundamental trade-off between the respective virtues of complexity and generalization'. On the one hand, the single case study enables the exploration of the context and complexities of a single political system but provides limited scope for generalisation. On the other hand, a statistical modelling approach to comparison facilitates robust generalisation, but provides less nuance around the specific political systems encompassed in the study. Ragin (1987) characterises two primary methodological orientations: variables-based and case-based strategies. The former tends to characterise quantitative research, investigating many cases – or adopting a large-N approach – with few variables. In contrast, the latter is associated with qualitative research, focusing on a limited number of cases but with a large number of variables. Peters (2013: 6) notes that these types of approaches tend to be characterised by 'thick description' that involves a sophisticated 'understanding of the social, cultural and economic context of politics'. Our position within this book is not that either of these approaches is superior, but that the choice in terms of different approaches to comparative research is dependent upon the research questions and perhaps more frequently the researcher's epistemological, ontological and methodological assumptions.

In our field of inquiry, there is an extensive use of survey techniques and quantitative analyses. Rich datasets, such as the European Social Survey, provide a mass of quantitative data on comparative understandings of trust, particularly trust in politicians and levels of government. The representative national-level survey is valuable insofar as it allows significant variations to be measured according to socio-demographic data, territory, ideology and party. It provides initial answers to probing questions such as: is there a propensity to trust one level of government over another? Are levels of government trusted (or mistrusted) according to different criteria, whether by level or by cross-sectional group? In a context of generalised mistrust towards politics and politicians, what implications might be drawn for democratic governance? Responses to these questions need to go beyond the simple charting of correlations between independent and dependent variables. However valuable they are, however, such approaches are limited to establishing general associations. More focused qualitative studies are required to answer questions that go beyond purely statistical associations, especially in the field of trust. Although some of the quantitative data on trust addresses the appropriate level of governance, there is relatively little data on transparency and both issues are rarely captured via interactions within the policy community or local civil society. As noted in the previous chapter, the trust–transparency matrix provides a heuristic device to guide the collection of qualitative data and enable the systematic comparative analysis of our cases.

Our study follows the comparative case study method. Our investigation begins with the simple question: what is the case? – the starting question for Ragin and Becker (1992). This apparently simple question has many possible answers. Cases can be theoretical or empirical, just as they can be understood strictly in terms of their own dynamics (in the constructivist tradition) or more generally for their capacity to rise up in general, whereby the single case is a tool for theorisation (the theoretical case study). Furthermore, to give some idea of the polysemy of the case study method, consider the following definitions that combine temporal, spatial and process-based dimensions. Framing the case in temporal terms, Bennett and George (2005: 5) define a case abstractly as 'an aspect of a historical episode', inviting the diachronic comparison across time and within the context of the single case study. Landman (2000), by contrast, frames cases in terms of space, taking the country as a single unit, an approach that is contested by many scholars, such as Dogan and Pelassy (1990), for whom it is important to 'segment before comparing', or drill down to identify variables below the level of the nation-state (for example, social class) or common processes (for example, political socialisation). In a variation, Collier (1993: 112) advocates 'within-case comparison', where two or more aspects of a specific case are compared, usually across time. Within-case comparison across time offers one use, especially with the rising sophistication of process tracing as a research method. Therefore, a conceptual imprecision remains as to whether the phenomenon observed constitutes one case, whether there is 'within-case comparison' or whether there are different cases. We agree with Nohlen (1994) that a case is constituted by the object of scientific investigation. It can concern a country, a political system, an institution, an organisation, a particular process, an event, a crisis, a war or a particular problem in a particular context.

A case study delivers precise knowledge about a case. It eschews generalisation but does gain breadth and depth of understanding, as Sartori (1994: 24) notes. Many researchers stress the problem of the complexity of a phenomenon that a detailed, qualitative case study necessitates. In the words of Collier and colleagues (2004: 248), such cases require 'thick analysis' or 'thick description'. We seek out a middle position; the ideal types outlined within the trust–transparency matrix help us elucidate similarities and differences in explanation and understanding of the trust–transparency nexus. Trust and transparency (either alone, or as linked phenomena) are best understood when framed in a broader (environmental, cognitive and relational) comparative context. Rather than a purely mechanical exercise, whereby causal mechanisms affect social or political processes through which an independent variable exerts a causal effect on another dependent variable, reasoning utilising ideal types allows researchers to identify regularities throughout the course of a research project. The approach is an abductive one (Keating and Della Porta, 2010); mechanisms emerge inductively, but can be studied using inference and deduction. It is the most promising angle for our study, which drills down into case studies, in a comparative context, with a view to making contingent generalisations.

Introducing our cases

The context for our case studies lies in the common process of state reconfiguration that has been identified as part of a European-wide trend, which, it is argued, has led to the redistribution of authority upwards to supranational organisations, most notably the EU, and downwards to

Table 3.1: Types of multi-level governance

Type I	Type II
General-purpose jurisdictions	Task-specific jurisdictions
Non-intersecting memberships	Intersecting memberships
Jurisdictions at a limited number of levels	No limit to the number of jurisdictional levels
System-wide architecture	Flexible design

Source: Hooghe and Marks (2003: 236).

regional and subnational territories (Rodriguez-Pose and Gill, 2003). This phenomena has been captured most prominently by the concept of multi-level governance, which emerged in the early 1990s in response to structural policy in the EU (Marks, 1992, 1993; Hooghe, 1996). The pressures from below have led to increased interest in territorial politics and governance: for example, Piattoni (2010: 9) notes that regardless of the specific causes of these pressures (regionalism or regionalisation), 'throughout Europe we witness a trend towards the devolution of certain functions to intermediate levels of government (or administration) that lie between the centre (the national government) and the periphery (municipal governments)'. Due to the practical limits of our research, the analysis in this book is focused on the subnational level and the key additional element of multi-level governance, the horizontal dimension. This refers to the blurring of the boundaries between state and society, or, as Bache and Flinders (2004: 3) describe it, the 'growing interdependence between governments and non–governmental actors at various territorial levels'. As noted in the Introduction, it is challenging to capture the multi-level dimension as it feeds into debates over trust and transparency, but the governance dimension is perhaps more accessible via our cases – if no less complex.

The concept of MLG has evolved in recent years, notably through Hooghe and Marks' (2001, 2003) influential distinction between Type I and Type II forms of MLG (see Table 3.1). They characterise citizens in Type I MLG as being located in 'a Russian Doll set of nested (general-purpose) jurisdictions, where there is one and only one relevant jurisdiction at any particular territorial scale' and which are usually 'stable for periods of several decades or more, though the allocation of policy competencies across jurisdictional levels is flexible'. In contrast, Type II MLG is fragmented into 'functionally specific pieces' which vary considerably in number and scale, and 'come and go as demands for governance change' (Hooghe and Marks, 2003: 236). The limits of our research mean that we are unable to explore the trust–transparency nexus at all levels described by Hooghe and Marks; for example, the national and international levels are largely beyond the scope of our study. However, we are able to explore what they describe as the regional, meso and local levels. Furthermore, as noted in the Introduction, our cases appear to provide varying examples of Type I and Type II MLG. The German federal system appears to fit most neatly into the Type I description, while the French and UK models of territorial governance provide more complex and variable pictures. Therefore, the different MLG settings that we find in our three countries provide one of the 'external' factors discussed at the end of Chapter 2, which need to be factored into our analysis of the trust–transparency nexus.

Before exploring the specific multi-level contexts of our three country-level cases, and the six subnational cases within them, it is useful to provide a broad overview of the distinctive models of territorial governance that can be identified across our cases. In order to compare our three cases, we are going to utilise the Regional Authority Index (RAI) originally developed by Hooghe and colleagues (2010) but which has since been updated and revised (Hooghe et al, 2016; Shair-Rosenfield et al, 2021). The RAI provides a useful framework for comparing the three models of subnational, intermediate or regional tiers of governance that we find in France, Germany and the UK. It draws on the study of federalism to disaggregate regional authority into the domains of self-rule and shared rule (Riker, 1964; Elazar, 1987; Keating, 1998, 2001; Lane and Ersson, 1999). Hooghe and colleagues (2016: 23) define self-rule as 'the authority that a subnational government exercises in its own territory' and shared rule as 'the authority that a subnational government co-exercises in the country as a whole'. The self-rule domain is made up of five dimensions (Hooghe et al, 2016: 25):

1. Institutional depth – 'the extent to which a regional government can make autonomous policy decisions'.
2. Policy scope – 'the breadth of regional self-rule over policing, over its own institutional set-up, over local governments within its jurisdiction, whether a regional government has residual powers, and whether its competences extend to economic policy, cultural–educational policy, welfare policy, immigration, or citizenship'.
3. Fiscal autonomy – 'a regional government's authority to set the base and rate of minor and major taxes in its jurisdiction'.
4. Borrowing autonomy – 'the centrally imposed restrictions on the capacity of a regional government to independently contract loans on domestic or international financial markets'.
5. Representation – 'whether a regional government has a regionally elected legislature; whether that legislature is directly or indirectly elected; and whether the region's executive is appointed by the central government, dual or autonomously elected'.

The shared-rule domain is also made up of five dimensions (Hooghe et al, 2016: 25):

1. Law-making – 'the role of regions in structuring representation at the national level; whether regions have majority or minority representation there; and the legislative scope of the second chamber'.
2. Executive control – 'whether regional governments have routine meetings with the central government and whether these are advisory or have veto power'.
3. Fiscal control – 'the role of regions in negotiating or exerting a veto over the territorial allocation of national tax revenues'.
4. Borrowing control – 'whether regional governments have no role, an advisory role, or a veto over the rules that permit borrowing'.
5. Constitutional reform – 'the authority of a regional government to propose, postpone, or block changes in the rules of the game'.

Each of these dimensions is measured to provide self-rule and shared-rule scores which combine for an overall RAI score. The self-rule (see Table 3.2), shared-rule (see Table 3.3) and overall RAI scores (see Figure 3.1) for our three country cases highlight the varied territorial models that provide the context for our analysis of the trust–transparency nexus at the subnational level. The French case provides a relatively clear example of a unitary state, with the Régions having a degree of self-rule across all dimensions, but shared rule is non-existent. This pattern is replicated at the lower levels of governance in the French case identified in the next section. The self-rule scores for Départements (9), Métropoles (8) and Communautés urbaines (8) are all relatively strong but the shared-rule domain remains absent (Hooghe et al, 2016). The German case is notable for the strength of the Länder in both the self-rule and shared-rule domains. This perhaps should not be a great surprise given the extensive competences that were provided for Länder in the 1949 Basic Law of the German Federal Republic and the 2006 reforms which broadened their legislative powers (Swenden, 2006; Behnke and Benz, 2008). Finally, the case of the UK provides a fragmented picture which has evolved considerably over the past 20 years. In England, the mayoral combined authorities that have emerged in recent years, which vary considerably in scope (as explored later), have less authority than the various forms of local government and the Greater London Authority, but significantly more than the regional institutions that were phased out at the beginning of the Coalition Government elected in May 2010. In contrast, Wales has gone on its own journey since the introduction of devolution in 1999, reflected in the initial self-rule score of 8.0 in 1999 and its increase to 13.0 in 2018, as highlighted in Table 3.2. The specific territorial models that have emerged across our three cases are explored in more detail in the next section.

Table 3.2: Regional Authority Index: self-rule dimensions

	Institutional depth	Policy scope	Fiscal autonomy	Borrowing autonomy	Representation	Self-rule
France: Régions	2.0	2.0	1.0	2.0	3.0	10.0
Germany: Länder	3.0	3.0	2.0	3.0	4.0	15.0
UK: mayoral combined authorities	2.0	1.0	1.0	1.0	3.0	8.0
UK: Wales	3.0	3.0	2.0	1.0	4.0	13.0

Source: Hooghe et al (2021).

Table 3.3: Regional Authority Index: shared-rule dimensions

	Law-making	Executive control	Fiscal control	Borrowing control	Constitutional reform	Shared rule
France: Régions	0	0.0	0.0	0.0	0.0	0.0
Germany: Länder	2	2.0	2.0	2.0	4.0	12.0
UK: mayoral combined authorities	0	0.0	0.0	0.0	0.0	0.0
UK: Wales	1.5	1.0	0.0	0.0	4.0	6.5

Source: Hooghe et al (2021).

The multi-level context of our case studies: France, Germany and the UK

United Kingdom: North West England and Wales

The introduction of devolution by the Labour Government in 1999 led to a fundamental recasting or reconfiguring of territorial administration within the UK. The creation of devolved institutions in Scotland, Wales and Northern Ireland, the introduction of an elected mayor in London and the initial regional agenda pursued in England challenged traditional conceptions of the UK as a highly centralised, unitary state. However, as Jeffery (2007: 92–93) notes, the UK 'was never the unitary state of textbook myth' and therefore devolution can perhaps best be viewed as the process of 'grafting

Figure 3.1: Regional Authority Index: combined scores

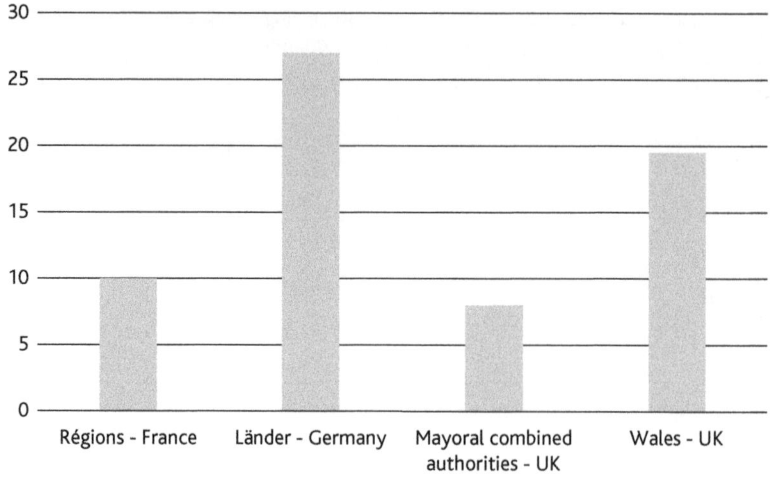

Source: Updated RAI scores, https://garymarks.web.unc.edu/data/regional-authority/

democratic processes' onto existing territorial administrative arrangements. In addition, Westminster governments since 1999 have adopted a piecemeal approach to the development of the devolution settlement, characterised by Ron Davies, the architect of devolution in Wales, as a 'process not an event' (Davies, 1999). The absence of what Jeffery (2009: 291) describes as a 'normative statement of purpose for the post-devolution state' has had a range of effects, including the haphazard further transfer of powers to the devolved administrations, a permissive approach to policy divergence, the absence of England from the devolution settlement and the failure to introduce effective arrangements for intergovernmental interaction, the latter starkly exposed by the Brexit process (Rawlings, 2017; McAngus et al, 2019; McEwan, 2020; McEwan et al, 2020).

The evolving nature of the devolution settlement within Wales has illustrated the wider approach to devolution adopted within the UK. The latest stage in the incremental development of devolution, the Wales Act 2017, shifted the devolved settlement to a 'reserved powers' model of devolution whereby the National Assembly for Wales, renamed Senedd Cymru in May 2020, can legislate on any matter that is not expressly 'reserved' to the UK Parliament at Westminster. This latest step followed previous key staging points, notably the 'Yes' vote in the referendum on the Assembly's law-making powers on 3 March 2011 (Stafford, 2011; Wyn Jones and Scully, 2012). The new legislation was intended to resolve the grey areas or 'silent subjects' in the previous devolved settlement where it was unclear whether the UK Parliament or the then National Assembly for Wales had competence. However, the extent to which the new legislation provided a stable settlement has been questioned. For example, a joint report published by the Wales Governance Centre and the Constitution Unit (2016) noted that many of the reserved matters identified in the legislation lacked a 'principled justification' and created a highly complex settlement. Furthermore, as Evans (2020) notes, calls for the further devolution of powers have not abated and the characterisation of Welsh devolution as a process continues to resonate.

Over the first two decades of devolution a key question for the Welsh Government and the wider policy community was whether the governance structures within Wales provided a sustainable and effective way to deliver public services (Cole and Stafford, 2015). Prior to devolution in 1996, the local government system was reformed, replacing a two-tier system of 8 county councils and 37 district councils with a single tier of 22 unitary local authorities (Thomas, 1994; Pemberton, 2000). Cole and Stafford (2015) note that these structures led to problems of scale and administrative duplication. Since 1999 the Welsh Government has explored a variety of potential solutions to these problems, from encouraging collaboration at the regional or meso level and the sharing of resources by local authorities to wholesale reorganisation. For example, in April 2013 the then First Minister for Wales, Carwyn Jones, established the Commission on Public Service Governance Delivery (Williams Commission) to explore potential options for reform. The Commission's (2014: 90) proposals were designed to 'ensure coherence and representativeness while reducing the risks of small scale and creating local authorities that are more efficient and resilient'. The Commission put forward four revised local government structures, but the high opportunity costs of wholesale reform, opposition within the Labour Party and the political capital required to drive through reorganisation meant that ultimately the proposed reforms failed. Therefore, the Welsh Government has returned to the option of collaboration as the mechanism to address the sub-optimal governance structures via the creation of corporate joint committees proposed in the Local Government and Elections (Wales) Bill, albeit delayed by the COVID-19 pandemic.

A coherent plan for the territorial governance of England has remained the missing piece of the devolution jigsaw in the UK since the late 1990s. Mycock (2016: 541) characterises the attempts to address this deficit as 'largely unplanned, piecemeal and pragmatic' and adopting an 'open-ended process that lacks strategic clarity in terms of the purpose, procedure or extent of the renegotiation of powers within England'. While one might argue that this description reflects the approaches adopted by successive UK Governments to devolution more generally, the process in England has been marked by 'a fudge of partial solutions and incoherent arrangements' since the late 1990s (Raikes, 2020: 7). In parallel to the introduction of devolution elsewhere in the UK, the

Labour Government under Blair and Brown pursued a reform agenda centred on newly established Regional Development Agencies (RDAs), alongside enhanced Government Offices for the Regions, and indirectly elected 'regional chambers' made up of local government leaders and key stakeholders. The failed 2004 referendum in the North East on elected regional government and an increased focus on city-regions and functional economic areas meant that by the tail end of the Labour administration the region as a spatial imaginary faded from the policy agenda (Ayres and Stafford, 2009; Ward et al, 2015).

Following the 2010 election, the Coalition Government, and then successive Conservative Governments, swept away the final elements of the regional agenda and replaced it with a rhetoric of localism, partly delivered through a patchwork of business-led Local Enterprise Partnerships (LEPs) and a small number of devolution deals creating combined authorities and 'city-region' mayors (Fenwick, 2015; Copus et al, 2017; Ayres et al, 2018; Johnston and Fenwick 2020). Sandford (2020b) notes that these devolution deals were negotiated in private between central government and local authority leaders. They effectively represented a trade-off for local authority leaders: in order to access what the then Chancellor, George Osbourne, characterised as a 'serious devolution of powers and budgets', local authorities were required to engage with local governance reforms via the introduction of combined authorities and an elected mayor (HM Treasury, 2014). Randall and Casebourne (2016: 6) argue that this initiative 'signalled the recognition by central government that meaningful devolution requires subnational structures that exist at an appropriate scale to take on tasks currently performed by Whitehall, and that these would likely require new forms of visible, accountable leadership'. Once these deals were agreed and published, they needed to be approved or ratified by all of the constituent authorities involved in the deal, and in several instances this led to the rejection of the proposals, effectively returning the plans back to square one.

The latter process has been subject to widespread criticism, including that it is fragmented and inconsistent, fundamentally elite-driven, limited in terms of the scope of power and level of funding devolved. From this perspective, rather than delivering the rhetoric of 'localism', the approach is much more about centralisation (Martin et al, 2013; Lyall et al, 2015; Pike et al, 2015; Etherington and Jones, 2016; Mycock, 2016; Wall and Bessa Vilela, 2016; Hambleton, 2017; Leach et al, 2018; Shutt and Liddle, 2019). Indeed, Blunkett and colleagues (2016) and Sandford (2017, 2020a, 2020b) question whether 'devolution' is the correct language to characterise this process. The former argue that devolution and decentralisation are inappropriate to describe the reform agenda, and instead characterise the new arrangements as 'a new partnership between central and local government (with power still firmly vested in the former, not the latter)' (Blunkett et al, 2016: 558). Sandford

Table 3.4: Types of local and subnational authorities in England

Two-tier local authorities	
County councils	24
District councils	181
Single-tier local authorities	
Unitary authorities	58
Metropolitan districts	36
London boroughs	32
City of London	1
Isles of Scilly	1
Subnational authorities	
Combined authorities	10
Greater London Authority	1
Total	344

Source: Department for Levelling Up, Housing and Communities and Ministry of Housing, Communities & Local Government (2021) 'Local government structure and elections' GOV.UK, [online] Available from: https://www.gov.uk/guidance/local-government-structure-and-elections [Accessed 09 December 2021].

(2020a: 41) argues that focusing on the language of 'devolution' risks painting the reforms as 'insubstantial or a deception'. Rather it is best to see English devolution deals 'not as developments in territorial governance, but as a series of contract-style agreements between central government and local public bodies, to pursue agreed outcomes in discrete policy areas where a common interest can be identified' (Sandford, 2017: 64). However, it is important to situate the combined authorities and city–region or metro mayors within the wider patchwork quilt of English governance arrangements (Townsend, 2019).

The combined authorities and elected city-region mayors introduced by the recent devolution deals have been implemented alongside differentiated local government structures, with much of England retaining a two-tier structure with functions divided between county and district councils (Fenwick, 2015) (see Table 3.4). The combined authorities (see Table 3.5) have emerged from a top–down process driven by the centre and characterised by a 'template-style, cut and paste approach' rather than the bespoke devolution promised by ministers (Wall and Bessa Vilela, 2016: 664). However, Sandford (2020b: 10) notes that although there is something of a 'menu' for the devolution deals, each deal also contains 'a few unique elements or "specials" (often consisting of commitments to explore future policy options)'. The Greater Manchester City Region, for example, is frequently portrayed as the 'trailblazer' in the devolution process, partly based on the history of collaboration between its constituent

Table 3.5: Devolution deals

Combined authority	Devolution deal agreed
Greater Manchester	3 November 2014 27 February 2015 8 July 2015 25 November 2015 16 March 2016
Sheffield City Region	5 October 2015 12 December 2014
West Yorkshire	18 March 2015 13 March 2020
Cornwall	27 July 2015
North East North of Tyne	23 October 2015 (rejected) 24 November 2017
Tees Valley	23 October 2015
West Midlands	17 November 2015 23 November 2017
Liverpool City Region	17 November 2015 16 March 2016
Cambridgeshire/ Peterborough	20 June 2016
Norfolk/Suffolk	20 June 2016 (rejected) (East Anglia: 16 March 2016)
West of England	16 March 2016
Greater Lincolnshire	16 March 2016 (rejected)

Source: Sandford (2020b).

authorities (Deas, 2014; Kenealy, 2016). This portrayal was further enhanced in February 2015 with the devolution of control of health and social care spending to the newly created Greater Manchester Health and Social Care Partnership (GMHSCP), which would operate alongside the Greater Manchester Combined Authority (Checkland et al, 2015; Walshe et al, 2016). Devolution deals for other parts of England have either struggled to gain agreement from constituent local authorities or been rejected by the UK Government. For example, the original One Yorkshire proposal in February 2019 was rejected because it would 'involve significant departures from the type of devolution deals that we have successfully put in place elsewhere in terms of geography, governance and purpose' (Yorkshire Post, 2019). However, out of the ashes of the failed One Yorkshire bid, a revised West Yorkshire proposal was agreed in March 2020 and Tracy Brabin was elected the first Mayor of West Yorkshire in May 2021 (Sandford, 2020b). Therefore, much like Wales, the journey of English devolution shows no sign of stopping, albeit without a clear destination.

Table 3.6: The administrative system of Germany

	Federal level (Bund)	
	Federal states (Länder)	
Area states (Flaechenlaender)		City states (Stadtstaaten: Hamburg, Berlin, Bremen)
(Rhineland Palatine, Bavaria, Baden-Wuerttemberg, Lower Saxony, Saxony, North Rhine-Westphalia, Brandenburg, Mecklenburg-Pomerania, Thuringia, Hesse, Schleswig-Holstein, Saarland, Saxony-Anhalt)		
Governmental districts (Regierungsbezirke)		
Rural districts (Landkreise)		Urban district (Kreisfreie Städte)
Collective municipalities (Gemeindeverbände)	Municipalities (Gemeinden)	
Municipalities (Gemeinden)		

Source: Author's elaboration.

Germany: Hesse and Saxony-Anhalt

Germany has a federal system of government, the main structure of which is presented in Table 3.6. The German case is one of joint decision-making between governments at the federal level, the Bund, and the regional level, the Länder: both the Bund and Länder levels influence the lives of ordinary German citizens. Unlike in strict dual federal countries, such as the United States (where federal and state government inhabit separate policy worlds), the traditional German model was one of overlapping responsibilities, with the federal government taking on an increasingly important role in all areas. Since the federal level entered into existence in 1949, competence and power has slowly moved to the federal level so that a creeping centralisation took place in the period from 1949 until 2006.

According to the Basic Law, it lies in the competence of the Länder to execute federal laws. Indeed, the Länder are constitutionally tasked to implement federal laws appropriately (Basic Law Article 84). There are also provisions for sharing competences between the federal level and the Länder within the so-called concurrent legislation, embodied in Article 72 Paragraph 1, 2, 4, and Article 74. In these articles, the federal government has predominance in the fields of penal law, coastal affairs, air pollution, noise, animal- and plant protection, education funding, admission to medical sector jobs, association law and labour law. But in Article 72 Paragraph 3 there is also provision for concurrent legislation with a predominance of the Länder, meaning that Länder may diverge from the legal text as proposed by the federal government. This exists, for example, in the issues of hunting, water, high school access, nature, and territory management.

Not all legislation is shared between the federal level and Länder, however. The federal level has its exclusive competences in Article 71 and 73 concerning external relations, defence, currency law, border control, citizenship, terrorism, atomic energy, gun control, air traffic and customs. As with the federal level, the Länder also have their exclusive competences, such as in Article 70 in the issues of education, culture, police, broadcasting and municipalities.

The German federal model is best described as a system of separate institutions sharing powers. Germany's political system represents a near-classical example of a system of MLG, whereby competences are split up between the federal level and Länder by the Basic Law, and policy preferences are 'uploaded' to the European level. The German model is one of multi-level policy-making, linking regional, national and European intergovernmental negotiations. The EU process known as the 'European Semester', for example, resembles the budget coordination model established with the 2009 reform of federalism in Germany. Though this EU dimension lies largely beyond the limits of this study, dynamics are nested in a broader pattern of multi-level governance.

The German federal model is tied into concepts of interdependence and intergovernmental coordination between the federal and Länder levels. In budget policy, for example, coordination is promoted by instruments of budgetary control that the federal and federated states must respect. While the Länder governments autonomously decide on spending public funds and are responsible for financing most public investments and service delivery, they depend largely on revenues from joint taxes (income tax, corporation tax, value added tax) determined by federal law and allocated between the federal and Länder levels and among individual Länder governments according to different formulae. Moreover, the federal constitution constrains Länder budget autonomy by limiting public debts, which should not exceed the amount of planned investments. When this rule was introduced in 1969, it was deemed to allow for a cyclical and anti-cyclical policy as a means to balance economic development according to Keynesian theory. The 2009 constitutional amendment established a so-called 'debt brake', a new rule limiting public borrowing by all levels of government, including the Länder. Formulated prior to the COVID-19 pandemic, this constitutional rule requires that the federal government by 2016 and the Länder governments by 2020 had to achieve virtually balanced budgets (their debt not exceeding

0.35% of gross national product – GNP). All Länder governments committed themselves to changing their own rules of budgeting in order to comply with the new paradigm of fiscal policy.

A further distinctive feature relates to the role of the second chamber, the Bundesrat, made up of representatives from the 16 Länder and which is much more powerful than the second chambers in the UK or France. Therefore, Länder governments have a say (consent or objection) within the Bundesrat about all legislation, though the Bundestag may override the objection of the Bundesrat. Legal experts determine if the law is a consent or objection law. In general, if a law touches Länder competences (powers), for example the case for public administration, then it is considered as a consent law, which signifies that the Bundesrat's consent is needed before the law enters into force. Hence, the Bundesrat can reject both kinds of law, but the rejection can be overridden by the Bundestag in the case of an objection law. If there are diverging standpoints between Bundestag and Bundesrat, a reconciliation committee (which consists of members from the Bundestag and Bundesrat and is not public) hammers out compromises (Lehnert et al, 2008).

Since 2006, there have been moves to strengthen the Länder. The 2006 Federal Reform provided the most systematic attempt to rearrange the competencies of the federal and state governments (see, for example, Scharpf, 2005; Gunlicks, 2007; Benz, 2008; Schneider, 2013; Stecker, 2016). Since the federal reform of 2006, there is supposed to have been a clearer demarcation of the responsibilities of the Bund and Länder governments. In the terms of our project, the federal reform of 2006 was intended to introduce greater transparency between levels and enhance the sense of political accountability of parties (and institutions). However, tensions exist within the German federal model. Since 2007, economic crisis has challenged the solidarity basis of fiscal equalisation and produced stand-alone strategies from stronger regions (Braun and Trein, 2014). If so-called cooperative models of federalism produced the stasis of the joint decision trap (Scharpf, 1988), the model of competitive federalism creates its own increasing tensions and incentives for stand-alone strategies from stronger regions (Benz, 2007; Benz and Heinz, 2017). Competition between regions has been diagnosed as one of the features of a more competitive model of federalism driven by competition for scarce resources and economic regionalism.

France: Bretagne, and Auvergne and Rhône-Alpes

France has a rich tapestry of multi-level government. Various subnational authorities have overlapping territorial jurisdictions and loosely defined spheres of competence. There are as many as six layers of public administration between the French citizen and Europe (commune, intercommunal structure, département, region, national government and EU). When formally introduced in 1982, decentralisation was declared to be the 'grand affair' of the first Mitterrand presidency. Ever since then, decentralisation in France has been pulled in somewhat different directions by the instruments of central steering, by processes of local and regional capacity-building and a very imperfect process of territorial differentiation and identity construction. Adapting a phrase used to refer to Welsh devolution, decentralisation is a process, not an event – but a process with no agreed end point or starting analysis. It has been the object of many political and institutional battles over recent decades. The main division is that between the traditionalists (*anciens*) and the modernists (*modernes*); the former favouring the territorial status quo (centred on preserving the rights of the 35,000 or so communes and 101 départements), while the latter support the alternative pole represented by the intercommunal authorities (Etablissements publics de coopération intercommunale – EPCI) and the regions.

Borrowing a metaphor from the federalism literature, as noted previously, the French model of multi-level government is more akin to a marble cake (random and fruity), rather than a well-ordered layer cake, with neatly distributed competencies between levels (Entwistle et al, 2014). However, the French case is constructed on various temporally distinct layers: the historic foundations of a Napoleonic state (resting on the underlying logic of the communes, the départements and a strong central administration, which deconcentrated its own organisation from the 1960s); the move towards regionalisation from the 1950s; the more recent development of the metropolitan councils (métropoles) and new forms of urban governance. There is no formal hierarchy between levels of local and regional authority (see Table 3.7). Since 2016, there have been 13 mainland regions (including Corsica), but they have lacked regulatory or law-making authority or an effective means of control over the other levels. The EU dimension adds additional complexity: territorially, as there has been a gradual shift from a regional narrative of strategic Europeanisation (whereby cities and regions use Europe to further their own ambitions and visions) to a practice of normative Europeanisation (whereby local and regional authorities are forced to adapt to a stronger EU-driven convergence) (Carter and Pasquier, 2010; Cole et al, 2015); politically, with the rise of Eurosceptic forces and discourses in mainstream French politics, from Melenchon to Le Pen, barely occulted by Macron's election as president in 2017; and functionally, as EU integration continues to challenge some important underpinnings of the French model of politics and policy.

French local authorities are general-purpose local authorities, whose management draws on two legal doctrines in particular: the free administration of local authorities, and the general administrative competency (Marcou, 2011; Steckel-Assouère, 2015). The first principle prevents any one local authority from claiming a hierarchy over any other. Second, the general

Table 3.7: France's local and regional authorities

Type	Number	Functions
Communes	34,968	Varying services, including planning permission, building permits, building and maintenance of primary schools, waste disposal, some welfare services
Tax-raising intercommunal corporations (EPCI). Includes: métropoles, urban communities; city-wide communities and communities of communes	1,254	Permanent organisations in charge of intercommunal services such as firefighting, waste disposal, transport, economic development, some housing, structure plans
Departmental councils	101	Social affairs, some secondary education (*collèges*), road building and maintenance
Regional councils (mainland France, Corsica and overseas)	18	Economic development, transport, infrastructure, state–region plans, some secondary education (*lycées*), training
Special statute authorities	5	The Corsican territorial authority has enhanced regulatory powers. The Lyon metropole exercises the functions of the Rhône department on its territory. Martinique and Guyane have special statutes as does the department of Mayotte

Source: *Les Chiffres-clés des collectivités locales*, Paris: Interior Ministry, www.collectivites-locales.gouv.fr/collectivites-locales-chiffres-2020

administrative competency allows local authorities (communes, départements and regions until 2015) to develop policies in fields they deem to further the interest of their constituents. Although the 1982 decentralisation laws also referred to the principle of the blocs de compétences, in practice communes, intercommunal public corporations and départements have developed policies across a broad array of sectors (Pasquier, 2014). The survival of almost 35,000 communes retains the fiction of local autonomy, but most communal functions have long been mutualised and in practice their functions are routinely administered by the intercommunal public corporations (EPCI) that now cover the entire French territory (Desage and Guéranger, 2011). The 101 départements have jealously repeated their claim to act as general-purpose local authorities, but in practice they have become delivery arms of the French welfare state, especially since the transfer of major social service delivery responsibilities in 2003–4. The 2015 NOTRE law rescinded their general administrative competency. While also recognised as having general purpose competency until 2015, the regions have been more interested in developing their capacity in areas of strategic management and planning (transport, economic development, education, research and innovation).

Even after the transfers of school ancillary staff in 2004, the regions remained lightweight, rather than heavy service delivery organisations.

The mechanics of subnational government thus described are pertinent since they are part of the problem of political mistrust, and poor administrative and organisational transparency. French citizens celebrate proximity (their support for municipal government and the figure of the local mayor), but express frustration at the weak political accountability and administrative transparency that characterise French central–local relations. These themes are developed in Chapter 6.

Conclusion

This chapter has provided an overview of both the logic that underpins the comparative research design adopted in our research and an introduction to our cases. The contrasting multi-level governance settings that characterise our three country case studies and the potential contrasts at the subnational level, at least in the UK, provides an indication of the specific 'external' factors that are likely to shape the trust–transparency nexus in our cases. A focus on the dimensions of multi-level governance or an analysis of the distribution of authority via a tool like the Regional Authority Index tells us much about the governance setting. However, this chapter has not explored other external factors or macro influences related to the wider political environment that we may expect to see shape trust and transparency. For example, the shape and role of the media, identity mixes, and perceptions of social and cultural capital that may characterise our subnational cases are missing from the discussion. As noted in the first section of this chapter and in Chapter 2's introduction of the trust–transparency matrix, these more discursive types of external factors and the internal factors or micro influences can only be identified by the fine-grained analysis of our case studies, and it is to this analysis that our book now turns.

4

UK: North West England and Wales

One of the central themes of Boris Johnson's speech on the morning of 13 December 2019, following his party's landslide election victory, was trust, and specifically the trust placed in his government by voters who had previously never voted for the Conservative Party. Despite Brexit's almost all-encompassing domination of the political agenda in recent years, the decline of political trust in the UK can be characterised as representing a longer-term phenomenon (Whiteley et al, 2016). It has been portrayed by the BBC's political editor, Laura Kuenssberg, as the latest in a long line of events over the past 20 years that have 'shattered' public trust in politics, from the Iraq War in 2003 to the high-profile MPs' expenses scandal in 2009 via the financial crisis in 2007–8 (Kuenssberg, 2020). Furthermore, Brexit has been supplanted from the political agenda – even if only temporarily – by the COVID-19 pandemic, and once again the narrative around the decline of trust has come to the fore. Although Jennings (2020) noted an initial 'rally-round-the-flag' effect of the crisis, trust has steadily been eroded. The question of transparency has had a lower profile in terms of both academic and public debate. The primary focus around questions of transparency in the UK context have been the measures introduced in the Freedom of Information Act 2000, which came into force in January 2000 (Worthy and Hazell, 2017). As explored in Chapters 1 and 2, exploring transparency and its interaction with trust requires a nuanced analysis which moves beyond formal mechanisms and methodological nationalism.

This chapter applies the trust–transparency matrix outlined in Chapter 2 on different levels of the trust–transparency nexus in the UK case – exploring political trust at the UK and the subnational levels, and finally the trust–transparency dynamics within and between civil society at the subnational level. The chapter develops a comparative analysis of North West England, centred on the Greater Manchester City Region and Liverpool City Region, and Wales. It draws on a wide range of secondary sources including existing published research and survey data, policy documents and 39 semi-structured interviews carried out between 2017 and 2018. The chapter is divided into four core sections. The first section explores 'thin' conceptions of political trust and transparency in the UK context, primarily drawing on public attitude surveys. The second section extends this analysis to the subnational level, focusing on political trust and transparency in North

West England and Wales. The third section reflects on the findings of this analysis within the context of the trust–transparency matrix and interplay between 'thick' forms of interpersonal and interorganisational trust and transparency within and between civil society actors in the study areas. The final substantive section concludes with a short section identifying the key themes highlighted by this multi-level analysis and situating this analysis within the trust–transparency matrix.

Exploring trust and transparency in the UK

In the UK there has been renewed interest in the analysis of political trust and related factors, such as political discontent, perceptions of the integrity of government and the impact of bad behaviour by politicians (Pattie and Johnson, 2012; Allen and Birch, 2015; Whiteley et al, 2016; Jennings et al, 2016, 2017, 2020; Clarke and Newman, 2017; Clarke et al, 2018; Jennings and Lodge, 2019; Rose and Wessels, 2019). Jennings and Lodge (2019: 776) note that public disaffection and discontent with establishment politics that shaped the Brexit agenda had been steadily on the rise for several decades and were further fuelled by events such as the financial crisis and parliamentary expenses scandal of 2009. Although a degree of mistrust, characterised by a dynamic of vigilance, can be characterised as a positive feature of a democratic society, the general trend in the UK has been characterised as one of a decline of trust and rise of distrust (Devine et al, 2020). These trends have been reflected in domestic surveys, such as the British Social Attitudes survey, but also international surveys, such as the Edelman Trust Barometer, Eurobarometer and European Social Survey. For example, Ed Williams, president and chief executive officer of Edelman's Europe, Middle East and Africa region, characterised the UK as a 'parable of distrust' in the organisation's 2020 Trust Barometer, with 36% stating that they had trust in government (Edelman Trust Barometer, 2020). Indeed, despite a brief 'trust bubble' in the wake of COVID-19, with trust in government increasing 24% between January and May 2020, by January 2021 the bubble had burst and trust had gone down by 15% (Edelman Trust Barometer, 2021). The Eurobarometer survey suggests that this reported decline in trust potentially varies quite considerably according to the level of government in question, a theme consistent with previous research (Denters, 2002). In the most recent Eurobarometer surveys in October/November 2019, for example, 72% and 70% of respondents stated that they 'tend not to trust' the national-level government and parliament respectively, whereas only 45% stated that they 'tend not to trust' regional and local authorities (Figures 4.1–4.3). Perhaps unsurprisingly, trust in the EU is fairly low, but levels of distrust of the EU in the most recent iterations of the Eurobarometer has actually been lower than the national level (Figure 4.4).

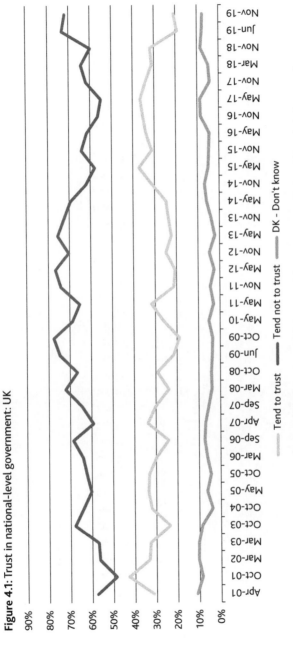

Figure 4.1: Trust in national-level government: UK

Source: European Union (2001–19) Standard Eurobarometer, Question wording: I would like to ask you a question about how much trust you have in certain institutions. For each of the following institutions, please tell me if you tend to trust it or tend not to trust it. The [NATIONALITY] government. (https://europa.eu/eurobarometer/surveys/browse/all/series/4961)

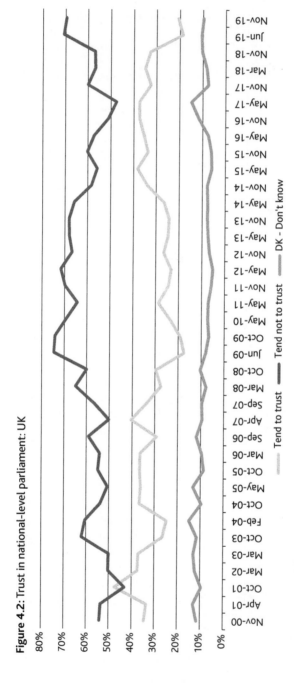

Figure 4.2: Trust in national-level parliament: UK

Tend to trust ——— Tend not to trust ——— DK - Don't know

Source: Eurobarometer 2000–19.

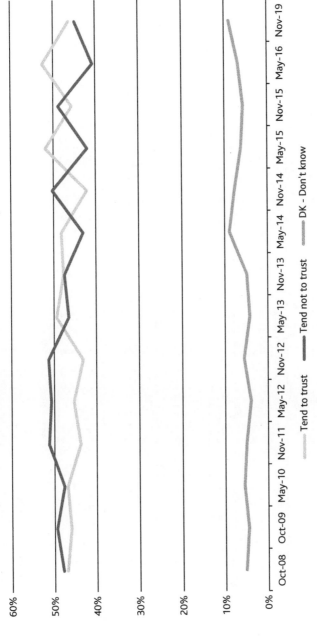

Figure 4.3: Trust in regional and local public authorities: UK

Source: Eurobarometer 2008–19.

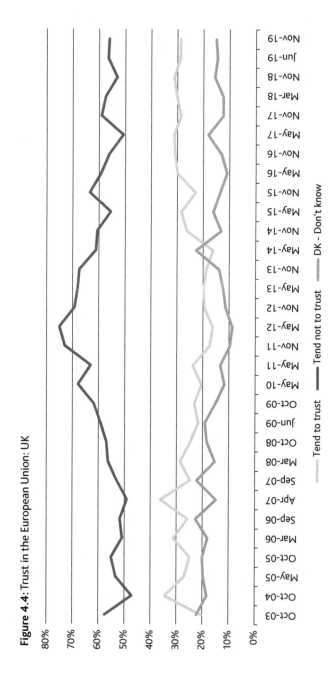

Figure 4.4: Trust in the European Union: UK

Tend to trust ——— Tend not to trust ——— DK – Don't know

Source: Eurobarometer 2003–19.

If this data is supplemented with additional sources, it is possible to provide a more fine-grained picture of trust related to the three component elements identified in Chapters 1–2 – perceived competence, perceived benevolence and perceived integrity – and integrated into the trust–transparency matrix. First, if we utilise levels of satisfaction as a proxy for a national government's perceived competence, the picture tends to reinforce the overall trend towards distrust, albeit with the same type of fluctuations highlighted above. The European Social Survey asks respondents to answer the question 'Now thinking about the national government, how satisfied are you with the way it is doing its job?' by ranking the government from extremely dissatisfied (0) to extremely satisfied (10). Figure 4.5 collates the scores of 0–3 as low satisfaction and 7–10 as high satisfaction, and results reflect a consistently higher proportion of low-satisfaction responses over the past two decades. Second, a variety of measures can be utilised to explore trust as perceived benevolence. In the 2018 European Social Survey, respondents were asked the extent to which they agreed with the statement 'the Government takes into account the interests of all citizens', and just over 40% responded 'very little' or 'not at all' (Figure 4.6). Although these responses are not perhaps as bad as one might expect, similar statements explored in the 2017 British Election Survey paint a much more negative picture (Table 4.1). Finally, a variety of measures can be utilised to assess perceived integrity. For example, the Ipsos MORI Veracity index explores perceptions of actors telling the truth. A collection of surveys between 2004 and 2013 conducted by the Committee on Standards in Public Life, responsible for advising the Prime Minister on ethical standards across the whole of public life, provides a relatively nuanced picture of perceptions of integrity. Figure 4.7 illustrates that UK citizens have very low expectations in terms of politicians telling the truth and, most starkly, owning up to

Figure 4.5: Now thinking about the national government, how satisfied are you with the way it is doing its job?

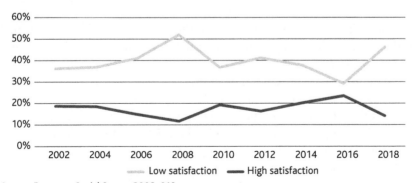

Source: European Social Survey 2002–018.

Figure 4.6: The government takes into account the interests of all citizens

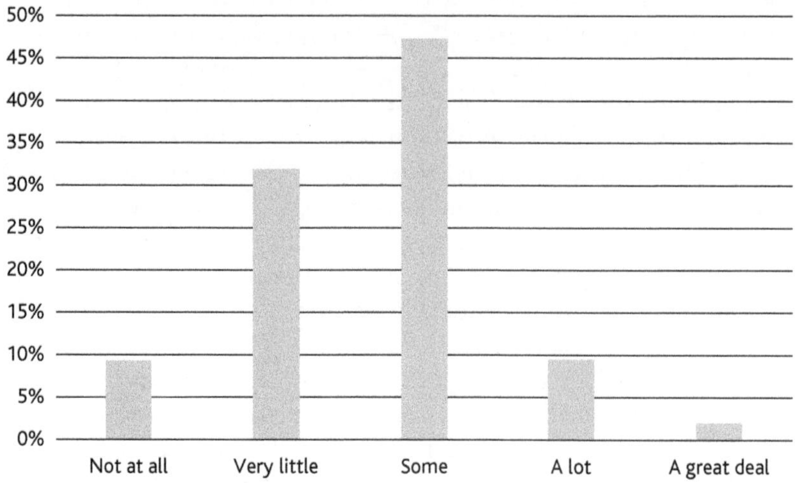

Source: European Social Survey 2018.

Table 4.1: Trust as perceived benevolence (%)

	Strongly disagree	Disagree	Neither agree nor disagree	Agree	Strongly agree	Don't know
Politicians don't care what people like me think	2.7	24.8	20.8	35.6	15.1	0.9
Parties and politicians in the UK are more concerned with fighting each other than with furthering the public interest	1.5	11.9	13.4	45.2	26.7	1.4
Politicians ignore the issues I really care about	1.4	23.2	24.4	35.8	13.9	1.4

Source: British Election Study, 2017.

their mistakes. Therefore, across all of the dimensions of trust identified in the trust–transparency matrix discussed in Chapter 2, the UK appears to perform poorly.

The range of data for examining transparency at the UK level is much more limited when compared to trust. The key focus of many studies has been assessing the effectiveness of specific transparency mechanisms, perhaps most notably FOI requests (Worthy and Hazell, 2017; Worthy et al, 2017). The World Justice Project published the Open Government Index 2015, which collated four dimensions to measure government openness: publicised laws and government data; right to information; civic participation; and complaint

Figure 4.7: Perceptions of conduct of MPs, 2012

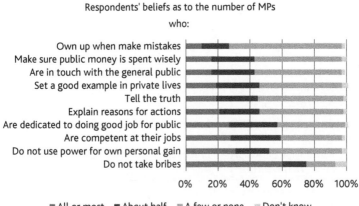

Respondents' beliefs as to the number of MPs who:

■ All or most   ■ About half   ■ A few or none   ▨ Don't know

Source: Survey of public attitudes towards conduct in public life 2012.

mechanisms. Based on responses to household surveys and in-county expert questionnaires, countries are scored from 0 to 1 (1 = greatest openness) (World Justice Project, 2020). The UK's overall rating of 0.74 placed it eighth in the global index and seventh in the WJP's European Union, European Free Trade Association and North America region (behind Sweden, Norway, Denmark, the Netherlands, Finland and Canada). The responses to the 'publicised laws and government data' survey questions provide a useful overview of public perceptions of information provided by the government, and the UK performs comparatively well (Table 4.2). Similarly, in terms of the 'right to information' measures, 57% of respondents were aware of FOI laws, although only 8% had actually requested information from the government. This confirms Worthy and Hazell's (2017: 29) assessment that there was little evidence that FOI had actually increased public participation. However, in contrast to the positive responses to the WJP survey, over 60% of respondents to the 2018 European Social Survey rated the transparency of decisions in politics as 'not at all' or 'very little'.

The OECD has developed the OURdata Index to benchmark the design and implementation of open data policies at the central government level (OECD, 2020). The index is based on responses from high-level government officials to the OECD Survey on Open Government Data which features questions designed to examine the three core pillars of the index: data availability, data accessibility and government support for data reuse (Lafortune and Ubaldi, 2018). In the original 2017 index, the UK was fourth in the OECD rankings (behind Korea, France and Japan) but the 2019 index saw the UK fall to twentieth. The UK score fell in all but one of the sub-pillars and was perhaps most marked in those areas which

Table 4.2: WJP Open Government Index 2015: publicised laws and government data (% very good or good)

	UK	EU + EFTA + North America
How would you rate the quality of information published by the government?	77	67
How would you rate the quantity of information published by the government?	75	63
How would you rate the accessibility of information published by the government?	68	59
How would you rate the reliability of information published by the government?	70	63

Source: WJP Open Government Index 2015.

Table 4.3: OURdata Index 2017 and 2019: UK

	2017	2019
OURdata Index overall score	**0.78**	**0.57**
Pillar 1: Data availability	0.83 (0.28)*	0.58 (0.19)*
1.1 Content open by default policy	0.31	0.23
1.2 Stakeholder engagement for data release	0.22	0.14
1.3 Implementation	0.29	0.21
Pillar 2: Data accessibility	0.83 (0.28)*	0.72 (0.24)*
2.1 Content of the unrestricted access to data policy	0.30	0.31
2.2 Stakeholder engagement for data quality and completeness	0.23	0.13
2.3 Implementation	0.29	0.28
Pillar 3: Government support for data reuse	0.69 (0.23)*	0.4 (0.13)*
3.1 Data promotion initiatives and partnerships	0.30	0.10
3.2 Data literacy programmes in government	0.28	0.23
3.3 Monitoring impact	0.11	0.07

Source: OECD Stat (*the score in brackets refers to the weight given to each pillar in the overall OURdata Index score).

required stakeholder consultation and engagement across the three pillars (see Table 4.3). The OECD report on the 2019 index stated that the UK drop 'can be explained as a result of a mix of different aspects, including reduced efforts towards user engagement across the whole policy process, and change of policy priorities from open data to analytical capacity within the public sector'. The report concluded that the significant drop in the UK's position in the index highlighted the need for 'solid governance frameworks, securing continuous policy implementation, as well as ensuring that changes in government and political priorities do not put open data initiatives at risk' (OECD, 2020: 21). Combined with the relatively poor perception of transparency illustrated in the 2018 European Social Survey, the OECD OURdata Index suggests that the picture might not be as clear as that painted by the WJP's Open Government Index and other measures, such as the Open Data Barometer, which the UK topped alongside Canada in 2017. However, it is worth noting that all of these transparency measures tend to operationalise fairly narrow conceptions of transparency – focusing on the availability of data – and therefore somewhat miss the nuances that are identified in the analysis of our qualitative fieldwork.

Comparing trust and transparency at the subnational level

Since the introduction of devolution in Northern Ireland, Scotland and Wales in 1999, there has been increased interest in exploring public attitudes to institutions and layers of governance below the national level. However, in comparison to data on trust and transparency at the UK level, data focused on the subnational level is relatively scarce and therefore analysing political trust and transparency at this level is challenging. Furthermore, the institutional context in England, as noted in the first section one of this chapter, has been extremely fragmented and changed considerably over time. Therefore, comparing public attitudes to the institutions and governance arrangements in North West England to those in Wales presents further challenges. This section draws on a range of existing data to examine each of the elements of the trust–transparency matrix, although in many cases this means utilising proxy measures and, in the case of the transparency dimensions, drawing on an initial analysis of interview data in Wales and North West England.

The extent to which citizens perceive the devolved and local institutions in Wales and North West England as competent can be illustrated utilising a range of different measures. The data related to the Welsh Government and Senedd Cymru is unsurprisingly more plentiful than similar measures of public attitudes in relation to the much younger institutions in North West England. For example, the National Survey for Wales, which began in January 2012, has regularly collected public levels of satisfaction in the Welsh Government and performance in key policy areas, such as health services and education. Figure 4.8 provides an overview of the mean response to the survey question of how satisfied respondents were with the job that the Welsh Government was doing in general, and in respect to health services and all aspects of the education system (0 = Extremely bad,

Figure 4.8: National Survey for Wales: satisfaction scores

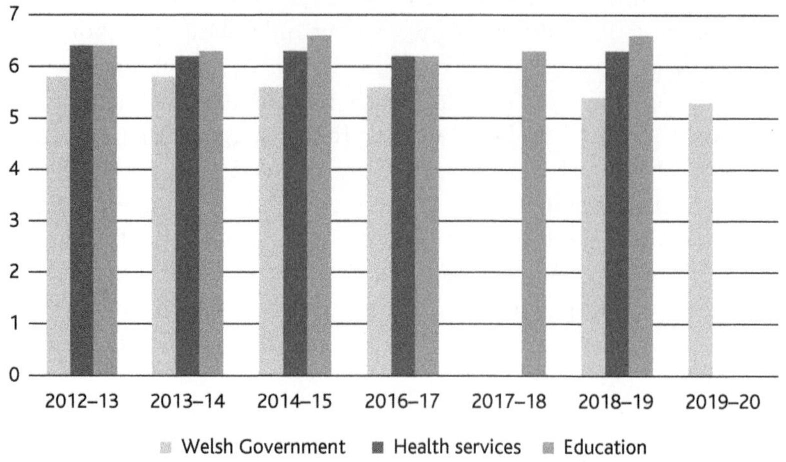

Welsh Government   ■ Health services   ■ Education

Source: National Survey for Wales 2012–20.

10 = Extremely good). The responses illustrate a consistent performance in all three areas which compare relatively favourably with similar scores for the UK Government. For example, in the 2018–19 National Survey for Wales the Welsh Government achieved a mean satisfaction score of 5.4, whereas the UK Government achieved a mean score of 3.75 in response to the same question in the 2018 European Social Survey. Similarly, mean satisfaction scores in relation to education and health services were marginally higher in Wales (6.3 and 6.6) than the UK (5.5 and 5.7) in the same surveys. These results appear to illustrate a fairly consistent picture of reasonable levels of trust framed as perceived competence. The data for the Liverpool City Region Combined Authority and Greater Manchester Combined Authority are less comparable with UK-level data, but findings from survey data collected by the Centre for Cities in February 2020 paint an intriguing picture. The survey asked respondents across city-regions in England what they felt was the most important thing that the respective mayors had achieved since taking office in 2017. In the case of Greater Manchester, over half of respondents stated 'don't know', although the stress placed by Burnham on addressing homelessness in GMCR appears to have resonated with respondents (Table 4.4). Interestingly, in the case of LCR, the confusing governance setting, where Steve Rotheram's position as Mayor of LCR continued to coexist alongside Mayor of Liverpool Joe Anderson, meant that collecting reliable data around satisfaction was hugely challenging. Given the infancy of the devolved institutions across English city-regions, the type of response highlighted in GMCR perhaps illustrates the insufficient knowledge or understanding of the activity of the newly devolved institutions, rather than the absence of trust as competence.

Table 4.4: Satisfaction with elected mayors

Andy Burnham has been the mayor of the Manchester city-region since 2017. What, if anything, do you think is the most important thing Andy Burnham has done during his time in office?

Tackling homelessness	17
Improved public transport	10
Cheaper/capped public transport	2
Being there for the city/people	2
Helped in the aftermath of the Manchester bombing	2
Pollution/air quality/eco-friendly actions	1
Raised the city's profile	0
Attracted investment/business/job creation	0
Safer city	0
Tackling poverty	0
Improved education/further education	0
Reduced/tackling crime	0
Other	8
Nothing	8
Don't know	52

Source: Centre for Cities (2020).

The perceived benevolence and integrity dimensions of trust once again reflect the very different settings in Wales and North West England, and analysis is hampered by the relative paucity of data. In Wales, survey data suggests that citizens trust the Welsh Government and members of Senedd Cymru to work in Wales' best interests more than their counterparts in Whitehall and Westminster (Table 4.5). The Welsh Election Survey 2016, for example, found that almost 60% of respondents trusted the Welsh Government to work in Wales' interests 'just about always' or 'most of the time', whereas the figure for the UK Government was just over 21% (see Table 4.5). Similarly, in the same survey when asked which level of government 'cared what people like you think', respondents ranked local councils and the Welsh Government higher than either the UK Government or the EU (see Table 4.6). These findings are consistent with existing research regarding the influence of scale on trust, and also reflect the relatively high level of support for devolution in the Welsh context. Although the data for the LCR and GMCR is inevitably scarcer, there is some evidence of a similar trend towards trusting the local or devolved level more than central government. For example, in a ComRes survey in GMCR conducted in 2017, 76% of respondents agreed with the statement that 'politics in

Table 4.5: How much do you trust the following to work in Wales' best interests? (%)

	Just about always	Most of the time	Only some of the time	Almost never	Don't know
UK Government	2.8	18.3	40.4	31.4	7.1
Welsh Government	16.4	43.14	25.2	8.1	7.2
Members of the Westminster Parliament	1.6	13.8	45.9	30.1	8.6
Members of the National Assembly for Wales	12.9	44.8	26.4	8	7.9

Source: Welsh Election Study 2016.

Table 4.6: How much do you think that each of the following care what people like you think? (%)

	A lot	Some	A little	None	Don't know
Local Council	4.9	25.8	30.2	31.4	7.7
Welsh Government	5.3	27.4	33.4	25.9	8
UK Government	2.1	14.7	32	42.9	7.6
European Union	1.5	9.4	20.7	59	9.4

Source: Welsh Election Study 2016.

Westminster is out of touch with life in Greater Manchester' and only 19% agreed with the statement that 'MPs in Westminster, rather than local politicians in Manchester, should have ultimate control over policy-making for the area'. This trust in more local representatives is perhaps illustrated in the policy areas respondents to the Centre for Cities February 2020 survey believed that the elected mayors in LCR and GMCR should be given more direct responsibility (Figure 4.9). This illustrated that in key areas, such as affordable housing and bus services, a majority of respondents favoured these policy areas being devolved further responsibilities.

In terms of the transparency of decision-making, policy content and policy outcomes in the LCR and GMCR, and in Wales, institutions across all three localities operate within the wider UK transparency-related architecture. For example, the Freedom of Information Act 2000 and the Local Government Transparency Code. The latter requires local authorities to publish information in a range of areas, including grants to voluntary, community and social enterprise organisations and an organisation chart (Department for Communities and Local Government, 2015). The LCRCA, GMCA and the Welsh Government websites all feature dedicated pages centred on accountability and transparency, and there are a wide range of similarities and contrasts across the three sites. The GMCA and Welsh

Figure 4.9: Which of the following policy areas do you believe the mayor of the Liverpool/Greater Manchester city-region should have more direct responsibility over?

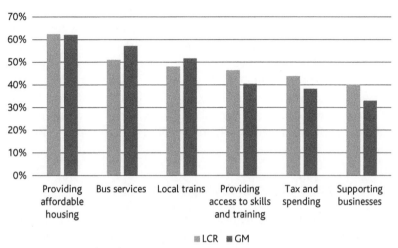

Source: Centre for Cities (2020).
The Mayor of Liverpool/Greater Manchester has some responsibility for skills and training, transport, housing, policing and crime, health and social care and promoting the city nationally and internationally. These responsibilities are currently shared with national government. Which of the following policy areas do you believe the mayor of the Liverpool/Greater Manchester city-region should have more direct responsibility over?

Government websites both feature sections collating key decisions, but there are noticeable differences: for example, the LCRCA website also provides an overview of FOI compliance statistics. The extent to which the provision of this information provides effective transparency is difficult to answer, and in many senses is linked to the question regarding public engagement with the institutions.

Interviewees from across a wide range of civil society organisations and the institutions themselves provided a somewhat mixed picture of transparency in terms of the wider public. A key factor in the Welsh context was the relatively weak media. A voluntary sector stakeholder noted that "working in the field I think there's a level of transparency, but I think the lack of Welsh media means to lots of people it won't be very transparent at all" (Interview WAL06). This issue was recognised by the National Assembly for Wales' Culture, Welsh Language and Communications Committee's (2018) report, *Read All About It*, which identified the decline of indigenous commercial news journalism and the widespread consumption of UK media, which generally ignores Wales and devolved institutions. The picture in North West England is somewhat different, with both LCR and GMCR having robust local media, such as the *Liverpool Echo* and *Manchester Evening News*, but with the processes being largely elite driven. An LCRCA official reflected that although initiatives had been taken to engage the public and transparency arrangements were in place, "I still don't think most people understand what a combined authority is ... they know the bits that impact on them as individuals" (Interview NW15). This point was underscored by the responses to the Centre for Cities February 2020 survey for the LCR, where although 89% of respondents confirmed that they were aware that the city region had an elected mayor, only 22% correctly identified that elected mayor as Steve Rotheram. However, it is important to note that this low level of recognition was likely exacerbated by the confusion caused by the fact that Liverpool City Council had a high-profile elected mayor, Joe Anderson, who was named by 24% of respondents as being the city-region mayor (Centre for Cities, 2020).

Civil society and the trust–transparency nexus

The context for exploring the nexus between 'thick' forms of interpersonal and interorganisational trust and transparency within and between civil society actors unsurprisingly varies across Wales and the North West city-regions explored in this chapter. The ensuing section engages in a comparison of Wales and the city-regions of North West England, focusing on the axes of the trust–transparency matrix presented in Chapter 2.

Although in the early days of devolution Welsh civil society was characterised as being fairly weak, organisations have increased their capacity over the past two decades of devolution, largely enabled by funding opportunities and a partnership-based approach provided by the Welsh Government (Entwistle, 2006; Bristow et al, 2009; Rumbul, 2016a). However, there have been concerns that this environment has tended to favour elite organisations, and that the dependency on Welsh Government funding and the small size of policy communities has led to an inherent timidity in expressing criticism of government policy (Hodgson, 2004a; 2004b; Rumbul, 2016b).

A key challenge facing civil society actors in the LCR and GMCR has been adapting to the shifting governance arrangements highlighted in the previous chapter. Although the wider North West region retained Voluntary Sector North West (VSNW), established in the late 1990s to provide support for the voluntary, community and social enterprise sector (VCSE), the largely top-down nature of the post-2010 devolution agenda led to the formation of the Greater Manchester Voluntary, Community and Social Enterprise Devolution Reference Group and VS6 in the Liverpool City Region. Beel and colleagues (2018: 254) argue that these initiatives epitomised 'a joint effort on the part of local civil society actors to exert agency at city-regional level and influence the process'. However, reviews of the VCSE sectors in both the LCR and GMCR highlighted the challenges created by spending cuts, in terms of both the funding of organisations and a significant increase in the demand for VCSE services (Jones and Meegan, 2015; Damm et al,

2017). Paradoxically, as noted by Jones and Meegan (2015), these pressures reinforced the value and role of the VCSE sector.

The degree of trust in different levels of government varied considerably in the Welsh case, and unsurprisingly the primary focus was on the devolved level, and specifically relations with the Welsh Government. The relationship was characterised by the variety of civil society actors involved in the fieldwork as being broadly positive: for example, a housing stakeholder (Interview WAL11) stated that there was "very much an open door" in relation to decision-making, and a business stakeholder similarly described "a depth of engagement that we have here which isn't replicated in any of the other devolved administrations" (Interview WAL08). However, there were some issues highlighted regarding the relationship between the Welsh Government and civil society. Perhaps the key criticism was that Welsh Government–civil society relations within Wales were characterised by "a cosy consensus" (Media stakeholder, Interview WAL17) and the perception of a "single nationalisation … in terms of thoughts and opinion that doesn't necessarily result in a robust critique" (Public affairs/think tank stakeholder, Interview WAL01). The role of the different dimensions of trust identified in the trust–transparency matrix in underpinning government–civil society relations provided contrasting results in the Welsh context. Perhaps most notable was the interviewees' view of trust characterised as the perceived competence in relation to both the Welsh Government and local authorities. An education stakeholder illustrated the issue raised across policy fields in relation to the Welsh Government, stating that "where there's a lack of trust it's to do with expertise" and the problem of "professional civil servants who have insufficient understanding of the education system as it actually operates" (Interview WAL14). However, there was recognition that competence, of both officials and elected politicians, varied between individuals within organisations, and there was a recognition, at devolved and local levels, that resources and capacity had been under strain in recent years.

In terms of the other dimensions of trust in the matrix, perceived benevolence and integrity, the responses of interviewees were more consistently positive. For example, a voluntary sector stakeholder reflected that "by and large we perceive them [the Welsh Government] as an honest actor" and although there were occasions when they had been disappointed by decisions, "I wouldn't put that down to dishonesty, I would have put that down to it's just a different view" (Interview WAL06). Therefore, the picture of trust in different levels of government within Wales is somewhat uneven, although distrust tends to be driven more by perceptions of expertise and competence than dishonesty.

The picture of trust in levels of government in the Liverpool and Manchester city-regions was shaped by the relative infancy of the devolved arrangements, particularly in the case of the LCRCA. A trade union stakeholder, for example, pointed out that the GMCA drew on the shared history of the Association of Greater Manchester Authorities (AGMA), and therefore reflected "a collaborative venture before devolution was even a twinkle in the eye of George Osbourne" (Interview NW09). In contrast, the LCRCA had "started from scratch on its devolution journey", which meant that on day 1 "Andy [Burnham, GMCR mayor] was clapped in by 200 staff into his offices and Steve [Rotheram, LCR mayor] came into an empty room with empty desks and literally had to start a staff infrastructure from scratch". These contrasting settings had a range of effects on relations between the local authorities within the two combined authorities, and relations between these layers of government and civil society stakeholders. Several interviewees in both cities highlighted that Greater Manchester authorities were better at "singing from the same hymn sheet", whereas disagreements tended to come to the surface in LCR.

While the logic of collaboration within the LCR was as compelling as in the GMCR for constituent local authorities, the absence of a shared history of collaboration and established norms of working made the city region somewhat more dysfunctional. This variation was also reflected in the combined authorities' relations with civil society actors, although there were further variations in perceptions and experiences across policy fields. A voluntary sector stakeholder, for example, remarked that officials working in health policy in the GMCR were "inviting us to the table earlier on in the conversations, so that we can start to influence some real change" and that there was "a real commitment to codesign and coproduction" (Interview NW06). The picture in LCR was less clear: for example, a voluntary sector stakeholder reflected that "we did sign a bit of a pledge about working and you know, they're all really good at engaging and stuff, but I'm not sure how that's going to play out really" (Interview NW10).

Due to the relative infancy of the combined authorities, the different dimensions of trust identified in the trust–transparency matrix were less clear in terms of providing the foundations for government–civil society relations. Interviewees generally responded that it was "early days" (Voluntary sector stakeholder, Interview NW10) and the "jury's still out" (Voluntary sector stakeholder, Interview NW01) in relation to the perceived competence of both combined authorities. However, those stakeholders who had been involved in early policy development were cautiously optimistic. Regarding the perceived benevolence and integrity of the combined authorities, the responses of interviews were relatively optimistic and often cited the personalities of respective elected mayors.

The general perceptions of trust in individual local authorities and the UK Government were more variable. In many senses, this can be characterised as reflecting perceptions of trust related to the 'multi-level' dimension of multi-level governance or, in other words, the perception of intergovernmental relations. A trade union stakeholder reflected that for the wider North West region, "if you rated local authorities on a scale of 1 to 10, you'd probably get everything between 1 and 10, but you get a lot of people clustered between 5 and 7" (Interview NW09). Relations with the UK Government provided an interesting picture of how trust had evolved between the levels of governance: for example, a GMCA official pointed out that the relationship with one Whitehall department had evolved over five years from "not quite adversarial" to "a very strong relationship" (Interview NW03). However, much like local authorities, the level of trust varied from department to department. A local government politician reflected that "some departments are okay and others you wouldn't buy a car off them, and it's a shame because I think the ministers, certainly the ones I've spoken to, want this to work" (Interview NW08). Although not the central focus of our fieldwork, it is clear that within the context of relations between different levels or tiers of governance, the picture of trust is quite varied and changeable.

If we move the focus away from government–civil society relations to the role of trust in shaping relationships between civil society actors within policy communities, we can identify many similarities in the experiences and perceptions of interviewees across Wales and the two North West England city-regions, but also some notable differences. In the Welsh case, a common theme identified by interviewees was the overriding perception that "everybody has Wales' best interests at heart" and in many cases this was driven by "a sense of nationhood that you don't get in an English region" (Business stakeholder, Interview WAL16). However, the drivers of collaboration were more often linked to the practical challenges facing civil society actors. An environment stakeholder pointed out that there was "a necessity to work together because of our resources, and because the Welsh Government and Assembly Members can't cope with hearing ten different voices" (Interview WAL07). There was also recognition that collaboration was a balancing act and that organisations were often collaborating with potential competitors. A key element in building trust between civil society actors can be seen to be the explicit recognition and understanding of each partner's 'red lines' and the limits of any collaboration. Despite this relatively positive picture of trust and collaboration in Wales, there were some interesting reflections on whether the most was being made of the closeness of the policy communities.

The character of relations between civil society actors in the LCR and GMCR, as noted, featured similarities and differences from the Welsh case. Notably, there were few references to a common narrative resembling 'Team Wales' but collaboration and partnership remained a strong feature. A voluntary sector stakeholder noted that in the GMCR "public and business sectors, and academics, increasingly are predisposed to be collaborative, both with each other, and with others" (Interview NW07). The stakeholder explained that this shift had been driven partly by the 2007/8 recession and the post-2010 austerity measures because "when your back's against the wall ... you have no choice, you can't carry on as you were, so you have got to consider alternatives". Much like the Welsh case, there was clear recognition of the limits and challenges of these collaborative efforts. However, the generally positive picture of collaboration between business and trade union stakeholders was replicated in the North West, with the latter noting that "we've developed good working relations, we know on some things we will collaborate and on other things we will respectfully differ" (Interview NW09).

The characterisation of the trust relations between government actors and civil society organisations, and between civil society actors themselves highlights the interplay of interpersonal and interorganisational forms of trust highlighted in Chapter 1. The relatively small size of Welsh policy communities played a key role in underpinning forms of interpersonal trust. The prevalence of interpersonal trust and the small scale of policy communities within Wales was characterised as being "a blessing and a curse" for policy-making. A trade union stakeholder provided a detailed explanation of the benefits and costs (Interview WA18):

> 'I'll do the downside first ... there has always been in Wales a kind of, the Welsh word for it is the crachach, the kind of self-appointed elite, whether that's party political or not, and usually not, there's certainly a small group of people who run the country. And if you're part of it, you're part it and everybody knows each other and they all influence each other informally. There's all the downsides of that, clearly there's groupthink and there's "oh well they're a bit of an outlier and we're all here thinking similar". How do you get influx of new thought and new areas of influence? ... The upside is we can respond to stuff really quickly, so trust is there from the start when you're working with people quite closely week in, week out. Because we're a small country we are working much more closely with chief execs, directors and organisations that if I was doing this job somewhere else I wouldn't be working as closely with them, so I wouldn't get to know them personally before a crisis hits.'

However, the downsides to this environment are perhaps more varied than simply the formation of "little cabals" of the "usual suspects" (Business stakeholder, Interview WAL08). The extent to which building interorganisational trust could act as a remedy for the breakdown of interpersonal trust was questioned. For example, the trade union stakeholder observed that they tried to "always disentangle the person from the office" and that "you build organisational trust from the knowledge of what happened the last time ... and where the red lines are" (Interview WA18). In contrast, a business stakeholder argued if personal trust existed with individuals in other organisations you have "at least the base to say 'right, well let's sit down and work on this issue together or at least let's have a conversation about this issue together'" but "where that individual trust isn't there, then you can't even get to that first base" (Interview WAL08). Therefore, as highlighted in Chapter 1, the dynamics between interpersonal and interorganisational trust can potentially play a key role in institutionalising relations.

The interplay of interpersonal and interorganisational forms of trust was replicated in the LCR and GMCR, albeit in a very different setting. A notable contrast was the greater stress placed on formal mechanisms to establish interorganisational trust, notably in the form of Memorandums of Understanding (MoUs). A local government politician noted that the MoUs had been "helpful to signify publicly and externally that we are an organisation willing to work in partnership with other players on particular things to improve the health of people in Greater Manchester" (Interview NW16). On a more practical level, a LCRCA official explained that MoUs were useful because "it stops being about individuals and personalities, and becomes something which is quite practical" (Interview NW15). In addition, a voluntary sector stakeholder involved in an MoU with CCGs (Clinical Commissioning Groups) in the LCR noted that they were "quite important ... because ... if some leaves tomorrow, so if one of my staff leaves or one of the CCG staff who we work with [leaves], it doesn't actually matter because we can go to the next person and say here's what we're working to" (Interview NW10). In some senses this illustrates the desire to make partnership working more resilient but could be seen to reflect the different stages in the development of institutions in Wales and the Liverpool and Greater Manchester city regions. Although MoUs are not absent in the Welsh context, they were not identified as key reference points for building trust.

The prevalence of formal mechanisms to build interorganisational trust in the LCR and GMCR did not mean that interpersonal forms of trust were entirely absent from the picture provided by interviewees. A voluntary sector stakeholder argued that "at the end of the day all of this is driven by people, so what I try to do is I try to develop as close a working relationship as I can" based on authenticity and honesty (Interview NW06). The stakeholder further explained that they trusted key actors, such as the then chief officer of the Greater Manchester Health and Social Care Partnership, Jon Rouse, and the elected mayor, Andy Burnham, because they had "a lot integrity". Similarly, another voluntary sector stakeholder observed that they did not "have very much trust at all in institutions" but based their trust on personal knowledge of people "watching them operate ... their honesty, and in our sharing of some very important values and ambitions for our city-region" (Interview NW07). However, the stakeholder went on to note that "one untrustworthy person ... can create an atmosphere which then affects wider relationships" and "can create a lot of mistrust". In many senses, one would expect to find similarities in the view of interpersonal relations in the LCR and GMCR when compared to Wales. However, despite the history of collaboration in GMCR, the characterisation of a small, almost insulated policy community that was a repeated feature of the fieldwork in Wales was comparatively absent. Although this does not mean that interpersonal trust was any less important, it highlights the contrasting ways in which it was framed in the different cases.

The perceptions of civil society actors in terms of the transparency of the decision- and policy-making process also varied considerably across the cases, and once again this reflected the distinctive journeys of the three localities. The general perception of Welsh civil society stakeholders varied quite significantly depending on their experience and the policy field within which they were working. A housing stakeholder, for example, stated that they felt that "on an official level transparency is really good, in terms of decision making that's always communicated in a pretty open way, if it's been a ministerial decision or whatever that's always done in quite clear terms" (Interview WAL11). However, in marked contrast, a local government officer argued that the experience was quite varied and that "there are certain decisions which frankly bemuse us, absolutely bemuse us, we don't know the genesis of some of the decisions" (Interview WAL02). This potentially reflects the quality of the relationships within different policy fields; for example, housing policy has been characterised by a strong partnership approach between the Welsh Government and key stakeholders. However, there was a consensus across interviewees that transparency was probably perceived differently depending upon proximity to the decision-making process. A voluntary sector stakeholder reflected this theme, explaining that "when you're working closely with it day-to-day perhaps there's a level of transparency that's not there for most of the people" and that this trend was exacerbated by the lack of an effective Welsh media (Interview WAL06). More generally, the weakness of the Welsh media was pinpointed as a problem in relation to providing accountability and transparency for non-insiders and to the wider Welsh public.

The Welsh Government's formal mechanisms designed to provide transparency, notably the publication of decision reports and cabinet minutes, were perceived as only partially opening up the decision-making process. For several interviewees, the Welsh Government's decision to no longer publish decision reports in September 2015 was indicative of its attitude to transparency. The then First Minister, Carwyn Jones, justified this decision by noting that "the vast majority of them were hugely mundane" and "you're talking about a huge amount of time in order to publish them, for documents that hardly anybody reads" (National Assembly for Wales, 2015). The decision was subsequently reversed in November 2015, but a public affairs stakeholder explained that the decision marked a "significant deterioration" in the Welsh Government's commitment to transparency (Interview WAL01). Despite the U-turn being welcomed by interviewees, several pointed out that "the way they are published now, I think makes them virtually worthless" (Education stakeholder, Interview WAL04). Similarly, although Cabinet minutes are published, the value of the information provided was questioned. This point raises the extent to which these formal reporting mechanisms around decision-making represent a 'nominal' rather than 'effective' form of transparency, as highlighted in Chapter 1 (Heald, 2006).

The other transparency elements of the trust–transparency matrix were also the subject of much debate by interviewees. Civil society stakeholders were relatively confident regarding the content of policies, but the primary platforms for delivering this type of information, notably the Welsh Government's website, were viewed less favourably. A business stakeholder, for example, argued that there "is an issue about the quality of what's put on the Welsh government website and the timeliness of it ... as it can be months after the fact that something goes up onto the website" (Interview WAL08). More broadly, the Welsh Government's failure to publish a detailed programme for government, including performance indicators, was seen as a step backwards in terms of transparency. Once again, this paints a somewhat mixed picture of transparency in terms of policy outcomes or effects.

In the English city regions, the perceptions of civil society actors of the transparency of the decision process reflected the contrasting journeys of LCR and GMCR. A voluntary sector stakeholder pointed out that in the LCR "it's early days" and it was unclear "what decisions are being made and when they're getting made" (Interview NW10). In comparison, a health stakeholder stated that "GM is in a much more mature place and maybe more confident" and "it's really important that people are transparent about that (when things go wrong) as well as when things go well, because you learn more from your mistakes" (Interview NW05). However, there was a clear disjuncture between the transparency of the formal and informal stages of the decision-making process. A local government official explained that they received "really good public reports from the Combined Authority in terms of what's been happening" but that "the informal decision-making processes still lacks some transparency" and sometimes there was not "a very clear rationale as to why that particular decision has been reached" (Interview NW11). The ability of the formal reporting mechanisms to capture the more informal aspects of the decision-making processes was a key theme. A trade union stakeholder highlighted this concern, stating that "if you attend the meeting of a combined authority you'd probably storm out thinking 'bah humbug this is a load of rubbish' because all the decisions are made behind closed doors" and the last meeting that they had attended only lasted 20 minutes (Interview NW09). Similarly, a local government politician argued that "if you try and resolve issues in public meetings then in a sense people dig their heels in a bit more" and therefore informal meetings were key to resolving "the tricky stuff" (Interview NW16). As noted above, in many senses these points reflect the much wider debate around the role of transparency in building trust, and the argument that too much transparency could undermine trust between different actors.

Given the relative infancy of the combined authorities in the LCR and GMCR, the views of interviewees regarding transparency of policy content and policy outcomes were relatively limited. However, there was more to be said about the state of the different mechanisms by which information about policy content and outcomes could be communicated. A GMCA official noted that "things have changed over the past few years in terms of most of the Greater Manchester decision-making boards, if not all of them, are live streamed ... and information is there if you want to access it". The official also explained that "we've had a kind of open-book approach to all of our programmes" and "if some things don't work, then they don't work but we will not try and fudge it" (Interview NW03). A voluntary sector stakeholder confirmed the general open nature of policy, noting that "there are plenty of facts and figures around and the committee papers contain a huge amount of data" and that key meetings were available to watch on the internet (Interview NW01). In addition, the media in the city regions was perceived as playing an important role, notably the largest local newspapers in each city region, the *Liverpool Echo* and *Manchester Evening News*. A local government politician stated that local media's "role is to accurately report what is going on, that doesn't mean we'll always agree with them, that doesn't mean we'll always appreciate the way they've reported it in a way that we don't think is fair, however, we have to respect the important role that they've got to do" (Interview NW13). In many senses the scrutiny provided by the local media in the LCR and GMCR can be seen as stronger than that highlighted in the Welsh case study.

In both Wales and the English city regions FOI requests were seen as part of the transparency architecture, but there were varied views on their effectiveness in promoting transparency of policy and decision-making. A local government officer in Wales described them as "a pain in the arse but it's a pain in the arse that we need" as they promoted "greater discipline to the way that people do business" (Interview WAL02). Similarly, a GMCA official explained that "one of the reasons why we try and get as much information as possible out there is so that we don't get Freedom of Information requests" (Interview NW03). In addition, an FOI application was characterised as something of a tool of last resort; for example, an environment stakeholder in Wales explained that "to be honest we'd probably tend to contact someone and ask for information rather than send the formal letter asking you know

I'm making a request under the Freedom of Information Act" (Interview WAL07). This point was reflected in the comments of a voluntary sector stakeholder in LCR who reflected that "it's a shame when a relationship breaks down that much that people start to ask for FOI ... but again that's probably just the old hippie in me saying just talk to each other and get it sorted out" (Interview NW10). Therefore, much like the Welsh case, FOI requests can be seen as a last-resort option that tends to come into play once informal channels have failed.

Applying the trust–transparency matrix: reflections on the UK

It is perhaps unsurprising that the UK case does not fit neatly into one of the ideal types outlined in the trust–transparency matrix presented in Chapter 2. However, applying the matrix to the different levels of analysis developed within this chapter provides an interesting picture of the interplay between trust and transparency within different settings. Firstly, if we adopt a 'thin' definition of 'political trust' and consider secondary data related to trust and transparency at the UK level, we are presented with a picture of low levels of trust and relatively high levels of transparency, albeit the latter quite variable and imperfectly captured. In simple terms, the UK's above-average performance in the admittedly limited measures of transparency, such as the WJP Open Government Index and OECD OURdata Index, does not seem to correlate with improved trust. Therefore, we might categorise the relationship between trust and transparency in terms of political trust at the UK level to fall broadly into the 'negligible or counter-productive effects' category of the matrix. However, it is important to note that this characterisation can potentially vary considerably over time and in relation to specific issues. For example, the initial response to the COVID-19 pandemic was characterised by relatively high levels of trust in the UK Government but this was steadily eroded by the perceived delay in locking down, shortages of personal protective equipment (PPE), and specific events, such as the much publicised trip by Dominic Cummings the chief adviser to the Prime Minister, to County Durham in March 2020 (Fancourt et al, 2020; Gaskell et al, 2020; Jennings, 2020).

The somewhat higher levels of trust in local and regional government appears to illustrate that scale is a factor in terms of shaping levels of trust. In other words, at least based on the limited data presented in this chapter, citizens tend to place more trust in layers of government that are closer to them, or, to put it simply, size matters. However, what is less clear is the precise role that transparency performs to these subnational forms of 'thin' political trust. A common theme in the interviews with civil society actors in both Wales and North West England was the point that although policy-making and decision-making was relatively transparent for them as 'insiders', for the general public or quite often for the individuals or groups that their organisation represented, it was undoubtedly much less the case. In both North West England and Wales, perhaps most central to this dynamic was a general lack of awareness or understanding of devolution among the general public. For example, in a Centre for Cities survey in early 2020, 22% and 72% of respondents were able to name Steve Rotheram and Andy Burnham as the mayors of the Liverpool and Manchester city regions respectively (Centre for Cities, 2020). Similarly, despite over 20 years of devolution within Wales, recent reports have suggested a continued lack of understanding of the responsibilities and role of the Welsh Government, specifically in relation to changing taxation powers (Owens and Jones, 2019, 2020). A key factor in this wider 'transparency' was the role of the media, and this was identified as a key problem in the Welsh context. However, given the high-profile role played by the devolved level in both the North West and Wales in leading the response to the COVID-19 pandemic, it is likely that, at the very least, levels of public awareness of these structures have increased.

The picture of the trust–transparency nexus changes somewhat when we focus our attention on 'thick' forms of trust which characterise relationships between civil society and government actors. In both North West England and Wales, the characterisation of the trust–transparency nexus moves closer to one of 'synergy', albeit one which varied considerably across sectors and territories due to the different dynamics of external and internal influences present. In general terms, transparency was characterised as a key element in building the core dimensions of trust. Openness and understanding were characterised as being key building blocks for positive perceptions of the competence, benevolence and honesty of both other civil society actors and government partners. Importantly, this did not necessarily mean that actors agreed on all issues, but that there was a transparency regarding the 'red lines' for different actors. What was notable was the importance of both internal and external factors, as discussed in Chapter 2, in shaping the specific character and dynamics of the trust–transparency nexus. There was a contrast within the UK cases; for example, in the North West greater stress was placed on the formalisation of relationships via compacts and concordats, partly due to a desire to recognise the rules of engagement but also in an explicit attempt to ensure that relationships were resilient and not entirely reliant on interpersonal linkages. Although these types of agreements were not entirely absent in Wales, it was notable that participants placed greater importance on interpersonal dynamics, partly due to long history of personal relations but also due to the perceived closeness of Wales. There were some echoes of this dynamic in the comparison made between GMCR and LCR in North West England, with relations in the former being perceived to be much more deeply embedded than the latter. Therefore, despite a relatively positive picture being presented across the different subnational cases in the UK, there was a sense that the factors which shaped the trust–transparency nexus varied across them, and this can partly be explained by the different stages that they have reached in their devolution journeys and the strength of their respective shared histories.

Conclusion

The multi-level analysis of trust and transparency within the UK developed in this chapter provides a relatively mixed picture. The UK level is characterised by declining levels of political trust driven by a series of events over the past two decades, from the Iraq War to the UK Government's handling of the COVID-19 pandemic. In contrast, at a national level the UK has been seen as an international leader in terms of promoting transparency and open government, and continues to perform well in international indexes, such as the World Justice Project's Open Government Index. Although there has been a decline in the UK's performance in other measures, such as the OECD's OURdata Index, it appears that at best transparency is a necessary but not sufficient factor in fostering political trust at the national level. The exploration of trust and transparency at the subnational level and within civil society also provides nuanced findings. On the one hand, devolved levels of government in Wales and the LCR and GMCR seem to receive higher levels of public trust, a finding consistent with the argument that trust is likely to increase the closer government gets to the people. On the other hand, the measures of trust at the subnational level are not without problems and transparency measures are almost entirely absent. The exploration of trust and transparency in civil society highlighted the importance of the wider context within which decision- and policy-making takes place. Trust relations between civil society and government actors, and between the civil society actors themselves, reflected the different stages that the three localities had reached in their respective devolution journeys and the depth of the shared histories which underpinned the interplay between interpersonal and interorganisational forms of trust. In general, what is quite clear from the analysis of all three levels in the UK is that the relationship between trust and transparency is far from straightforward and that these dynamics appear just as likely to diverge within states as between them.

5

Germany: Hesse and Saxony-Anhalt

For a long time German public opinion displayed high rates of trust in Chancellor Angela Merkel and her CDU party, as well as the federal government. In recent years, however, there have been signs of a general decline in trust, though the evidence in Germany is much less conclusive than in the UK or France. This chapter provides data to support the existence of a solid foundation of political trust in Germany at all territorial levels of the political system. At the same time, the data (whether that of private enterprises, like the Edelman Trust Barometer, or public institutions, such as Eurobarometer) casts doubt on the enduring features of trust in the national government, the parliament or political institutions in general. The chapter overviews national trends of trust and transparency in Germany. It then offers a closer comparison in the two distinct Länder of Hesse and Saxony Anhalt. Hesse is an affluent, dynamic land with a rising population, and is home to the dynamic metropolis Frankfurt, as well as a vibrant business community and associative life. Saxony-Anhalt, on the other hand, is economically stagnant with a shrinking population and problems of multicultural community integration.

The chapter follows a similar comparative logic to that undertaken in France and the UK. In the case of Germany, the trust–transparency nexus is understood mainly in terms of political accountability, administrative transparency, party politics, policy issues regarding trust and transparency in the two Länder and the operation of civil society. These themes cut across commonalities and divergent aspects of Hesse and Saxony Anhalt. All these themes tie into the nexus between trust and transparency. Parties and actors that are accountable to civil society and political institutions play an important role for the production and deterioration of trust. The chapter concludes by situating the German case in relation to the trust–transparency matrix.

Exploring trust and transparency in Germany

In order to interpret secondary data on trust and transparency in Germany, it is necessary to situate this discussion within the dominant national intellectual and methodological traditions that have shaped the discourse around these concepts. In the prevalent German political sociology tradition, 'institutional trust', defined as the trust of citizens in institutions, is generally quantitatively oriented. Much like the conceptualisation of 'social trust' in Chapter 1, trust is more generally understood at the individual level of analysis and therefore is broken down into horizontal trust (between individuals), vertical trust (between individuals and institutions), or social trust (the individual in a social setting) (Schaal, 2004). Trust represents the individual's belief that a ruler is representing their interests and the interests of others. Rather as in the other cases, however, most data is provided at an aggregate level; hence, we make general inferences to bring into line this chapter with the other country-specific ones.

One such general inference has been the challenge to political trust represented by the rise of the right-wing populist party Alternative für Deutschland (AfD), and in particular its success at the 2017 federal election and 2019 Länder elections. The AfD's breakthrough and persistence has been partly explained by the weakening of trust in political institutions (Reinl and Schäfer, 2020). However, Weisskircher (2020: 620) notes that explaining the rise of populism in Germany is a multifaceted affair, and therefore reducing the rise of AfD to short-term factors or a momentary decline in political trust is problematic. For example, he notes that long-term factors, such as the economic shape of Germany following unification, attitudes to migration and a perceived deficit in representation in the east of Germany, can be identified as driving AfD's popularity in certain regions. The 2020 Edelman Trust Barometer captures this relatively negative picture of Germany in terms of trust in the competence of government and a stark pessimism regarding the future of the German economy, with only 23% of respondents stating they were optimistic about their economic future (Edelman Trust Barometer, 2020). However, what was notable in the 2021 Edelman Trust Barometer was not only that the Government received one of the biggest COVID-19 'bounces' between January and May 2020 (+19%) but also that by January 2021 this 'trust bubble' had not burst to the same degree as other states. In Germany, trust in government had declined by 5% between May 2020 and January 2021, compared with 15% in the UK (Edelman Trust Barometer, 2021). Furthermore, the picture provided by European longitudinal surveys provides a somewhat mixed and fluctuating picture.

The Eurobarometer survey results for Germany, much like the UK, illustrate that perceptions of trust vary considerably based on the level of government in question. For example, in the November 2019 surveys, just under 48% and 54% respondents stated that they 'tend to trust' the national level government and parliament respectively and over 74% of respondents stated that they 'tend to trust' regional and local authorities (Figures 5.1–5.3). At least two points are immediately notable in these results. First, despite the attention given to AfD in recent years and the concern regarding a decline of trust in political institutions, these results are considerably higher at all levels than those outlined for the UK in Chapter 4. Second, whereas trust in national-level institutions has regularly fluctuated, trust at the local and

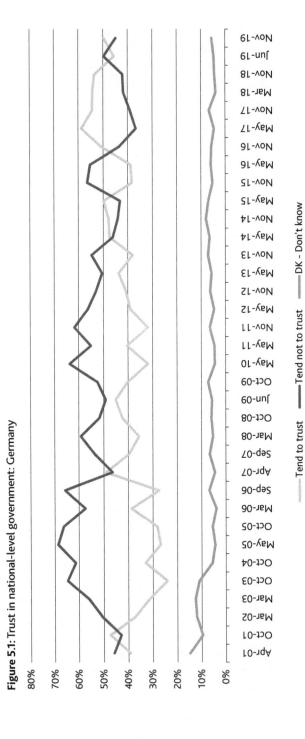

Figure 5.1: Trust in national-level government: Germany

Tend to trust ——— Tend not to trust ——— DK - Don't know

Source: Eurobarometer 2001–19.

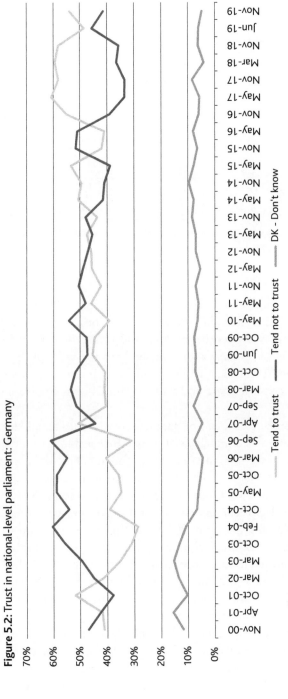

Figure 5.2: Trust in national-level parliament: Germany

Source: Eurobarometer 2000–19.

Figure 5.3: Trust in regional and local public authorities: Germany

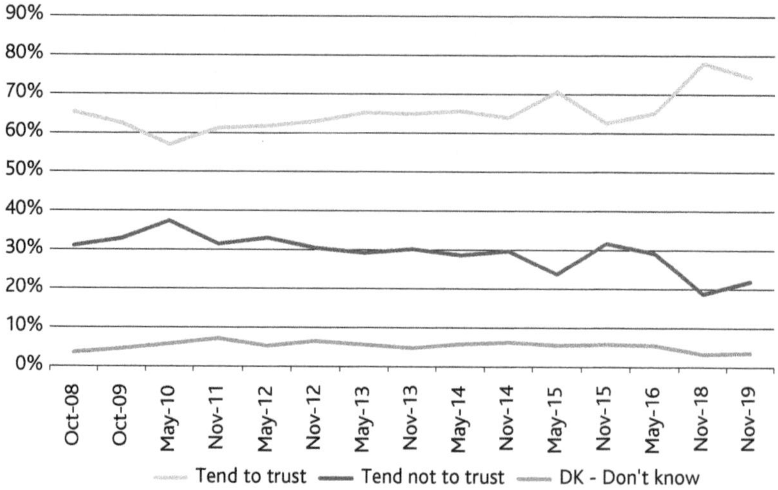

Legend: Tend to trust — Tend not to trust — DK - Don't know

Source: Eurobarometer 2008–19.

regional level has remained remarkably consistent. Since 2008, the number of respondents stating that they 'tend to trust' local and regional public authorities has rarely dipped below 60% and in recent years has climbed over 70% (Figure 5.3). Perhaps unsurprisingly in the wake of the financial crisis, trust in the EU has fluctuated considerably, but notably since 2016 – the post-Brexit era – support and trust in the EU has been consistently high (Figure 5.4).

The Eurobarometer data can be supplemented with further survey data to explore the different dimensions of trust. Once again, if we utilise levels of satisfaction as a proxy for a national government's perceived competence, the results paint a similar narrative to the Edelman Barometer highlighted earlier. The results of the European Social Survey question 'Now thinking about the national government, how satisfied are you with the way it is doing its job?' illustrate that from 2010 to 2016 high satisfaction scores (7–10) increased steadily before declining in the 2018 survey (Figure 5.5). This negative picture is even more clearly reflected in the responses to the German Longitudinal Election Study panel survey collected between 2009 and 2017, which presented a pessimistic set of responses to the statement 'the situation of ordinary people is not getting better, but worse' (Figure 5.6). Over 52% of respondents agreed with the statement, with only just under 20% disagreeing. However, the picture in relation to COVID-19, as highlighted by the 2021 Edelman barometer, is a much more positive picture. The Federal Press Office's June–July 2020 survey illustrated a very high degree of confidence in the response to the COVID-19 pandemic, with over 86% of respondents

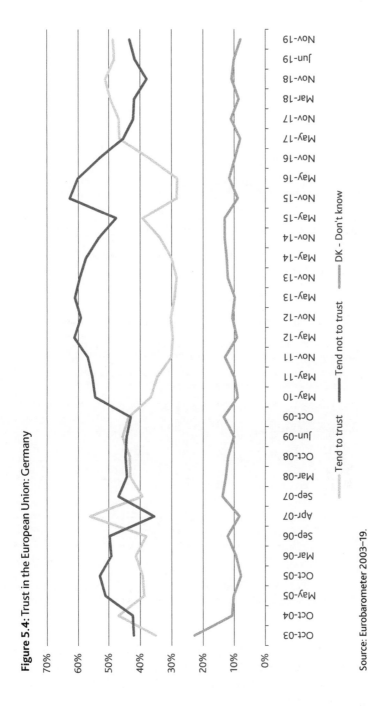

Figure 5.4: Trust in the European Union: Germany

Tend to trust ——— Tend not to trust ——— DK - Don't know

Source: Eurobarometer 2003–19.

Figure 5.5: Now thinking about the national government, how satisfied are you with the way it is doing its job?

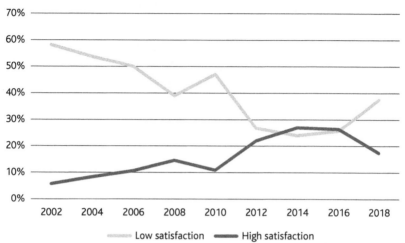

Source: European Social Survey 2002–18.

Figure 5.6: The situation of ordinary people is not getting better, but worse

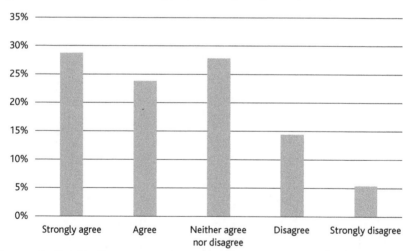

Source: GLES (2019). Rolling cross-section election campaign study with post-election panel wave, cumulation 2009–2017 (GLES). GESIS Data Archive, Cologne. ZA6834 Data file Version 1.0.0, https://doi.org/10.4232/1.13370.

agreeing with the statement that 'politicians in Germany are doing most of the right things when dealing with the Corona crisis' (Figure 5.7).

In terms of benevolence measures, much like the UK, we can utilise a proxy question in the European Social Survey asking whether government takes into account the interests of all citizens – a majority (almost 66%)

Figure 5.7: Politicians in Germany are doing most of the right things when dealing with the Corona crisis

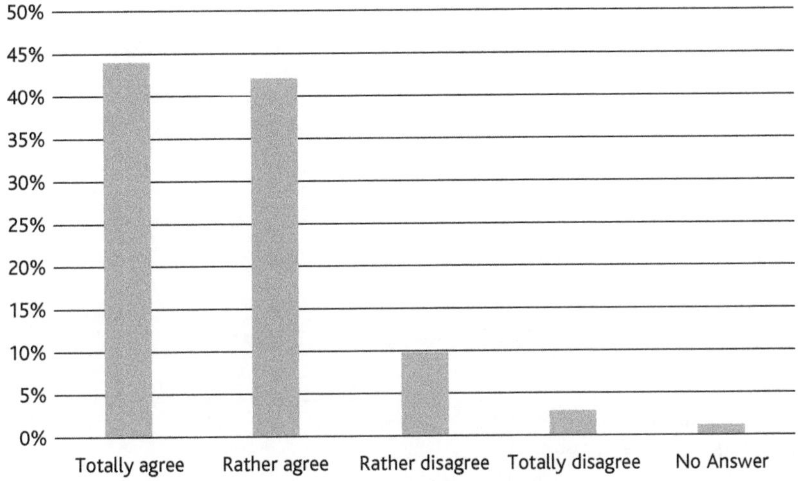

Source: Presse- und Informationsamt der Bundesregierung, Berlin (2021). Trust in state and society during the corona crisis (June/July 2020). GESIS Data Archive, Cologne. ZA7675 Data file Version 1.0.0, https://doi.org/10.4232/1.13654.

replied 'some' or 'a lot' but a sizeable minority (just over 33%) replied 'very little' or 'not at all' (Figure 5.8). Responses to a similar question in the German Longitudinal Election Study panel survey collected between 2009 and 2017 appear to show a similar theme, with just over 37% of respondents strongly agreeing or agreeing with the statement that 'politicians are not interested in citizens' (Figure 5.9). Unlike the UK, finding proxy measures for perceived integrity has been challenging but the Transparency International Corruption Perceptions Index, based on the perceptions of experts and business executives reported in a variety of surveys and assessments of corruption, gave Germany a score of 80, which equated to a global ranking of ninth (Transparency International, 2020). This placed Germany ahead of both the UK and France, and alongside the best performing Western European countries.

Transparency represents a key theme within political science in Germany, as mapped out in the work of Steffani (1971). Steffani (1997: 18) argues that any political system consists of two rather distinct processes: that is, the process of the formation of the political will and the process of making the political will binding for everybody. In both processes transparency through debate, speeches and communication is key for political decisions. Similarly, Ascher Barnstone (2005: 1–2) explains that the emphasis placed on transparency in the Federal Republic of Germany in political, societal and architectural terms represented 'a weapon against the past'. Furthermore, she argues that

Figure 5.8: The government takes into account the interests of all citizens

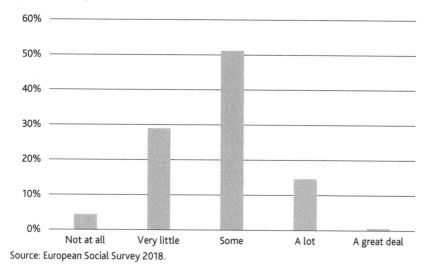

Source: European Social Survey 2018.

Figure 5.9: Politicians are not interested in citizens

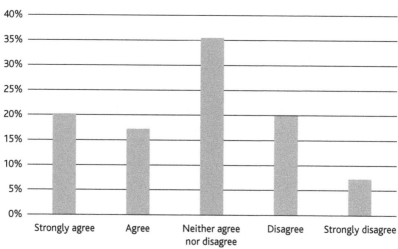

Source: GLES (2019). Rolling Cross-Section Election Campaign Study with Post-election Panel Wave, Cumulation 2009–2017 (GLES). GESIS Data Archive, Cologne. ZA6834 Data file Version 1.0.0, https://doi.org/10.4232/1.13370.

this collective memory and desire for transparency has meant that 'neither the failed experiments in radically transparent governance, nor the lack of a truly transparent society, or open and accessible parliament have dulled enthusiasm for the concept in the political realm' (Barnstone, 2005: 232). Indeed, a desire for transparency is reflected in the responses to high-profile scandals, corruption and accidents, such as Stuttgart 21 (Brettschneider and Schuster, 2013), the VW emissions scandal, the expansion of Frankfurt/Main airport (Geis, 2005), the building of the Elbe Philharmonic Concert Hall in Hamburg and the construction of Berlin-Brandenburg airport. Increasingly, transparency is framed as much by public demand and citizen participation as by political elites (Christmann and Taylor, 2002).

The data examining transparency in the German context, much like the UK, is relatively limited but in recent years a range of legislation has been introduced, including the Federal Freedom of Information Act 2006 and the Open Data Act 2017, which required all agencies of the direct federal administration to proactively publish all data as open data (Group of States against Corruption, 2020: 21). In addition, at the Länder and local level there has been some far-reaching transparency-oriented legislation. For example, the Hamburg Transparency Act of 2012 has been characterised as a pioneering piece of legislation shifting the focus to more proactive forms of openness (Deutsche Gesellschaft für Internationale Zusammenarbeit, 2019). These positive developments are perhaps reflected in Germany's performance in the World Justice Project's (WJP) Open Government Index 2015 collating four items: publicised laws and government data, right to information, civic participation, and complaint mechanisms. Germany's overall score of 0.72 placed it fifteenth in the global index and eleventh in the WJP's region (World Justice Project, 2020). Notably, the responses to the questions centred on 'publicised laws and government data' in the WJP's general population poll were often slightly below the WJP region average (Table 5.1). However, the 'civic participation' responses were frequently well above the regional average. This appears to confirm the emphasis that has been placed on the civic dynamic in relation to transparency in Germany.

The reality of transparency in Germany is perhaps not quite as positive as the picture painted by the WJP Open Government Index and recent legislation at both the Federal and Länder levels. Ahead of Germany's presidency of the Council of the EU, the Corporate Europe Observatory and LobbyControl eV published a jointly authored report that was critical of the Federal Government (Corporate Europe Observatory and LobbyControl eV, 2020). The report argued that ahead of the presidency the Federal Government had been 'too readily available' to be lobbied by big business and industrial interests, from the car and gas industries to big tech companies like Facebook, while smaller civil society had been left out in the cold (Corporate Europe Observatory and LobbyControl eV, 2020: 69). Although one might expect this line of reasoning, it ties in with arguments made elsewhere. For example, the Group of States against Corruption (GRECO) report on Germany adopted in 2020 noted that their evaluation team met some interlocutors who stated that certain federal agencies adopted a 'basic stance against the disclosure of information' and made a raft of

Table 5.1: WJP Open Government Index 2015: publicised laws and government data (% very good or good)

	Germany	EU + EFTA + North America
How would you rate the quality of information published by the government?	68	67
How would you rate the quantity of information published by the government?	60	63
How would you rate the accessibility of information published by the government?	58	59
How would you rate the reliability of information published by the government?	56	63

Source: WJP Open Government Index 2015.

recommendations related to strengthening transparency around lobbying (GRECO, 2020: 22). Finally, the OECD OURdata illustrates that, based on the relatively narrow definition of transparency as 'open data', Germany lags behind many European countries, finishing twenty-fifth in the 2019 statistics (OECD, 2020: 22). However, the adoption of the Federal Open Data Act had a significant impact on the 'data accessibility' dimension of the index (Table 5.2). It could be argued that these statistics reflect a wider challenge in that it is relatively straightforward to introduce the formal or legal dimension of transparency, but 'real transparency' is more challenging to realise (De Coninck and Förste, 2014).

Comparing trust and transparency at the subnational level

Although Germany is, in formal constitutional terms, a federation, its society is highly nationally integrated. The standard reading is that a national level of identification and regulation underpins political trust. The model of territorial organisation is based on a tradition emphasising equal public services. The region, as a distinct political entity or identity, is therefore alien to the German political system. There are, from a legal–political point of view, either Länder or the federal government. Regions may exist in a cultural sense, but regional identity is more often than not tied to a vernacular dialect that does not spill over into the political realm. Sometimes the dialects spoken in opposing regions are so close to each other that both entities understand each other better than they understand the German language. However, if linguistic borders exist, they do not play a role in politics.

Defining the region in German terms is deeply problematic. On the one hand, most German regions are artificial creations, as the federal structure

Table 5.2: OURdata Index 2017 and 2019: Germany

	2017	2019
OURdata Index overall score	**0.41**	**0.5**
Pillar 1: Data availability	0.43 (0.14)*	0.50 (0.17)*
1.1 Content open by default policy	0.08	0.19
1.2 Stakeholder engagement for data release	0.14	0.08
1.3 Implementation	0.21	0.23
Pillar 2: Data accessibility	0.54 (0.18)*	0.81 (0.27)*
2.1 Content of the unrestricted access to data policy	0.19	0.33
2.2 Stakeholder engagement for data quality and completeness	0.07	0.20
2.3 Implementation	0.29	0.27
Pillar 3: Government support for data reuse	0.25 (0.08)*	0.20 (0.07)*
3.1 Data promotion initiatives and partnerships	0.14	0.12
3.2 Data literacy programmes in government	0.11	0.08
3.3 Monitoring impact	0.00	0.00

Source: OECD Stat.

(*the score in brackets refers to the weight given to each pillar in the overall OURdata Index score).

was imposed to a degree by the Western allies after the end of World War II. Bavaria stands apart from the other regions, in that it combines a historical community with deep roots, a strong sense of identity and distinctive political institutions and movements. On the other hand, there is a cultural regionalism, for example, concerning the Francs and the people from Baden, who consider themselves to constitute regions. However, these vernacular cultures do not have any recognised state structures. Dialect and ancestors alone connect politicians to the culture and identity of either the Baden or Franc regions. These are mutually exclusive, so that it is not possible to be a Franc and a Baden at the same time and place.

The context provides other examples of national regulation, as in the case of the newspapers in Germany. Though newspaper titles might refer to specific regions in Germany, the general focus of the press lies in national politics, economy and culture. Most newspapers also have a branch for the region, but even then reporting is rarely principally concerned with that region. For example, the Frankfurter Allgemeine Zeitung (FAZ) contains the city of Frankfurt in its title, but it is also a national newspaper and by no means "only" a regional newspaper (Interview HE01).

There has been some discussion in Germany about the role of administrative and political transparency at the subnational level. In the broader public administration literature, one understanding of transparency is as a form of (new) public management; applied to subnational entities, transparency appears as a mechanism for ranking and rating the Länder. Such mechanisms are important in Germany, especially in the case of budgetary policy. As the experience in US federalism indicates, the transparency of budgets turns out to be more effective than legally binding budget rules. As a rule, voluntary compliance is motivated by 'naming and shaming'. The system prevalent in Germany of reports and indicators provides transparency on the quality of budget policy and its potential effects, so that Land parliaments, voters in Länder, rating agencies, banks, and even other EU member states can assess the policy of a Land. Though the proceedings of the Stability Council (the national-level body for coordinating budgetary policies) are confidential, individual Land governments are exposed to pressure from different sides to meet benchmarks. The effectiveness of this soft control mechanism is reinforced by the timing of the annual stability reports to be submitted to the Council. They are due each year right before the budget processes at the federal and Länder level enter into the parliamentary phase. Although budget processes are, in theory, not connected to each other, the federal and Länder governments and their parliaments now have comparative indicators available showing how their budget policy has developed in the last two years and how it can be assessed for the current year and the following two years. This public information has a regulating effect on the demands of Länder departments and parties in parliament requesting funds.

The stability reports on the budgets, in particular on the expenditures of Länder governments and the system of indicators and benchmarks, constitute a new element in German federalism. As mentioned earlier, the expectations or recommendations of the Stability Council cannot be legally enforced, however. Moreover, in spite of the legal possibility of decisions being taken with a qualified majority, the Stability Council acts in practice on the basis of a consensus. The procedure works in practice rather like the EU's 'Open Method of Coordination', benchmarking best practices, and exercising 'informal' peer group influence. Therefore, coordination results less from a deliberative process among peers than from the pressure of comparative evaluation.

The trust–transparency nexus in two German regions

In the German case, as in the UK and France, two regions within each state were chosen as comparators. These were Hesse and Saxony-Anhalt (constructed later than that of Hesse and of a more artificial nature). Though the contemporary German state structure was established in 1949, the state of Hesse had its roots long before then. On the other side Saxony-Anhalt was created after German unity in 1990. Of course, this leaves out the question if the German state after 1990 was a different state than before 1990; but, in formal terms, the former East German Länder were simply absorbed into the existing Federal Republic. Maintaining the Federal Republic as the form of German unity was deemed to ensure maximal continuity and to recognise the institutional stability and high level of trust accorded to the political regime. However, such unconditional absorption was in time resented by important parts of the Eastern German population.

Consistent with the introductory discussion, society and politics in Hesse and Saxony-Anhalt form part of an overarching German political culture and the situation is hardly equal to the situation of multinational or decentralised unitary states like Spain or the UK. Nonetheless, both Länder have distinct histories, party configurations and place-specific dynamics that are now presented as important contextual features for understanding the trust–transparency matrix.

Part of the contrast between these two regions lies in their differing types of institutional capacity. In the Western Länder or regions, institutions were already in place when Eastern Länder declared to abandon Soviet rule and step over to the West German institutions and the Basic Law. For other East European states these institutions needed to be built up anew and maintained, whereas in the (West) German case institutions had already existed since the end of World War II in 1945. This abstract notion of the persistence of trust is one whereby Eastern German Länder were designed with Western Germany in mind, creating a sense of mistrust towards and sometimes nostalgia for the pre-1990 regime. Institutional continuity is much greater in the case of Hesse, the established, historic Land, than in Saxony-Anhalt, in permanent institutional reconstruction. While in Hesse there were only minor modifications of the local government structure, there have been repeated reforms in Saxony-Anhalt. Phrased in a different way: trust in the political institutions of the former West German state is well exemplified in Hesse, but such associations make less sense in the case of Saxony-Anhalt, a latecomer to the Federal Republic of Germany.

The Land of Saxony-Anhalt was created by the German Democratic Republic (GDR, East Germany) and it was incorporated with very minor changes into the area of validity of the Basic Law upon unification. One part of the current Land ('Anhalt') existed as a province in the German Reich and the Weimar Republic, while the other territorial parts belonged at that time of the Reich and Weimar to the Land of Saxony. A province was the lowest administrative unit in the decentralised unitary state of the Weimar Republic; during the German Reich after 1933, all regional entities were equal, irrespective of whether regionalism played a role.

The expert interviews we carried out were structured in a way that allowed a comparison between regions and states – that is, for the case of Germany, Hesse and Saxony-Anhalt. We assured our interview partners that we would rigorously respect confidentiality. For the two cases of Hesse and

Saxony-Anhalt we identified three types of actor for interviews about trust and transparency in the two different Länder, according to the purposive sample adopted elsewhere: namely, government officials, parliamentarians and civil society actors. In the first group interview partners were mostly reluctant to accept our interview requests and we obtained only a small number of replies. In Hesse and Saxony-Anhalt, we deduce that it was hard for government officials to state that they do not trust a person or an institution. Here was a practical illustration of the institutional–individual dilemma and the interplay of contrasting principles such as confidentiality. This situation was similar in both regions, which were directly comparable in this respect.

The second group of interviewees were related to parliamentarians of Saxony-Anhalt and Hesse, as the democratic representatives of these Länder. Here the petition committee of the Landtag was the major access point, where citizens are able to get in contact with any political institutions of the relevant Land. However, only the opposition parties in Saxony-Anhalt and Hesse agreed to conduct interviews. Members of the governing parties were as reluctant as the government officials of Saxony-Anhalt and Hesse; trust excluded transparency in this instance. Opposition deputies did consent to be interviewed for the project, hence our parliamentary panel was somewhat skewed towards representatives of the opposition parties. In contrast, our third target group of representatives of civil society groups (including journalists, religious organisations and non-governmental organisations) were much more open to be interviewed.

Several prominent themes emerged from the interviews in the two regions, the most important of which concerned political accountability. The interviews revealed mistrust between the land parliaments and governments, a classical restatement of competition between the executive and legislative branches of government. There is a distinct possibility that such a mechanism was exaggerated, especially insofar as the respondents were drawn from the petitions committee and members of parliament from opposition parties (Interviews HE02, HE09, HE10, SH01, SH02). But it is equally likely that opposition deputies were expressing a more general frustration with regional political executives. The territorial structure itself was referred to only marginally by some interview participants (Interviews HE06 and SH08) and certainly did not feature as an element of general contention. Distributive politics, on the other hand, were present, in the form of the need for fairer policy delivery, especially in the social policy field by civil society actors (Interviews SH04, HE05, SH05). Indeed, the structure of society was mentioned by both older and younger residents in the sample (Interview SH09).

One solution for the problem of political accountability lies in a clearer separation of powers at the Land level. For one interviewee (Interview

HE01), a further strengthening of trust in Land political institutions would require a clearer separation between parliament and government instead of parliamentary majority and minority. But the reverse development has been taking place. The phrase 'new dualism' in Germany refers to the increasing practice of parliamentary scrutiny being limited, in practice, to the opposition parties (Detterbeck, 2010: 43). New dualism replaces the academic term of 'old institutionalism', whereby support and control of government is the work of the entire parliament, across parties. In a situation where there is increasing partisan division into government and majority, 'new dualism' signifies the introduction of a de facto majoritarian logic into the operation of the Land parliaments. In parliamentary government, as in German Länder, the government rests on the political party's majority in the respective Land parliament (Landtag). Logically, the increased polarisation between Land majority coalitions and their oppositions aggravated mistrust among parliamentary representatives and changed the nature of parliamentary scrutiny.

An additional institutional theme that emerged from the interviews related to the role of the petitions committee, bodies that are designed to enhance the role of citizens and encourage political participation. The petitions committee in each Landtag is foreseen by the Land constitutions. It is the place for citizens to criticise the administration. If a citizen approaches the petition committee and the committee accepts the citizen's complaint, then the committee has to check the complaint. In theory, the petition committee is a means of control of government by parliament (Zeh, 1989). But in practice the majority in government also has the majority on the petitions committee of the Landtag, limiting its capacity for neutral scrutiny (Interviews SH01 and HE02). The petitions committees have become toothless institutions, caught between the governmental majority and opposition minority in the new dualism. In terms of accountability, the danger is that the mechanism is underpinned by a party-based logic, a criticism voiced by interviewees in both Hesse and Saxony-Anhalt.

If political institutions were criticised for lack of transparency, several interviewees identified the types of policies that needed to be adopted to enhance trust in political institutions. Policies designed to enhance output efficiency were deemed likely to enhance trust in political institutions, especially those policies aimed at relaxing the job market. For one interlocutor (Interview HE02), increased spending on social and employment policies would increase trust in political institutions. According to this argument, if citizens had more local job opportunities, they would not need to change their domicile, hence trust could be built up more easily. This argument represents a form of place-based legitimacy. It translates into possible hypotheses where economic development is a predictor for trust in political institutions. The distinction between exchange and community-based sense of place is reasonable here. The exchange-based understanding of trust operates in terms of jobs as goods that can be distributed, with the expectation that those who have jobs will trust the government more than unemployed persons. For community-based trust, on the other hand, there is a much weaker link with political institutions and their capacity to broker exchanges. There is no relationship between trust in politics and the provision of public goods. Applied to the two regions, there is a much weaker tradition of exchange-based trust in Saxony-Anhalt than in Hesse, which has had the time since the end of World War II in 1945 to build up exchange-based trust practices (Gabriel and Zmerli, 2006). Saxony-Anhalt has much less rooted traditions of exchange (of goods and services, or political fortunes) that shaped the German model in the western part of Germany in a region such as Hesse from 1945 until 1990. It might at best be an exemplar of community-based trust, in the sense of a strong sense of place.

Exchange-based reasoning is also easier in Hesse because this Land has had a consistently high economic performance. There is a much weaker economic performance in Saxony-Anhalt and much less confidence in the brokerage capacity of political institutions. The solidarity within German federalism is at work in these two regions. Hence, Hesse contributes to the fiscal equalisation scheme between Länder and Saxony-Anhalt receives money from the fiscal equalisation mechanism. But economic transfers have not served to lessen the sense of rivalry between East and West Germany, or to rally citizens in Saxony-Anhalt to celebrate the virtues of a redistributive system of fiscal federalism. Herein lie the limits of solidarity. Even though people in Saxony-Anhalt benefit from many mechanisms like fiscal equalisation, there is no easy correlation between trust in government and the provision of public services (in this case of social assistance). As a result, it is extremely difficult to make the case for output legitimacy, whereby effective public policies foster trust.

In a variant of the institutional and policy debates, party politics played an important role in calibrating trust and mistrust. We observe two important points of similarity from Hesse and Saxony-Anhalt. First, parties operate in a nationally focused system. The political context for the two Länder was similar as both are embedded in the German context. The political parties themselves are similar in Hesse and Saxony-Anhalt to those at the federal level or in other Länder – except Bavaria, which explains in part why Bavaria was not chosen as a case for the comparison. The German party system is one key element of national cohesion, or has traditionally been considered so. Even the AfD is an all-German party and its leading figures are from the western part of Germany. The party Die Linke has its strongholds in Eastern Germany as it is the successor party of the Party of Democratic Socialism (PDS), itself the successor of the Sozialistische Einheitspartei Deutschlands (SED), the state party of the German Democratic Republic. Furthermore,

Bavaria has always had the Christlich Soziale Union (CSU) as the main party of the conservative right. Apart from the exceptions of the CSU and Die Linke, however, German parties are highly nationally integrated, as opposed to the nationally disintegrated ones that can be observed in some other federations, whereby parties at the decentralised level are markedly different from the parties at the national level. In Canada, for example, there are, at least from an organisational point of view, different parties at the provincial level than at the national level, although in some instances the parties have similar names.

Second, across both regions there were points of convergence, especially the need for the democratic parties to combine in order to exclude the right-wing party, the AfD, from regional government. An all-party coalition – the so-called 'Kenia' coalition of the CDU, Social Democratic Party (SPD) and Greens – was formed in 2016 in Saxony-Anhalt to avoid the prospect of the AfD entering into government. In Hesse, also, parties have converged in their resistance to the AfD entering office. One interviewee (Interview SH08) contrasted the situation in Hesse and Saxony-Anhalt, however; in the western Land, the CDU–Green government had all the allures of a modern and constructive engagement to contain the far-right, whereas the anti-AfD coalition in Saxony-Anhalt was fighting a deeply defensive battle. All in all, the presence of a right-wing party such as the AfD is a measure of mistrust in political institutions of the current German political system. Beyond our regions, this stance was even held in conservative Bavaria. Respondents thereby converged.

Germany is a country where there is very little tradition of minority government, at the federal or the Land level. Hence it was acknowledged, in several interviews, that there was a need to build coalitions to govern the regional governments. Across Germany, a variety of coalitions exist in Länder governments. But coalitions also produced a lack of transparency and political accountability. The party dimension played itself out in different ways in the Länder of Hesse and Saxony-Anhalt, particularly by these variable party coalitions at the Land level and the politics of coalitions. The two Länder represent forms of the asymmetry that is typical of German party systems at the subnational level. While Saxony-Anhalt first experimented with SPD–Green coalitions, Hesse was the land that allowed the Greens to break into government for the first time.

Saxony-Anhalt is a German Land with its own specific characteristics, one of which is its reputation for engaging in original political experiments. It was the first to experiment with the so-called 'Magdeburger Model', referring to the alliance that took place from 1994 until 2002, whereby an SPD–Green government under Prime Minister Hoeppner (SPD) was supported by the PDS (later renamed as Die Linke). The toleration was remarkable, because at the time the social democrats (SPD) at the federal level had avoided any cooperation with Die Linke, a stance that continues to this day. The 'Magdeburger Model' was then emulated in the city-state of Berlin between 2001 and 2002, with an SPD-led government tolerated by the PDS. Saxony-Anhalt thus diverged from the 'normal' pattern of party politics. True, there were coalitions between 2002 and 2016, but the 'normal' coalition of CDU and FDP governed for only four years during this period. There was a much longer period of 'grand coalition' between the CDU and SPD, a coalition that is seldom formed at the subnational level in Germany.

The Landtag of Hesse is rather more typical of the political history of Germany. Unlike in Saxony-Anhalt, the governments of Hesse have demonstrated a long-term stability: for example, Georg August Zinn (1950–69) was in office for a total of 19 years. But Hesse is also typical in that it was one of the first Länder in Germany to experience the governmental participation of the newly formed party, the Greens (Die Grünen). Hence Hesse has been, at the same time, traditional and innovative in its coalition politics at the Land level. All major political parties have been present in the Landtag, from the former party of German refugees (GB/BHE), long since disappeared, to the Greens, which were first established in a Land government in Hesse. The Land was typical, insofar as the liberal party (Free Democratic Party – FDP) entered coalitions with the Social and Christian Democrats. The close connection between the Landtag and the government of Hesse illustrated an important trait of German politics.

This overview suggests a weak transparency of governing coalitions. In addition to encouraging coalition formation, the German pattern of multi-level governance introduces mechanisms that blur forms of individual political accountability by politicians. Citizens' trust in parties has been damaged by the positioning of individual politicians/parties, whereby representatives of parties turn either to their federal or their Land profile, depending on the issue at hand. Building trust in party representatives as a whole is complicated by these variable alliances. Interviewees from among the political representatives emphasised the contingency of their own situation and the weight of Länder- and federal-level constraints. Building territorial capacity was complicated by changes in coalitions and incongruent state- and federal-level alliances. The German electoral system itself fed this sense of mistrust with parties. It allows two-level interpretations, depending on whether the broad national or more regional-level issues are considered. There is a German version of the second-order election thesis (Dinkel, 1977), whereby the steady stream of Länder elections is primarily of interest insofar as they impact upon national political issues (and how they modify the balance of forces in the second chamber, the Bundesrat). Usually, the parties in power in the federal government will claim a successful Land election as a reference for 'good' federal performance. On the other hand, governing parties at the federal level take losses in the Länder as a feature of special Land circumstances, in order to avoid negative repercussions of poor Land performance at the federal level (Völkl, 2016: 244).

Hence, in the German case, underpinned by a national frame of regulation, the deeper questions of trust and transparency are also answered with reference to the history of the German nation and especially the division between East and West Germany that continues to shape mentalities. The salient theme emerging from the interviews is the need for the more transparent organisation of formal governing arrangements.

Trust and transparency in civil society in Hesse and Saxony-Anhalt

In this section, we drill down into responses from our civil society interviews in the two regions. Relations within civil society revealed contrasting patterns, to some degree rooted in distinct historical trajectories. The Land of Saxony-Anhalt joined the Federal Republic of Germany (FRG) in 1990, with its first free state election occurring on 14 October 1990. The FRG was an entity that has existed since World War II and the Land of Hesse had existed even before the Federal Republic of Germany (the Land Hesse was establishment on 19 September 1945, while the Basic Law entered into force the on 23 May 1949). Hesse is therefore an older entity than Saxony-Anhalt – and this plays itself out in terms of aspects of trust and transparency in political institutions and civil society. In Hesse, there was a recognisable civil society at the time that the Federal Republic entered into force in 1949. In the case of Saxony-Anhalt, on the other hand, political institutions and civil society had to be rebuilt almost from scratch as a consequence of the new democratic situation in Saxony-Anhalt. Communist elites were and still are present as political actors, both in the administration and in civil society.

Drilling down into the interview corpus, there are notable differences between the two Länder that partially reflect broader distribution of economic capacity in the two cases. The backdrop to discussions of third-sector trust was Germany's model of cooperative federalism, centred on close relationships between social partners in the case of labour and welfare policy (Benz, 2008). Representatives of companies interviewed in Saxony-Anhalt declared that they did not maintain any particularly close or distant relationship with the parties in government and in parliament. The relationship was described as professional towards all actors. No actor was treated with particular favour; connections were more of a more personal nature than based on institutional or party-political logic. The principal complaint from the civil society interviewees lay in the number of coalition partners, making it far more difficult to target individual parties to raise specific concerns. Relationships were described in terms of the necessary and legitimate representation of interests, rather than framed in terms of trust. In this respect, interests, rather than trust, are the issue. From a business perspective, representing business interests forms part of the German bargaining tradition and does not involve concepts such as trust or transparency.

Trust might even be classed as an empty signifier, the main issues for firms were the autonomy of the system of social partnership and wage negotiations. Strongly invested with patterns of collective negotiations and bargaining, representatives of the employers resisted any involvement of political actors in their salary negotiations with employees. If trust is an empty signifier, transparency gained more traction, being understood in terms of clear guidelines for how businesses can obtain financial support or assistance through the public budget (Interview SH07). In general, transparency was not considered to be a problem, because it already existed (Interview SH03) or because it was necessary, in terms of relations between political actors and the public (Interviews SH03 and HE03). An open and transparent deliberation process would allow the people to decide about the issues at stake (Interview HE03).

Whereas the representative of economic enterprises saw hardly any changes in existing relationships between social partners, such as employers and trade unions, the prevailing belief in interviews was that there had been a weakening of trust regarding politics and politicians, and that this was in part due to the economic situation since German unification. In former East Germany, there had been a loss of trust because unification had not delivered the expected economic benefits. This testimony mirrors that of surveys, which demonstrate a rising mistrust in political institutions in Eastern Germany which has led to support for extreme parties. For example, the vote shares of the left-wing party Die Linke and the right-wing AfD have been particularly strong in the eastern part of Germany. In Western Germany, in contrast, cities and municipalities have continued to prosper and have grown more rapidly than in the East. German unification, which occurred three decades previously, had still not been digested by the East. The trust-related events of the past decade, such as the rise of the AfD and the robust performance of Die Linke in the eastern Länder, might be read as a delayed processing of German unification.

In terms of community-based trust, the effects of German unification were still being felt in Saxony-Anhalt. Many young people had moved west, leaving an aging population in Saxony-Anhalt, with increased life expectancy. There were indirect consequences for the political system. The Federal Republic prides itself on its acceptance of rules, its orderly behaviour and its transparent political processes. The evolution in Saxony-Anhalt, however, was a move away from this model, towards more closed communities, rather more distrustful of outside forces than commonly associated with the German model. In our project, many requests for interviews were left unanswered, itself producing a negative response in relation to transparency. The support for AfD now resembles the support of the party Die Linke in earlier times as a manifestation of community-based trust and suspicion of the West. It is important to note that in the former Eastern Germany, the events of 1989 caused genuine upheaval, whereby existing institutions were overthrown. This collective memory remains strong and makes East Germans less likely instinctively to trust the political institutions, seemingly designed for another set of circumstances and interests. In 1989, people in the GDR were not so sure what they wanted, but they were rather sure that they no longer wanted the GDR. In the opinion of one interviewee (Interview SH03), this memory of past institutional collapse continues to undermine the belief in political institutions and administration in general.

The consensus view from the interviews in Saxony-Anhalt was that trust is shrinking in all aspects of life. This mistrust embraces churches, the medical sector, the police and other institutions (Interview SH04), though it has not produced a destabilisation of the entire political system (Interview HE01). From an economic point of view, Saxony-Anhalt is doing worse than Hesse in any Länder ranking, but the economic situation (inner cities, streets, working conditions, and so on) is still better than in the former GDR. Only the perceived situation has become worse, because of the out-migration, particularly of women, from rural areas. This perception has to be contrasted with the real situation. We can deduce that redistributive policies do not play a major role in the production of trust in political institutions. In general, the real economic situation or the content of political order does not play a major role, but the process of how the decision is taken most certainly does. One alternative would be more direct, democratic forms of participation, but this pathway would produce its own repercussions (Interview SH06).

The German cases are replete with examples of proximity trust, whereby closeness to citizens is revealed as a measure of the trustworthiness of politicians. These general sentiments back up the headline findings from the Eurobarometer surveys. One factor affecting proximity trust in a negative sense lies in the withdrawal of local public services. In both Hesse and Saxony-Anhalt, several interviewees suggested a pattern of diminishing trust on account of remote service delivery. In Saxony-Anhalt, there have been continuing changes whereby local government entities have become bigger in size and scope, but catering for a declining population (Interview SH03). For one interlocutor, trust in public service delivery has suffered as a result. It takes more time and more effort to get into touch with local or municipal politicians or to access municipal or local services (Interview 3), let alone medical and social services.

From a formal point of view, access to public services is equal across Germany, but in practice, localities and municipal structures face diverse challenges that play upon their capacity to deliver. The case of the remote delivery of public services was identified in the German interviews, especially in sparsely populated Saxony-Anhalt. The problems are similar in Germany to those identified in our French regions: for example, the difficulties in recruiting medical doctors in rural areas, on account of remuneration and lifestyle. There are fewer rural public services, which feeds a vicious cycle whereby it is predicted that the rural population will decrease in the rural areas of Saxony-Anhalt, while the population of the urban areas, such as the cities of Magdeburg and Halle, will increase until 2030. The response of local government has been to involve citizens in its procedures for political decision-making (Interview SH10), but trust remains low. Indeed, the loss of trust in Saxony-Anhalt serves as a proxy for other German Länder, especially in former Eastern Germany, where the same phenomena of voting patterns and a shrinking number of municipalities or local government units exist.

If proximity trust remains a vibrant sentiment, then reviving trust is likely to lie within the realm of local and/or municipal politics where politicians or persons in the positions engaged in local self-administration are faced directly with citizens. Hence one actor praised the importance of 'socially thick, face-to-face relations' by referring to Warren (1999c: 348). When dealing with citizens, the municipal level has more freedom than the Länder, because the Länder have to obtain the consent of the Bundestag to change the status quo, especially in relation to taxes. On the other hand, more autonomous sources of taxes are available to the municipalities, though we must bear in mind that all German political institutions are obliged to respect a 'compulsory negotiations system' (involving social partners) (Scharpf, 1988).

For one interviewee (Interview SH08), endowing cities and municipalities with more financial freedom is essential if trust is to be revived. There is not much evidence that local tax-raising increases levels of mistrust: one interlocutor pointed out that in Hessian municipalities, local politicians had raised taxes yet managed to get re-elected, because they were able to create trust for their tax plans (Interview HE06). Municipal and local politicians achieved re-election, despite promising higher taxes, by being clear and transparent about their tax plans and by communicating with the citizens (Interview HE06). On the other hand, there is no evidence that granting more money to the cities and municipalities would produce more trust in political institutions. Likewise, there are no clear answers from the interviews about whether institutional design (the size of cities and municipalities) can affect political trust. In general, the interviews provided the expected picture and lobbied for the intermediary groups they stand for.

The trust–transparency matrix in Germany

It is perhaps unsurprising that the German case does not fit neatly into one of the ideal types outlined in the trust–transparency matrix presented in

Chapter 2. However, applying the matrix to the different levels of analysis developed within this chapter provides an interesting picture of the interplay between trust and transparency within different settings. As in France and the UK, each position on the matrix found some support.

First, if we consider secondary data to be related to trust and transparency at the all-German level, we are presented with a picture of comparatively higher levels of trust than in the other countries, and a fairly recent preoccupation with transparency, in the narrow terms of freedom of data on administrative performance as defined here, that has challenged more traditional notions of political accountability.

The German fieldwork offered some interview evidence to support the 'synergy' position on the upper-left hand on the quadrant (see Table 2.2). Verbal accounts of the importance of new public management mechanisms of transparency were confirmed in academic literature over the past decade (for example, see Holtkamp, 2008: 424). The notion of the new public management has spread in many European states and also in Germany, no longer a laggard in this respect. Germany arguably represented the strongest case to support the trust with transparency thesis evoked in Chapter 3. The drivers of transparency have been trends in international public management (soft transfer and naming and shaming), as much as older themes of political accountability and participation.

In the German case, we found little support for the 'blind faith' position. German democracy is strongly influenced by rules of political accountability (a form of transparency) and a legal culture based on rules and legal norms. Blind faith would run counter to these fundamental traits of the German polity. On the other hand, the linked concept of 'confidential trust' held much more analytical purchase, especially within the social partnership between business and labour communities. Confidentiality is a core principle of interactions within the intergovernmental networks that organise German politics. In the nationwide Stability Council, for example, negotiations on the Land and federal budgets are confidential. Regional ministers of finance have not only to explain the Land budget vis-à-vis their own parliament, but also, behind closed doors, in front of colleagues of the other Länder in the Stability Council. In this way, the Stability Council holds Land governments accountable if they diverge from a solid budget policy. Tensions were observed between these various forms of transparency: notably, political accountability to parliament becoming less influential than the mechanisms of policy transfer by the Open Method of Coordination style of exercising peer pressure through adherence to key performance indicators and targets.

The third ideal type postulates that high levels of transparency cause or at least fail to address the negative perceptions of an individual or organisation as being low in competence or incompetent, uncaring and dishonest. Therefore, we characterise this essentially negative-sum ideal type as being defined by 'negligible or counter-productive effects'. There is not much direct evidence for this. The example discussed earlier in relation to local politicians making transparent pledges to raise taxes in the interests of safeguarding public services would appear to go in the opposite direction.

The fourth position of dual dysfunctionality encompasses all the other dimensions and is the sum of mistrust. There is also some evidence to support this, especially at the level of parties and the rise of anti-elite populist movements (AfD in Saxony Anhalt, for example), which have drawn part of their appeal from the belief that key decisions on migration were taken by Merkel alone, without the participation of the Land and local governments likely to be most affected. A lack of transparency undermined trust. Other examples might include the 'boundary spanning' positioning of German politicians as representatives of varied local and national interests, which might be criticised on grounds of transparency as, more generally, the practice of maintaining distinct alliances at the subnational and national levels. Finally, as a whole, Germany fares better in terms of maintaining or preserving trust than either France or the UK, but the specific case of the 2015 decision to welcome migrants on account of Germany's asylum traditions caused controversy and was referred to in several interviews.

Conclusion

The survey of trust and transparency in Germany provides confirmation of broader trends from the other countries, namely the continuing importance of proximity trust, the rise of transparency as a general phenomenon, especially in terms of administrative processes, naming and benchmarking, the challenge of administrative transparency for older parliamentary traditions, with their classic doctrine of political accountability, and the continuing pertinence of national norms and legal reference frames. In both cases, interviewees pointed to forms of proximity trust, as in our other cases. While drawing any causal conclusions would be difficult, no trust can grow when there is no local or municipal identity.

Contrasts between the two regions are in part a function of spatial legacies and their distinctive historical paths. In the case of Saxony-Anhalt, in particular, we observed a form of dual dysfunctionality, whereby mistrust is aggravated by decisions that were perceived to lack transparency and legitimacy: such was the case of the decision taken by Chancellor Merkel in 2015 to do whatever it takes to welcome the wave of migrants from Africa and the Middle East. The choice to vote for anti-system parties challenges the persistence of trust within the political system. Deprived Saxony-Anhalt is characterised in terms of community trust, rather than the more representative exchange-based trust that underpins interactions in Hesse. Trust in politics is a dwindling resource. While trust in Hesse is based on an exchange-based model, Saxony-Anhalt follows the logic of a community-based way of creating trust. If the latter is more representative of Germany as a whole, a future based on trust–transparency synergy at a national level requires close attention to healing the territorial tensions that continue 30 years after German reunification.

6

France: Auvergne-Rhône-Alpes and Bretagne

This chapter applies the trust–transparency matrix outlined in Chapter 2 to the case of France. It draws on a nationwide survey conducted in October 2016, as well as 38 interviews carried out in the two regions Auvergne-Rhône-Alpes and Bretagne from 2017 to 2018. The first section provides an overview of the received literature on trust and transparency, while the second presents cross-national survey findings that portray France as, in most cases, a critical case of mistrust. In the third section, we present findings of the nationwide survey conducted by YouGov, while the fourth section drills down into the interviews in the two regions. After a discussion of civil society, the chapter situates France in the overall context of the trust–transparency matrix and concludes by assessing the challenges that lie ahead in terms of rebuilding trust and role of transparency.

Exploring trust and transparency in France

France has often been deemed a low-trust society. Classical American, British and French scholars converged in the traditional reading of a divided French political culture pitting the 'two Frances' against each other, afraid of face-to-face contact and hiding behind impersonal rules (Crozier, 1963, 1970; Hoffmann, 1963; Hayward, 1973). Such representations have proved stubbornly persistent. This dyarchic culture has variously been diagnosed in terms of a revolutionary tradition, marked by conflict between church and state, between centre and periphery, between Paris and the provinces (Cole, 2017). Central authority has been contested throughout much of France's 200-plus years of post-revolutionary history. There is an undercurrent of political violence, whereby power is won in Paris. The fulcrum of mistrust occurred in the post-war Fourth Republic, which experienced 28 governments in 12 years of existence before succumbing to the colonial conflict in Algeria (Williams, 1964).

The first decade of the Fifth Republic confounded these prognostics. The founding decades of the Fifth Republic witnessed a restoration of trust in national political institutions; specifically, the institution of the French presidency (Ambler, 1975), after the chaos of the latter years of the Fourth Republic. The French presidency, directly elected since 1965, provided an incarnation of political authority (Andrews and Hoffmann, 1981; Wright, 1989) and still represents the key political office. The political modernisation represented by the Fifth Republic was accompanied by profound changes in French society and economy. In one work, Mendras (1989) diagnosed a second French Revolution, where the sense of 'Us versus Them' had withered along with the diminishing influence of the Catholic Church, the Communist Party and the armed forces, the transformation of family life and the general diffusion of the cultural liberalism. May 1968 represented the coming of age of the 'baby-boomer' generation born just after the war. At the individual level, social change reflected the rise of individualism and individual choice in relation to moral issues such as abortion and divorce. Politically, the post-May 1968 period witnessed the increasing saliency of post-materialist politics and movements, reflected first in the revived Socialist Party and later on by the breakthrough of movements such as the Greens.

Such optimism was damaged by the end of the 'trente glorieuses', the three decades of continuous economic growth that ended abruptly with the oil crises of the 1970s (Fourastié, 1980). France experienced a full alternation in power (between right and left) in 1981, and novel forms of political power-sharing via 'cohabitation' (1986–88, 1993–95 and 1997–2002). By the turn of the century, however, not only was France in decline economically (Baverez, 2003; Smith, 2004), but it had to face a series of political shocks best exemplified by the presence of far-right leader Jean-Marie Le Pen in the second round of the 2002 presidential election. Arguably, the Fifth Republic has never really recovered from this 'strange affair' (Cole, 2002).

Hence, the crisis of trust that appeared in the early 2000s and which is linked with individual, intermediary and institutional levels of analysis. Economists have observed a deeply rooted pessimism among French citizens as a whole (Senik, 2014). In its 2020 report on Well-being in France, for example, the Centre pour la recherche économique et ses applications identified France as a distinct laggard in terms of happiness and well-being; with the same level of education, health, employment prospects or life expectancy, the French citizens were less happy than their counterparts in other European countries (Senik, 2014; Perona and Senik, 2021). This individual-level doubt manifested itself, for example, in the high proportion of French citizens declaring their hostility to any vaccine during the COVID-19 crisis (Vignaud, 2021). This latter example contributes to understanding how trust operates as a facet of civil society, a theme developed later on in the chapter. The diminishing social trust dimension represents a long-term evolution and is nested in broad patterns of social change (Todd, 1995). Senik (2014) identifies a loss of sense and a challenge to a status–conscious society (société de statut) as being the driving forces of social mistrust. Psephologists such as Mayer and Perrineau (1989) earlier on identified correlations between the support for the far-right National Front (Front national – FN) and low levels of interpersonal trust beyond the immediate family.

Third, the crisis of trust is a crisis of democracy (Boy and Chiche, 2010). As underscored by Rouban, Boy and Chiche (CEVIPOF, 2009) in their analysis of the first 'Barometer of political trust', the distrust of politics that appeared at the end of the 1970s has grown considerably, evolving into a rejection of the 'system', testified by the rise of anti-system forces such as the National Front and growing abstention rates. Running since 2009, the CEVIPOF'S Trust Barometer provides an exhaustive database on general attitudes towards trust. The period mapped by the CEVIPOF (2009–21) is one of democratic dissatisfaction. In 2009, those considering that democracy is functioning well were still in a majority (CEVIPOF, 2009, 2014, 2020). By 2010 opinion had shifted: a majority (57%) held the view that democracy in France was not functioning well, a figure that had risen to 73% by late 2014 (CEVIPOF, 2014). These attitudes were aggravated by a general mistrust towards 'politics' and 'politicians': by the time of the 2014 survey, mistrust mobilised 39% of respondents and distrust 33% (CEVIPOF, 2014). The trust in organisations question consistently revealed that political parties were the least trusted of all polled organisations, hovering at around 10% of trust throughout the period (Cheurfa, 2017; Cheurfa and Chanvril, 2019). The data also suggested that the concepts of left and right had lost their meaning and that neither left nor right could be trusted with the country's future (CEVIPOF, 2014). Emmanuel Macron's election as President in 2017 is best understood in this context of a broad-brush rejection of politics and political organisations and a calling into question of the left–right cleavage (Cole, 2019). By 2018, however, trust levels were once again declining and the 2018–19 Yellow Vest ('gilets jaunes') movement provided a spectacular reminder of the hollow bases of the social contract and linked with a much older literature on governability (Hoffmann, 1994; Bedock, 2019; Tran, 2021). France has a long history of mistrust and of a political culture alternating between remote, sometimes authoritarian rule, and sporadic revolts, sometimes described in terms of a revolutionary tradition.

There have been flashes of optimism, soon eclipsed by events and the feeling of democratic disenfranchisement. The 2017 electoral success of Macron and his party, La Republique En Marche!, for example, reflected Converse and Dupeux's (1962: 2) characterisation of 'spasms of political excitement' around flash parties in the French political system. However, a little over a year later the gilets jaunes movement emerged from outside traditional partisan structures and challenged the legitimacy of some state apparatuses and the agenda of the Macron regime (Tran, 2021). Kipfer (2019: 212) notes that the 'gilets jaunes' are slightly older than average, disproportionately white and drawn from a core of working-class occupations but importantly have little prior experience with political parties or unions. Therefore, in many senses they reflect the wider anti-politics and anti-establishment agenda which has characterised populist movements across Western Europe and the US in recent years. Grossman and Sauger (2017) identify a 'hatred' of politics, fed by the routine of excessive promises and shattered experiences, extending into a mistrust of professionals and the media (Agacinski, 2018). There has been a transformation in views of the leading institutions, the political parties in particular, now viewed as objects of disdain and distrust. The central political institution of the presidency has declined in prestige, exacerbated by the introduction of the five-year presidential term in 2002. Neither Sarkozy (2007–12) nor Hollande (2012–17) were able to secure re-election, the latter being unable even to progress to the second round (Drake and Cole, 2021).

There has been nowhere near the same degree of attention paid to transparency. The rise of transparency as a distinct part of the political agenda has elements in common in the French and other cases. First, transparency is a synonym for the anti-corruption drive in the scandals related to party funding and personal enrichment in the 1980s and 1990s. This remains the prevalent framing of transparency, largely interpreted in terms of the moralisation of political life: one of the first decrees of President Macron was accordingly entitled transparency and the moralisation of the political profession (Cole, 2019). The prevalent framing has centred on the rise of transparency as a form of anti-corruption, best represented by the creation of the office of Financial Public Prosecutor in 2013 and the then socialist government's laws regulating conflicts of interest. Transparency as a means of combating conflicts of interest was a recurrent theme in interviews. This broad trend is directly linked to debates about transparency and trust; investigating magistrates have contributed to the underlying sense of mistrust and malaise in the operation of France's political system, especially parties and the financing of political campaigns (Adut, 2004).

Other understandings of transparency present in the Meijer framework (Chapter 2), especially that of administrative modernisation, fit the French case well. At an interorganisational level, the demand for enhanced transparency is not new. It was being articulated as part of the state reform programmes of the 1980s, especially the transformations enacted by premier Rocard (1988–91) and later consolidated by governments of the left and right (Chevallier, 1988). The themes of One Stop Shops, of public sector partnership contracts, of simplified 'global' budgets and of tighter performance management regimes brought the French case somewhat closer to that observed in the UK and elsewhere (Bezès, 2012). The specific French interest in policy instruments provides an additional dimension whereby transparency, in terms of goals and implementation, became a leitmotif for modernising reformers in central state bureaux (Lascoumes and Le Gales, 2005; Lascoumes and Simard, 2011). New public management doctrines have been increasingly influential, at least since the Sarkozy period (2007–12). Long a laggard, public administration specialists began to diagnose a move from public service to public management in the 1990s, represented by the use of targets, the introduction of new budgetary formulae (Révision générale des politiques publiques, Loi organique sur les lois de finance) and a timid move towards performance indicators.

Third, in terms of open access for data, the French administration has been innovative in terms of the digitalisation of public services and promoting open data, a theme we address below. Finally, transparency has been understood in terms of calls to clarify 'who does what' in discussions of the decentralisation and administrative reform processes. It is this latter dimension that we mainly address in the ensuing discussion.

Survey findings on trust and transparency

In the international comparative surveys, mistrust is the overriding sentiment to describe the French case. For example, the 2020 Edelman Trust Barometer painted a relatively negative picture of government leaders with 69% of respondents agreeing with the statement 'I do not trust in our current leaders to resolve the problems of our country' (Edelman Trust Barometer, 2020). This negative picture of political trust in France was illustrated in the Eurobarometer surveys in October/November 2019, for example, with 71% and 66% of respondents stating that they 'tend not to trust' the national-level government and parliament respectively (Figures 6.1 and 6.2). Similarly, trust in the EU was relatively low, with almost 58% responding negatively, although it is worth noting that as recently as 2008 the EU was relatively well trusted (Figure 6.3). In stark contrast to this picture of distrust at the national and supranational levels, regional and local authorities in France received a relatively high degree of trust, with almost 60% stating that they 'tend to trust' subnational levels of government (Figure 6.4).

On the three dimensions of competence, benevolence and integrity, the French case is one of deeply rooted mistrust. First, if we once again look to levels of satisfaction as a proxy for a national government's perceived competence, the European Social Survey results around satisfaction with the national government paint a consistently negative image (Figure 6.5). Indeed, for the last decade the low satisfaction (0–3) has been around 50% and above, and remarkably in 2014 over 17% of respondents scored the national government 0 out of ten. Second, if we look at the range of measures that can act as a proxy for perceived benevolence we also see a very negative set of results. The 2018 European Social Survey question asking the extent to which respondents agreed with the statement 'the Government takes into account the interests of all citizens' produced by far the weakest set of results of our three countries (Figure 6.6). Over 61% of respondents stated 'very

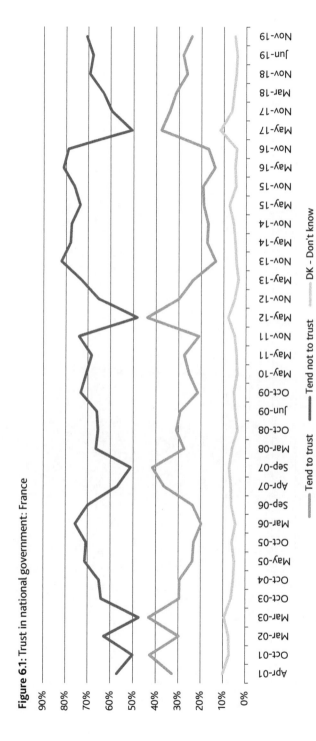

Figure 6.1: Trust in national government: France

Source: Eurobarometer 2001–19.

Figure 6.2: Trust in national parliament: France

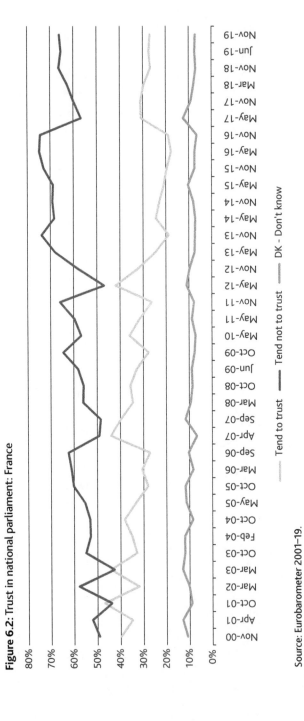

Tend to trust ———— Tend not to trust ———— DK - Don't know

Source: Eurobarometer 2001–19.

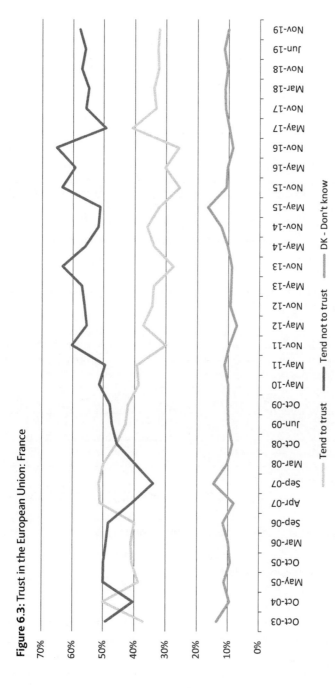

Figure 6.3: Trust in the European Union: France

Tend to trust ⎯ Tend not to trust ⎯ DK - Don't know

Source: Eurobarometer 2003–19.

Figure 6.4: Trust in regional and local public authorities: France

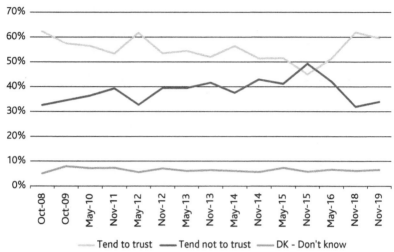

Source: Eurobarometer 2008–19.

Figure 6.5: Now thinking about the national government, how satisfied are you with the way it is doing its job?

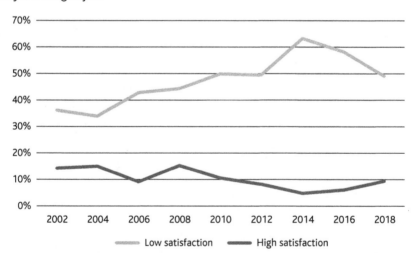

Source: European Social Survey 2002–18.

little' or 'not at all' – significantly higher than both the UK and Germany. Finally, measures of perceived integrity are once again relatively thin on the ground, but the Transparency International Corruption Perceptions Index, based on the perceptions of experts and business executives reported in a variety of surveys and assessments of corruption, gave France a score of 69, which equated to a global ranking of twenty-third (Transparency

Figure 6.6: The government takes into account the interests of all citizens

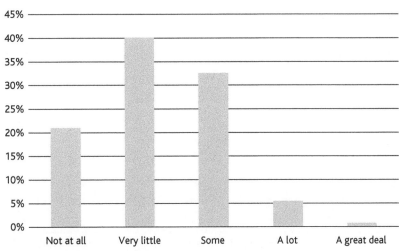

Source: European Social Survey 2018.

International, 2020). Once again, this places France behind the UK and Germany, and therefore across all the dimensions of trust identified in the trust–transparency matrix discussed in Chapter 2, France appears to perform the worst of our three countries.

The figures in Table 6.1 confirm the CEVIPOF's Trust Barometer, which, in its study of trust and key political institutions, identifies proximity as a key quality of trust. In relation to the general question 'do you trust the following institutions a great deal, somewhat, not much, or not at all', the survey consistently places municipal government ahead, followed by the intermediary local and regional authorities, the national government, the presidency, the National Assembly, the EU and organisations such as the G20. In the February 2020 edition, for example, the most trusted institution was the municipal council at 60% (6% up from 2018). When the question is reframed in terms of individuals occupying institutional positions, the conclusions are similar: the mayor of the commune is trusted more than other elected politicians, such as the département councillor, the regional councillor, the Deputy, the Senator, the President, the Prime Minister or the Euro–deputies. The support for the commune is deeply ingrained. That trust is enhanced by proximity is an intuitive finding that is backed up in our survey. In relation to the question 'which level is closest to the needs and preoccupations of the population?', the commune (28%) emerges as the institution that is perceived to be closest to the needs and concerns of the population, ahead of the national government (16%), the region (14%), the département (13%) and the EU (4%). The communal level scores high on the logic of proximity: but the specific question asked by the CEVIPOF

Table 6.1: Correlation analysis results

Variables	Government	Municipal	Region	Department	EU	None
Age	–	–	xxx	–	xxx	xxx
Social class	–	–	–	–	–	–
Left–right scale	xx	x	xxx	xxx	xx	x
Gender (female)	xxx	–	–	–	x	–
Education	xxx	–	–	–	–	–
Party ID	xxx	x	xxx	–	xxx	xxx
Region	xx	–	xxx	x	–	–
Constant	1.52	1.50	1.33	0.40	0.21	5.23
R^2	0.15	0.02	0.08	0.03	0.06	0.13

Source: YouGov. DK and 'other' responses for Party ID and left–right scale included in model but not reported. Sig $*p < 95.0\%$; $**p < 99\%$; $***p < 99.9\%$.

AGE: negative correlation (–0.32 ***) for the 25–32 cohort and the region; **positive correlation** between younger cohorts and the EU (0.35 *** for 18–24; 0.21*** for 25–44). Others non-significant.

LEFT–RIGHT: negative correlations at the extremes (right-wing –0.44 *; very right-wing –0.75**). Others non-significant.

GENDER (female): **negative correlation** with central government (–0.65**) and EU (–0.08*). Others non-significant

EDUCATION: Positive correlation between advanced education and trust in central government 0.55***. Others non-significant.

REGION: Positive correlations with central government for Paris (0.50**) and south-east (0.31*) regions; **negative correlations** with region between Paris (–0.28 **) and south-east regions (–0.33***). Others non-significant.

PARTIES: Positive correlations between Socialists and Central Government (2.26***), Socialists and regions (0.60***), Socialists and EU (0.20**), Republicans and central government (1.04***), Republicans and regions (0.59***), Left Party and central government (1.09 ***), Left Party and regions (0.54**), Greens and central government (1.09***), Greens and regions (0.66***), Democratic Movement (MODEM) and central government (0.98***), MODEM and the regions (1.15***).

is a very general one related to the functioning of political institutions, rather than their competencies in specific areas. It informs us little about policy priorities or, indeed, territorial or socio-demographic effects.

If we examine the relatively narrow interpretation of transparency as open data and FOI, France is frequently characterised as an early adopter. Indeed, its own National Action Plan 2018–20, published as part of the Open Government Partnership – which it joined in April 2014 – stated that 'the principles of accountability and transparency in public action permeate France's judicial and institutional arsenal' and can be traced back to Article 15 of the 1789 Declaration of the Rights of Man and Citizen (République Française, 2018). In addition, France's Law on Free Access to Administrative

Table 6.2: WJP Open Government Index 2015: publicised laws and government data (% very good or good)

	France	EU + EFTA + North America
How would you rate the quality of information published by the government?	65	67
How would you rate the quantity of information published by the government?	No data	63
How would you rate the accessibility of information published by the government?	54	59
How would you rate the reliability of information published by the government?	No data	63

Source: WJP Open Government Index 2015.

Documents was created in 1978 and considered part of the first wave of FOI reforms. In recent years further reforms have strengthened this regime: for example, the creation of a dedicated agency in February 2011, Etalab, to oversee the promotion and implementation of open data policy, and the Digital Republic Bill, adopted in December 2015, which incorporated an 'open by default' policy (Transparency International, 2017). To an extent, these commitments are echoed in the international indexes focused on open data, although the French results in the WJP Open Government Index 2015 are undermined by an absence of data (Table 6.2). However, the results in the OECD OURdata Index identified France as one of the leading countries in the world in terms of open data policies, second only to Korea in the 2019 index and outperforming the UK and Germany by a significant margin (Table 6.3). For example, the OECD report on the 2019 Index noted that 'as an early adopter of Open Government Data policies, France has one of the most highly developed central open government data portals (data.gouv. fr) among OECD countries' (OECD, 2020). Therefore, if transparency is defined narrowly as open data, France can be characterised as an international exemplar. The extent to which this performance is reflected in terms of broader dimensions of transparency is perhaps more open to question.

Trust and accountability: findings from the YouGov survey, 2016

The ensuing data reports findings from a major nationwide survey of trust and transparency in France's system of multi-level government that was carried out from 7 to 11 October 2016. The key headline finding from the survey was a generic one: it revealed a deep mistrust in the functioning of French democracy, including in the new regions, the specific target of the

Table 6.3: OURdata Index 2017 and 2019: France

	2017	2019
OURdata Index overall score	**0.85**	**0.9**
Pillar 1: Data availability	0.83 (0.28)*	0.89 (0.30)*
1.1 Content open by default policy	0.26	0.31
1.2 Stakeholder engagement for data release	0.30	0.29
1.3 Implementation	0.27	0.28
Pillar 2: Data accessibility	0.94 (0.31)*	0.94 (0.31)*
2.1 Content of the unrestricted access to data policy	0.31	0.28
2.2 Stakeholder engagement for data quality and completeness	0.33	0.33
2.3 Implementation	0.30	0.33
Pillar 3: Government support for data reuse	0.78 (0.26)*	0.88 (0.29)*
3.1 Data promotion initiatives and partnerships	0.29	0.29
3.2 Data literacy programmes in government	0.23	0.33
3.3 Monitoring impact	0.26	0.26

Source: OECD Stat.
(* the score in brackets refers to the weight given to each pillar in the overall OURdata Index score)

enquiry. This phenomenon is discussed later. A secondary core finding of the 2016 survey was that trust and mistrust are mediated by scale. Though deeply ambivalent or hostile to all institutions, when forced to choose, citizens looked to local, urban and national levels of government over the proposed alternatives. Turning to the 60% of citizens who feel that at least one institution can be trusted, the national government was considered to be most trustworthy on most policy issues. Support for the intermediary levels of subnational government (13 regions and 96 département) is sector- and place-specific, but provided a thin form of legitimisation. The key absence was the EU, barely identified at all as a significant actor even in fields where it manifestly performed a core role (Kohler Koch and Quittkat, 2013). It therefore makes sense to refer to the territorial scales of trust, whereby the city, the département, the region, the national government and the EU attract support or hostility in line with different forms of justification, namely proximity (communes), specialised service delivery (département and regions) and generic institutionalism (national government).

Two types of statistical relationships might be explored. The wider political science literature has identified a range of potential factors underpinning trust, such as citizen satisfaction with policy, economic performance, the prevalence of political scandals and corruption and the influence of social capital (Parker et al, 2014). Such an exercise, which would ideally require longitudinal or time-series analysis, lies beyond the boundaries of this chapter, which engages in a more limited comparison of institutional dynamics at two levels of analysis: public opinion and territorial communities. The more modest question is addressed here of whether trust towards political institutions is the reflection of macro-level sociological variables.

Assuming that trust is a property of socio-demographic markers would require a strong correlation between socio-demographic variables and levels of trust. There is a variety of plausible causal explanations, based on age, gender, social class, education, region and family situation. Literature on social capital (Putnam, 1995), cultural capital (Bourdieu, 1986), political participation (Sintomer and De Maillard, 2007) and co-production (Parrado et al, 2013) would all point to the expectation that levels of political trust correlate strongly with social properties. Existing accounts of the French data identify some relationship (albeit weak) between demographics and trust; for Rouban (2016), distrust is linked to the level of education, socio-economic status, age and political affiliation. The highly educated, the wealthy, the elderly and supporters of moderate parties are more trusting than other groups, though 'trust' in politics has been declining in all categories.

If cross-sectional analysis is to bear out these strong relationships, the evidence will need to demonstrate strong correlations between specific social traits and attitudes towards trust. The analysis presented in Table 6.1 is inconclusive in this respect. Our survey suggested that demography has a significant impact of some sort on trust in all of the institutions, but the nature of the effect varied. Older people trusted département (the general councils) and regional authorities more than those under 45, though age had no effect on trust in the national government or city/communal authorities. On the other hand, youth was associated with higher trust in the EU, which corresponds to the established finding that young people are typically associated with lower levels of Euroscepticism (Gabel, 1998; Hooghe and Marks, 2005). The main finding is that some characteristics were statistically significant predictors of trust in one institution, but not another. Women, for example, are typically less trusting of the national government and the EU than men once all of the other factors in the model are controlled for. Gender had no effect, however, on trust in any of the other institutions. Education had some effect; those with a university degree are typically more trusting of the government. Social class, perhaps surprisingly, has no significant effect on political trust in this survey. From this survey, it is impossible to identify a particular group as typically being more or less trusting than another in governmental institutions. Instead, trust needs to be examined within the specific context of the institution in question.

In the correlational analysis presented in Table 6.1, political ideology (left–right scale) and party identification appear as significant variables, which suggests that political trust is more a function of political concerns than sociological characteristics. These are significantly related to trust in every institution examined, often with substantial effects. Typically, those who identify positively with political parties are more trusting of political institutions than those who do not – with the exception of those who identify with the National Rally (Rassemblement national, RN, formerly Front national). This suggests that not identifying with a political party is indicative of a form of political alienation in France, reflecting the dissatisfaction of individuals with the political options available to them. The 2017 presidential election campaign. won by the centrist Macron who defeated the FN's Le Pen, with neither the Socialists nor the Republicans reaching the run-off, revealed the depth of anti-party sentiments in the French electorate. These findings elucidate why distrust in parties has aggravated the crisis of trust in democracy. Simply put, parties matter; the evidence from this survey suggests that the weakening of party identification has negative spill-over effects for trust in democracy as a whole.

The 2016 YouGov survey ($n = 3,003$, conducted in October 2016) also asked penetrating questions about transparency. It was designed in part to investigate the relationship between trust and accountability in the political system; we treat accountability as a proxy for transparency, as is the case for part of the literature. In the survey, two questions on accountability were the same as those asked in the European Social Survey, along with a bespoke question. These questions were envisaged as testing opinion in relation to three levels of analysis: the democratic principle of accountability in what Lijphart (1999) would call a majoritarian democracy; the practice of conflicts of interest and financial transparency (Mény, 1986; Frears, 1988); and the role of interest groups in public affairs. The survey findings uncovered demands for more accountability: 70% of those surveyed wanted to know more about the role of interest groups in the political process. More than two thirds (69%) considered that existing laws regulating financial probity and conflicts of interest were insufficiently robust. Almost 9 of out every 10 citizens surveyed believed that organisations ought to be accountable, rather than trusted to deliver without close scrutiny. In the finer detail, 61% considered accountability to be 'very important'. An examination of how this varied by region, education, gender, social class and party identification found that there were no significant differences in the belief in the importance of institutional accountability in these traits. The one area where there was a notable difference was age: while the differences were not large, the younger the respondent, the less important they felt institutional accountability was. Of the under-25s, 69% felt that institutional accountability was very important, compared with just over three quarters of those aged 35–44, and 87% of the over-55s.

The 2016 survey asked questions on conflicts of interest and the role of interest groups, two of the core dimensions of the transparency agenda in France. There was a near convergence across region, gender, party

Table 6.4: A demand for tougher laws to regulate conflicts of interest: To what degree do you consider that the laws surrounding information on financial matters and forbidding conflicts of interest are sufficient? (%)

	All (n = 3003)	Bretagne (n.164)	Auvergne Rhône-Alpes (n = 541)	Nouvelle Aquitaine (n = 237)
Entirely or fairly satisfactory	17	12	17	12
Fairly or entirely inadequate	69	78	66	69
Don't know	14	10	17	19

Source: YouGov survey (n = 3,003), October 2016.

identification and generation in relation to demanding tighter controls on conflict-of-interest practices. Around the time of the survey, the dispute over Lux Leaks and the holding of assets in offshore accounts and companies raised public awareness of the thin boundaries between public and private. While not explicitly framed in terms of corruption, the dangers of amalgamation are great, insofar as such practices feed the essentially anti-political sentiment of 'tous pourris', on which populists from Le Pen to Trump have prospered. Interestingly, in our survey, National Front supporters vied with those supporting the Europe Écologie les Verts (EELV) as the most robust advocates of tighter controls. These sentiments were also captured in interviews.

Table 6.4 reveals some differences between two of our regions, the Bretagne sample being more strongly of the opinion that laws needed to be tightened up than the more hybrid sample in Auvergne-Rhône-Alpes. One of the most striking findings of the project, however, is evidence of a public–practitioner misfit: around two thirds (69%) of our interview panels considered that existing laws regulating financial probity and conflicts of interest were sufficiently robust, almost exactly the reverse proportion to that expressed in the opinion survey.

The survey also asked a question about the role of interest groups, also previously used in the European Social Survey (ESS). The question framing was aimed to make explicit views on the acceptability, or otherwise, of the role of interests and experts in processes of policy formulation. Rather unsurprisingly, the role of lobbies – at all levels – is beyond the comprehension of most citizens (Table 6.5). Lobbies and interests are viewed as part of the process of secret government and the exercise of power beyond institutions: much policy elaboration occurs behind closed doors, via expert committees and multi-organisation partnerships (Robert, 2018). Interests formed part of the black hole in the French context, where there is a traditional suspicion of lobbies, yet a rich associative life existing within and around all four levels of government that are identified in the

Table 6.5: Confusion about the role of interest groups in public affairs: Do you feel that you are sufficiently well informed about the role of interest groups in public affairs? If no, would you like to know more? (%)

Level of interest about the role of interest groups	All (n = 3003)	Bretagne (n = 164)	Auvergne-Rhône-Alpes (n = 541)	Nouvelle Aquitaine (n = 237)
Yes, sufficiently well informed	5	4	6	3
No, but interested in finding out more	65	70	63	66
No, no interest in finding out more	19	17	18	18
Don't know	11	7	13	14

Source: YouGov survey (n = 3,003), October 2016.

survey. We observe a noticeable difference between the sampled regions, with Bretagne being the most favourable to knowing more about the role of interests, which might be interpreted as a form of civic belief consistent with existing representations, while the evidence is weaker in Nouvelle Aquitaine and Auvergne-Rhône-Alpes.

The 2016 survey contributed usefully, in a fairly precise sense, to the broader corpus of attitudinal surveys on trust and transparency. Such surveys can suggest regularities, but do not by themselves deliver interpretations. Trust cannot simply be read from statistical indicators. Hence, alongside the nationwide survey, the research enquiry was simultaneously pursued at the level of interactions within territorial policy communities in two French regions, Bretagne and Auvergne-Rhône-Alpes, selected in order to represent distinctive regional cases, in line with the recommendations of Przeworski and Teune (1970). The ensuing section now considers the arguments used in the interviews around trust in political institutions and extrapolates conclusions therefrom.

Comparing trust and transparency at the subnational level

In this section, we investigate trust as a mode of operation within territorial (regional) policy communities, as captured by purposive panels in two French regions. Zooming into the policy communities and public opinion in two regions, the main question that it is possible to answer is whether territorial tensions undermine pre-existing forms of trust among territorial policy communities. A subsidiary question is whether mistrust has increased between elites and the masses. It is acknowledged that the type of trust being investigated here is distinct from that in the mass survey. It comes closer to thicker interactions as surmised in the metaphor of community. It corresponds to the ontological imperative to address primarily that which can be known (Moses and Knutsen, 2012).

What do the existing hypotheses tell us? The literature focusing on territorial governance from an identity-based framework looks to regions as historic, cultural and political entities (Keating, 1998). More instrumental accounts looked to the material capacity of regions and their ability to deliver competencies. The case selection reflected this basic dichotomy: one historic 'strong identity' region, Bretagne; and a second 'new' region, created in 2015 as a result of the merger between the Rhône-Alpes and Auvergne regions. In the ensuing analysis, the French region of Bretagne is interpreted as a strong identity region with a history of trusting relationships and trans-partisan territorial advocacy; while Auvergne-Rhône-Alpes is described as a vast region of more recent creation, which was marked during fieldwork by steep political conflicts and administrative turf wars. The linkage with the previous section is ensured by focusing on the institutional/organisational dimension of trust and transparency: through interview-based retracing and some limited lexical cluster analysis, opening up the way to elite–mass comparisons in the final section.

One of the most distinctive regions of France, Bretagne has a strong sense of its position within French society (Sainclivier, 2004; Morvan, 2017). It is a modestly populated region, with around 3 million population (almost 4 million if the historic capital Nantes were to be included in the analysis). The received literature describes Bretagne as a second-order strong-identity region with a distinctive territorial model (Cole and Pasquier, 2015). Our second region, Auvergne-Rhône-Alpes, is a vast region that spans eastern and central France and includes 12 départements, with a population of 6,622,000. It is a new region, created as a result of the merger between the Rhône-Alpes and Auvergne regions in 2015, producing an entity with considerable weight and influence (the most economically powerful region outside of Île-de-France and Paris). The previous Rhône-Alpes region was celebrated in the 1990s as part of the Four Motors of Europe (with Catalonia, Baden-Württemberg and Lombardy), to signify the alliance of regional economic powerhouses adopting an active transregional European policy (Borrás, 1993; Weyand, 1996; Vavakova and Wolfe, 1999). The scale argument is far more complex than in Bretagne; it is a reconfigured region in the context of a strengthening metropolitan form of government, via the creation of the Lyon metropolitan council in 2015. If Bretagne remains a small, cohesive region without a major metropolis, Auvergne-Rhône-Alpes is a vast region, "the size of Ireland or Holland" (Interview AURA03).

In their work on validity in qualitative research, Adcock and Collier (2001: 541) admit that qualitative researchers ultimately rely on using their 'knowledge of cases to assess alternative explanations'. Interviews are the main source of primary data for understanding the role of trust and transparency in relationships within territorial policy communities on the basis of case-specific knowledge. Interviews ($n = 38$) occurred with comparable members of the policy community in the two regions on the basis of a semi-structured interview schedule which shared several questions with the mass survey, centred on the conditions for political trust and transparency, the appropriate level of decision-making in multi-level governance, the role of interests and trust and the functioning of democracy.

According to established models, there is prima facie evidence to treat Bretagne as a strong trust region. In analysis of the responses to the 2016 survey, the regional level was invested with more trust in the Breton case than in the larger region of Auvergne-Rhône-Alpes. Whereas 47% of the sample trusted the regional council to ensure territorial development in Bretagne, the figure declined to 36% in Auvergne-Rhône-Alpes. Analysis of the coded questionnaire responses (that accompanied the 2017 face-to-face interviews) in Bretagne demonstrated quite clearly a preference for a regional level of regulation among members of the panel. In the word cluster analysis with NVivo (Table 6.6), the region is clearly clustered with the historic entity of Bretagne and the Bretons, as well as there being as a close linkage with low-level democracy and participation involving localities and associations. Auvergne-Rhône-Alpes, on the other hand, is characterised as a weak trust region on account of a deficit of administrative transparency, as well as sharper political tensions, though it enjoys higher material capacity. In the qualitative data analysis with NVivo, the Auvergne-Rhône-Alpes region is clustered with the départements, region(s), the economic development function, local government, budgets and competencies. There is a less salient link to the specific region, of new creation, than in the case of Bretagne, though the region as a general category featured prominently.

During fieldwork, three types of explanation emerged as factors undermining territorial trust: political conflicts, spatial tensions tied to processes of metropolitanisation and administrative complexities. The pervasive and usually rather under-specified influence of a Breton model is a constant that is often asserted in written accounts and interviews (for example, Lucas, 2011; Créhange, 2019). The authors have analysed this in detail elsewhere (Cole and Pasquier, 2015). The main question during fieldwork became that of the end of the Breton model, or at least the lessening distinctiveness of this emblematic region. It is important not to reify a territorial model; features that figure prominently at one stage in history are not necessarily transferable to different sets of circumstances. In the traditional Breton model, for example, the cross-partisan linkage

Table 6.6: Word clusters around trust and transparency in Bretagne and Auvergne-Rhône-Alpes

Breton clusters	Associated words	AURA clusters	Associated words
Breton and the Bretagne region (*n* = 2,908)	Bretagne, Breton, trust, power, region, economics, politics, interests, groups, scale, local, construction, participation	Public authorities (*n* = 1,425)	Departments, Auvergne-Rhône-Alpes, region, economic development, local government, budgets, France
Metropolitan dynamics (*n* = 1,704)	Metropolis, policy competencies, policies, local authorities, evaluation	Trust (*n* = 1,233)	World, evaluation, democracy, power, politics, public policy, policies report, employment, level trust, firm
Territorial political capacity and multi-level government (*n* = 1,945)	European, regional, territories	Transparency and public policy (*n* = 1,130)	Level, interests, citizens, citizen, transparency, politics, competencies, services, territory, local authority, territories, service
Global and European context (*n* = 1,359)	Europe, world, regions, cities, services, municipalities	Metropolis (*n* = 446)	Metropolis, place, communes, commune
France, transparency and democracy (*n* = 483)	France, transparency, democracy	Civil society (*n* = 350)	Regional economic and social council, regions, departments, powers and associations

Source: Author's elaboration on the basis of the Bretagne and Auvergne-Rhône-Alpes interviews. All French words translated into English. The cluster analysis feature of NVivo uses Pearson correlations to identify linguistic associations within the corpus, allowing us to re-group the core interview themes by region and to interpret the relationships between them. There is no hierarchy between these clusters of words, but the feature allows for interesting patterns of co-occurrence, association and variance within the text.

between parties and territorial institutions appeared as the core element of territorial cohesion. The consensual Breton model was an inaccurate pointer to the state of relations in 2018. Interviewees voiced a certain scepticism about the continuing pertinence of this cross-partisan model. In the view of one such interviewee (BRET 08): "The Breton partisan model is an old Christian democratic tradition, which says nothing today to those who are under 50." The evidence pointed to an ebbing of all types of parties as cohesive forms of territorial control – in Bretagne, as elsewhere in France and Europe. Bretagne was no longer insulated against the weight of the far-right National Rally (Rassemblement national) and subject to the same broader pressures in terms of political disaggregation and social disaffection as other areas of France, as demonstrated by the 'gilets jaunes' movement (Tran, 2021). Likewise, the centrist consensus that had characterised the former Rhône-Alpes region had withered well before the forced merger of the region with that of Auvergne in 2016. The deep mistrust revealed during the 2017 interviews was due as much to the consequences on the ongoing institutional merger (between the two regions) as to the change of political majority, from Socialists to Republicans in 2016.

Spatial conflicts and territorial tensions undermined reputed trust in both regions. In the light of the 'gilets jaunes' movement, there is the now dense literature on peripheral France (Guilluy, 2010; Charmes, 2019) and controversies over whether spatial inequalities lie behind new forms of social fracture (Bedock, 2019). Both of our test regions experienced the social movements known as the 'gilets jaunes'. In the case of the Lyon metropolis, Charmes (2019) demonstrates a strong correlation between living in certain rural and small town communities, socio–economic deprivation, sympathy for the 'gilets jaunes' and the breakdown of trust in political and social institutions.

Small towns such as Annonay in the south and Villefranche-sur-Saône to the north of the Lyon metropolis experienced strong protests on the roundabouts in a marked anti-metropolitan movement. In the case of Bretagne, Rennes also became the site for such protests, though less so than Bordeaux, Toulouse or Nantes. These anti-metropolitan and anti-establishment political and social protests were widely diffused across the country, hence it is difficult to identify as a specific territorial effect. These findings damaged the overall cohesion of the territorial capacity approach; more generally, drilling down into the purposive samples for linkages of territorial interactions and trust proved inconclusive.

Such territorial tensions were also highly visible within the larger region, centred on the role of the Lyon metropolis. The prevalent framing of Lyon was as a dynamic metropolis, with strengths in services, insurance, pharmaceuticals, health and manufacturing. In the words of one interviewee (Interview AURA03), Lyon lies "at the hub of a transnational region, with links to the four motors, to the Lyon-Turin fast train liaison, to Switzerland". Another (Interview AURA05) diagnosed a "great diversity with a real economic punch". In the case of Lyon, the prevalent framing was in terms of material capacity: "the Lyon metropolis represents a formidable resource and opportunity" (Interview AURA08); and international prestige: "the metropolis looks firmly to the international arena and is at the heart of a vibrant network" (Interview AURA02). On the other hand, the city of Lyon was an object of considerable controversy. There is a more complex pattern of territorial cleavages than in Bretagne. In the opinion of one Auvergne panel member: "the Lyon people will not like what I'm going to say, but Lyon has an overpowering weight and squeezes out all other territories" (Interview AURA01). Similar sentiments were very widespread among interviewees, and indicative of an underlying spatial tension between the Lyon metropolis and the rest of the region.

Third, administrative complexities performed an independent role. The unease expressed in many of the 2017 interviews in both regions reflected a perceived lack of transparency in interactions. Fieldwork revealed how administrative complexity can be an independent factor of mistrust. Who does what is a vital question in terms of basic transparency and competition between bureaus can have a debilitating effect in terms of organisational trust. The complexities of the main local government reforms under the Hollande presidency were barely understood, even by regional or metropolitan councillors themselves. Such tensions were especially apparent in the new region of Auvergne-Rhône-Alpes. For example, although a 2015 law identified the regional councils as lead authorities in terms of economic development, the Lyon metropolitan council had specific, legally based rights in terms of economic planning. Turf wars ensued and relations between regional and city-based actors were bitter, to an extent reflecting different political majorities in the region and the city of Lyon.

Turning to the interviews themselves, we explored the role of trust and transparency in relationships within territorial policy communities. To be clear, the exercise was one of identifying interpretative associations, rather than organisational networks, which lay beyond this study. To paraphrase the dominant theme of the interviews, interaction requires trusting relationships between actors and is the precondition to accepting placing relationships in the public domain. In terms of our interview panels, trust was generally more highly valued than transparency, at least in terms of small group trust, or interpersonal trust in small communities; it provided the glue for the iterative games of interorganisational relationships. On the other hand, trust is mediated in an interactional sense: a recurrent theme in interviews was that transparency is also a precondition for trust between actors, at least in terms of common understanding of the rules of the game (Interview AURA21). The unease expressed in many of the 2017–18 interviews reflected a perceived lack of transparency in interactions. Among interviewees from all backgrounds, especially in Auvergne-Rhône-Alpes, there was an almost total consensus that the criteria for the 2015 territorial reform lacked transparency and that the main stakeholders were not involved in the process.

Let us pursue somewhat further the question of transparency. While a majority of interviewees in the French regions agreed that organisations ought to be accountable (one of the survey questions), the dangers of excessive transparency emerged as a constant theme in the interviews, to the extent that one interlocutor spoke of "disruptive transparency" (Interview BRET15), while another affirmed that "100% transparency serves no purpose and is counterproductive" (Interview AURA10). In a slight variation, another stressed the dangers of excessive transparency, arguing in favour of "maintaining confidentiality around sensitive programmes" (Interview AURA17). Another dimension emphasised in interviews was that calls for more openness fuel suspicion of the behaviour of politicians. Above all, transparency has been mobilised as part of the agenda of populist parties and a sceptical electorate. In both regions, our survey demonstrated a discursive gap between the operation of policy communities and public opinion, indicative of the high degree of *mistrust* that emerged in the survey. This gap was more important than any distinction between the regions.

Zooming back to the policy communities, we conclude that in both cases (but especially in the stronger Auvergne-Rhône-Alps region) territorial trust and mistrust are in part a function of complexity and interdependency. In practice, new forms of interdependent relations fail against basic benchmarks of transparency, an argument best illustrated by two examples from the field of decentralisation. First, the background to the survey was the territorial reform of 2015. Redrawing the regional map in 2015 was mainly justified by the Hollande administration in terms of size, to align the 13 new regions with the European norm represented by the 16 German Länder. Large regions such as Nouvelle Aquitaine, Grand Est and Auvergne-Rhône-Alpes were intended to reinforce the message that size matters for strategic reasons in a more integrated European space. The process of redefining the regional map manifestly lacked transparency. Territorial actors complained of not having been consulted. Three different versions of the regional map appeared in quick succession; neither the regional councils as institutions, nor the citizens were associated with redrawing the regional boundaries. Even the powerful local government associations complained of being excluded. The lack of transparency was a recurrent theme in gatherings of academics and practitioners in 2015.

Second, the complexities of the two main reforms under the Hollande presidency – the 2014 MAPTAM (La loi du 27 janvier 2014 de modernisation de l'action publique territoriale et d'affirmation des métropoles [the law on the Modernisation of territorial public policy and the metropolitan councils]) and 2015 NOTRe (loi portant nouvelle organisation territoriale de la République [the Law on the New Territorial organisation of the Republic]) laws – were barely understood, even by regional or metropolitan councillors themselves. The economic development process known as the Regional Development Plan (Schéma Régional de Développement Economique d'Innovation et d'Internationalisation – SRDEII) provided evidence in this respect. Although the 2015 NOTRe law identifies the region as the lead authority in terms of economic development, the Lyon metropolitan council has specific, legally based rights over economic planning. It became apparent in interviews with the Auvergne-Rhône-Alpes region and the Lyon metropolitan council that both players had to agree; otherwise the Prefect decides, which both sides wanted to avoid. But relations were hardly trusting; in the opinion of one specialist in the region, the Lyon metropolitan council held the upper hand and produced its own urban plan without formally consulting the region. However, most councillors did not understand these complex manoeuvres, or were not aware of them, with only "25 out of 200 regional councillors able to understand the complexity of the new economic development provisions and the respective roles of the region and the Lyon metropolitan council" (Interview AURA04).

Actors within the territorial policy communities had lost their grasp of complex new arrangements. In both regions, trust was undermined by fuzzy governance and a lack of transparency as part of the process.

Civil society and trust–transparency dilemmas

A comparative study into civil society invites several remarks in relation to the case of France. Once bidding for a comparative education project, the UK members of the team were confronted with the definitive there is no such thing as civil society in France. Official narratives emphasise territorial integrity and ideational unity, the former to recall that France is one and indivisible (the general will embodied in a state), the latter to affirm the universal character of the French Enlightenment and the republican consensus (more observed in orthodox political discourse than in reality). Both unitary constructions refer to past cleavages setting Church against State and Paris against the provinces. More contemporary controversies continue to turn around these two overarching frames that each question the legitimacy of civil society as a distinct sphere of influence. The recent (at the time of writing) controversy in relation to the role of Muslim associations provided a case in point.

Mainstream French intellectual traditions have been hostile to the interplay of interests. The prevailing interpretation, well articulated by Mény (1986), is that the French State has historically been less tolerant towards autonomous groups than in comparable countries. Organised group activity was forbidden during the French Revolution. Only in 1884, with the repeal of the Loi le Chapelier, were professional groups allowed to organise, but they remained weak (Guiliani, 1991). Although the 1901 law fully legalised associations, from the outset there was a bias in favour of 'good associations' that were inclined to work with the State in the pursuit of the general interest (Barthélemy, 2000). The State sets itself above special interests, but it recognises the need for dialogue with social partners. Through subsidising voluntary associations, trade unions and professional associations, public authorities (central and subnational government) bring social organisations into their public policy orbit. Baumgartner (1998) refers to these groups as being colonised by the state.

In formal legal terms, voluntary associations or clubs must be registered under a law dating from 1901 as 'non-profit-making' associations if they are to assured legal protection (Courtois, 1991; Defrasne, 1995; Barthélemy, 2000); '1901 Associations' are required to adopt certain organisational characteristics, such as having written statutes and a management board, and are obliged to register their existence with the prefecture. This enables a fairly precise representation of the extent of civic participation in voluntary associations. What types of groups seek to influence policy outcomes? In a major survey of lobbying activities in the 2012 parliamentary election, Courty and Gervais (2016) identify the types of actors involved in lobbying candidates as including consultants, associations, trade and employers' unions, professional lobbyists, firms, foundations, think tanks and religious organisations congregations. The sectors involved in lobbying, as measured by solicitations reported by candidates in the 2012 legislative elections, included the economy, health, human rights, education, environment and energy, work, social policy and transport, cultural policy and defence. The groups highest profile involved included Terra Nova, the police unions, France Nature Environment and the Social Forum. Finally, Courty and Gervais observed that lobbyists based in Paris had few links with those operating in Brussels, the capital of the European institutions.

Drilling down, there are three alternative perspectives that attempt to capture State–society relations in France (Jennings, 2000; Levy, 2001; Cole, 2008), each of which is elucidated in our interviews. First, republican corporatism (Muller, 1984; Jobert and Muller, 1987), which lays emphasis on the close ties between civil servants and members of the professions, especially in fields such as medical and pharmaceutical standards. In his study of middle managers in the French civil service, Page (2012) brings to light extensive evidence of informal interactions between mid-ranking civil servants and powerful representatives of economic and professional lobbies in what can best be described as policy communities that exclude politicians (hence the book's title *Policy without Politicians*). In his innovative study of the origins and implementation of ten statutory regulations – five décrets (governmental decrees) and five arrêtés (ministerial orders) – Page identified a larger than expected role for interest groups in originating regulations. In six out of ten cases surveyed, the initiative that produced a new or modified regulation lay with an interest group, and only in four cases did the initiative come from the central government department or in response to implementing an EU directive. In the cases covered by Page, the scarcity of information is the critical resource; expertise lies within specialised groups, or with policy entrepreneurs who move between government and interests, and work on the same agendas waiting for policy windows to open. Such a conclusion was backed up in our interviews in Auvergne-Rhône-Alpes: one interview with a veterinary services professional confirmed the policy community view that transparency of deliberation would undermine the trust necessary to ensure effective cooperation. Beneath the cloak of a tight network, in practice professions occupy a key role in determining standards – or in lobbying the EU.

A second approach emphasises the strengthening of local and regional levels of subnational government, which has created new arenas for group influence and activity. There is a fragile functional interdependency between local and regional councils and charities providing services in the field of housing, medical assistance and food. Most voluntary associations exist at a local, or subnational level. The system of regional and local authorities providing financial support for associations means that even groups bitterly opposed to the local authority often depend upon grants for their continued existence. Most French associations are in a weak position with regard both to elected authorities and governmental agencies. They depend upon the latter for both financial support and information. The relationship between local associations and the town hall in particular is a complex one; the mayor claims to personify the general interest, whereas local associations can only claim to represent one fraction of the population. To implement policy effectively, however, the town hall needs a network of associations in all different spheres of local society. In practice, funded associations are de facto implementing agencies for public policies across a very wide range of areas.

The role of associations (formerly speaking, the '1901 associations') in the delivery of public services is one of the more paradoxical features of French politics. Funded in part by grants from municipal, departmental or regional authorities, such associations are unwilling clients of local authorities, subject to brutal political shifts, as in the case of Auvergne-Rhône-Alpes, with the change of political majority in 2016. Questions of trust and mistrust are germane to the interactions between local and regional councils and voluntary associations. Two types of civil society actor interviewed in 2016–17 revealed how poor relations between the new regional majority and association had become. Interviewees from a housing charity complained of being shut out of access to decision-makers with the change of political majority in 2016, and of losing funding shortly after. For their part, trade unionists regretted that existing networks had been disrupted on account of the 2016 territorial reform, which merged the Auvergne and Rhône-Alpes regions. In this case, transaction costs were greatly increased by the absence of clear institutional venues, and the territorial variety dimension added to the prevailing sense of mistrust. There was a breakdown of civil relations between political majorities and the main associations. There was no such brutal rupture in the case of Bretagne, which retained its institutional continuity, and traditionally close interaction between the regional council and key associations.

There is spill-over into the third dimension, the impact of the traditional repertoire of direct action on trust–transparency relations (Tilly, 1986). Evidence emerged during fieldwork of the corrosive effect of the repertoire of direct action, fundamentally based on power relations and the threat of violence, giving rise to movements such as the 'gilets jaunes' (Tran, 2021). In most European democracies, groups that resort to street demonstrations will generally tend to exercise the least pressure, except where demonstrations are massive, and highly symbolic of widespread support. In France, however, such methods have a long history (Fillieule, 1997). Direct action tactics have become a regular feature of group activity, superimposed upon a distant memory of a revolutionary tradition (Tarrow, 1994). French farmers, fisherman, railway workers, lorry drivers and students have perfected strategies designed to cause maximum possible disruption to the normal functioning of French life. The apparent success of such procedures has further encouraged their protagonists. For groups such as farmers, direct action tactics go alongside behind-closed-door negotiations between interest group representatives and state officials. The stratified society produces a labour market that is disputed by insiders and outsiders (Smith, 2004), making more difficult the adaptation of a social model to the challenges of globalisation and international markets.

Some of the most prominent new social movements have been closely associated with the pan-global, anti-globalisation protests that have gathered pace since the failure of the Seattle round of trade talks in 1999. Anti-globalisation groups such as the Social Forum have undoubtedly influenced the climate within which French politics is carried out and have created a major headache for the main left-wing party, the Socialist Party. The behaviour of groups such as the ZADists, fiercely opposed to the building of a new airport at Notre Dame des Landes near Nantes and the demonstrations against the police during the 2018–19 'gilets jaunes' protests showed that violence is never far beneath the surface as part of the collective action employed by these groups. The vigour of these new social movements since the 1980s is testament to the difficulty encountered by existing party structures to articulate new social and generational demands. It is part of the broader processes of mistrust and misfit that are now discussed.

Applying the trust–transparency matrix

As with the other cases, mapping the French example against the trust–transparency matrix reveals distinct dynamics. In the left-hand quadrant of Table 2.2, there appear to be few examples of high trust, high transparency or explicit trust–transparency synergy. Certainly, French politicians such as Hollande and Macron have sought to link greater transparency (via open data and measures to challenge conflicts of interest) with rebuilding trust. There is some evidence from interviews that transparency of the rules of the game is a key element for understanding functioning relationships. From the French case, at least, it is difficult to establish this as a general principle. Bureaucratic turf wars – illustrated throughout the troubled year of 2020 – countered the demand for greater transparency that had accompanied Macron's election in

2017. During the COVID-19 crisis, calls for more transparency underpinned mistrust and demonstrated a lack of positive-sum relationships. The theme of transparency and its linkage with trust is nonetheless a feature of the Macron period, at least in terms of intention. The creation of the Citizens' Convention on the Environment (Convention Citoyenne pour le Climat, 2021), reporting in 2021, provided a precise example on new forms of citizen engagement. Above all, the 2019 'Great Debate' represented a successful exercise in public deliberation in an effort to resolve an institutional and political crisis, in the form of the 'gilets jaunes' movement of 2018–19.

In line with the central focus of the evidence from France, there was less direct evidence of these mechanisms at the regional or local levels; consistent with the survey findings, exercises in deliberation are nationally driven, further elucidating the paradoxes revealed in our 2016 survey. The upper right-hand side of the quadrant of Table 2.2 denotes high trust, low transparency that we describe as 'blind faith'. We found little evidence to sustain this position, given the solid foundations of mistrust. We also identified a variety that we labelled as the 'confidential trust' hypothesis. It refers mainly to interactions within relationships and across organisations. Interview evidence clearly supported the classic position that relationships needed to be maintained as confidential, and that transparency would disrupt such relationships. Trust within organisations and communities remained as a form of secretive government – even when there was the internal requirement for agreement on the rules of the game.

The lower left-hand side of the quadrant refers to low trust, high transparency, which we labelled 'Negligible or counterproductive effects'. The COVID-19 crisis provided ample, if rather paradoxical, evidence that the more practices and procedures were brought into the public domain, the less trust or confidence was expressed in the government; the democratic experiments under Macron also fell somewhat into this category. Whether transparency promoted trust was contextual; the 2019 'Great Debate' witnessed Macron regain the political initiative, while the hesitations and reversals during the COVID-19 crisis gradually sapped political trust (even when an effort was made to promote transparency).

The lower right-hand side of the quadrant – Dual dysfunctionality – finally, is the sum of mistrust. Rather than being substantiated by any specific episode, it represents the history of mistrust in interpersonal, collective and institutional relations which has produced a narrative of weakened state capacity and bureaucratic stasis, especially prevalent in the disputes over the absence of administrative transparency and the weight of bureaucratic turf wars during the 2020–21 COVID-19 crisis. This overview strengthens the received view of a challenged French democratic order, with a strong sense of mistrust and hatred of political representatives, coexisting with a mistrusting society (Algan and Cahuc, 2007) and a mode of collective action that looks to the street to arbitrate disputes. This overview would be incomplete without referring to the complex relationship with the French State, implied in the survey findings: the State is simultaneously detested, yet absolutely central as a reference point.

Conclusion

Mistrust is the overwhelming phenomenon that emerges in this study. Mistrust emerged as the salient feature of our 2016 survey, dominated the 2017 presidential campaign and continued to feature prominently in the CEVIPOF barometer three years later. Findings from the French case are consistent with the more general trends across Europe (even before the COVID-19 pandemic). There are powerful causal narratives around the loss of trust in democratic politics, described in Chapter 2. Such mistrust spills over into direct action in the form of sporadic social movements, such as the 'gilets jaunes' in the case of France in 2018–20 (Tran, 2021). Most fundamentally, we observed little difference among public opinion in the different regions in relation to trust and mistrust of politicians. In both empirical cases, there was some evidence of elite–mass distancing, backing up evidence of mistrust of elites uncovered in the survey.

Can transparency restore trust? We agree with Grossman and Sauger (2017) that political distrust is not equivalent to suspicion. The former reflects a demand for a better democracy and might help to improve it by leading to more oversight, for example, of campaign financing. Much reform in the French case has been designed to introduce more transparency to address the problem of combating mistrust. The common trend in our three countries – and beyond – can be summarised as a long-term move from confidential trust to trust with transparency. But there are powerful forces that work to undermine any simple relationships; the growing number of sources of information has made citizens more demanding, for example, without implying greater knowledge of the results of political actions. Social networks have encouraged people to retain information that supports their opinions, hence weakening the public debate and fuelling mistrust. Debates on transparency do not in themselves respond to the broader challenge of reviving democracy. Transparent standards are necessary, but not sufficient for rebuilding trust. The empirical data collected for this chapter spanned two recent periods of French and European politics. A year of mixed messages in relation to the COVID-19 pandemic – and deep unpopularity – underlined the challenges that lay in terms of rebuilding trust and the role of transparency. We now address the complex trust–transparency relationship in our concluding chapter.

Conclusion: reflections on the trust–transparency nexus

The health of trust – in its various configurations and conceptualisations – and questions as to whether it is in decline, have been a consistent feature of academic research across a wide range of disciplines since the 1960s. Interest has often centred on assessing the impact of specific events or crises on the state of trust, for example, the 2007–8 financial crisis and the rise of populism across the world (Ziller and Schübel, 2015; Algan et al, 2017; Hosking, 2019; Geurkink et al, 2020). The COVID-19 pandemic which engulfed the world from early 2020 sparked further interest in trust-related research, as Devine and colleagues (2021: 276) note, in terms of the impact of the presence or absence of trust on government responses to the pandemic, but also the impact of the pandemic itself on trust. A key feature of this wide-ranging literature has been attempts to understand the role that political trust performs and the impact of its presence or absence. For example, Devine and colleagues (2020: 2) note the key distinction between trust, mistrust and distrust. They point to the characterisation provided by van der Meer and Zmerli (2017: 1) that trust plays the dual role as the 'glue that keeps the system together' and the 'oil that lubricates the policy machine', and mistrust or 'political scepticism' can underpin engagement and accountability. The key challenge occurs when this mistrust evolves into feelings of distrust towards the political system, threatening disengagement and disorder. A further feature of this literature, and perhaps almost more important given the dominant contemporary narrative, has been the search for mechanisms or processes that can help rebuild or restore trust. It is within this space that the research on civil society outlined within this book was situated, and specifically given the existing literature's primary focus on the national level, whether these themes vary as much within states as between them.

The primary objective of the project outlined in this book was to analyse the dynamics between trust and transparency – the trust–transparency nexus – in a comparative context, examining the extent to which these dynamics may differ as much within states as between them. Although the fieldwork was completed before the COVID-19 pandemic, the nuances of the trust–transparency nexus and the importance of contextual factor highlighted in Enria and colleagues' (2021) work, also resonated in our fieldwork. Each of the previous three chapters, drawing on Worthy and Grimmelikhuijsen's

(2012) characterisation of external and internal influence, explored the key factors which shaped processes of building and maintaining trust between civil society actors within the wider context of increasingly complex forms of multi-level governance. In order to facilitate this comparative analysis we operationalised a trust–transparency matrix, outlined in Chapter 2, which identified four ideal types of trust–transparency relationships: synergy, blind faith, negligible or counterproductive effects and dual dysfunctionality. Drawing on the arguments put forward by Meijer and colleagues (2018), the application of the matrix was not intended to provide a calculative tool for the formal measurement of the causal relationship between the two variables, but to provide a heuristic device to enable the systematic comparative analysis of the cases. This final concluding chapter will bring together the findings of the case studies and reflect more broadly on both the potential conceptual and empirical contributions of the research.

Comparing national trust and transparency profiles

The initial analysis of political trust at the national level within our three states provided the broad context for our detailed exploration of 'thin' and 'thick' forms of trust at the subnational level, and specifically in the context of relations between civil society actors. It is important to emphasise again the contrasting character of political trust in this broad context, characterised helpfully by Hooghe and Zmerli (2011: 3) as a 'kind of general expectation that on the whole, political leaders will act according to the rules of the game as they are agreed upon in a democratic regime' and the thicker forms of trust drawing on interpersonal and interorganisational forms of trust, which will be explored in the next section.

Drawing on a wide range of secondary data, the case study chapters provided pictures of political trust in France, Germany and the UK which largely match the dominant narrative around the decline of trust, particularly in France and the UK. The Eurobarometer data on trust in national government, for example, highlights that although all of our countries have experienced some fluctuations over the past two decades, the general trend over recent years is that the gap between France and the UK, and Germany has grown (Figure 7.1). Moreover, the chapters highlighted that if we explore in greater depth different dimensions of trust – competence, benevolence and integrity – the picture of all three cases is not particularly positive. To an extent, this is confirmed by high-profile studies, such as the Edelman Trust Barometer and CEVIPOF Trust Barometer, which have consistently painted a picture of a decline in trust. Intriguingly, the 2021 Edelman Trust Barometer noted that the COVID-19 pandemic created a 'trust bubble' and, although this bubble has appeared to burst in the UK, it shrank to a smaller degree in Germany, and actually grew between May 2020

Figure 7.1: Trust in national government

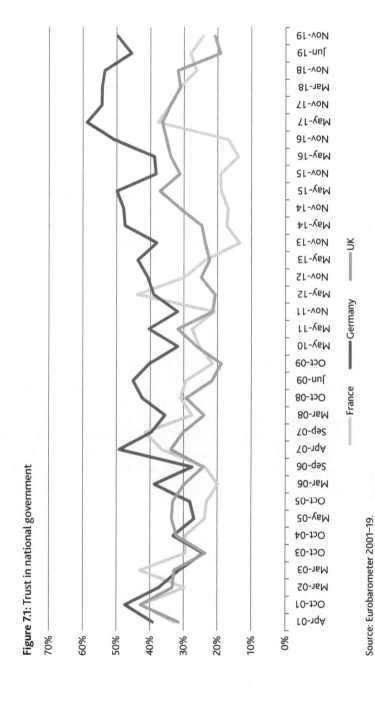

France ———— Germany ———— UK

Source: Eurobarometer 2001–19.

Table 7.1: Edelman Trust Barometer: trust in government

	January 2020	May 2020	January 2021	May 2021
France	35	48	50	51
Germany	45	64	59	55
UK	36	60	45	53

Source: Edelman Trust Barometer (2021).

and May 2021 in France (see Table 7.1). Although the performance of our respective countries is likely to continue to shift dependent on perceptions of government performance in dealing with the pandemic and the vaccination programme, for example, according to the May 2021 Edelman Barometer, trust had once again grown in the UK but declined in Germany.

In all of our states finding comparable data related to transparency was challenging, particularly compared to the rich range of secondary data available on trust-related issues. The majority of international sources featured in our chapters, such as the WJP Open Government Index and OECD OURdata, utilise a relatively narrow conception of transparency centred on the availability of data to the general public. As highlighted in Chapter 2, much like trust, transparency is a multidimensional concept that can encompass a multitude of phenomena and therefore focusing on the extent to which states have introduced measures to ensure data availability and accessibility is perhaps only part of the story. However, these formal measures provide an interesting picture of our three states. For example, despite embracing aspects of transparency, Germany performs fairly poorly in the WJP Open Government and OURdata indexes, and France and the UK perform fairly well. However, when this data is compared to public attitudes on transparency within the respective countries, an interesting picture emerges. Responses to the question 'How much would you say that decisions in [country] politics are transparent, meaning that everyone can see how they were made?' in the 2018 European Social Survey provide a contrasting result (see Figure 7.2). Despite coming second in the OECD's OURdata Index in 2019, over 70% of respondents in France stated that decisions were 'Not at all' or 'Very little' in terms of transparency. Therefore, there appears to be a disjuncture between formal steps towards open government, such as FOI legislation and a proactive approach to making data available, and public perceptions of openness more broadly.

Exploring the trust–transparency nexus at the subnational level

A key starting point for the project was the observation made by Grimmelikhuijsen and colleagues (2013: 584) towards the end of their

Figure 7.2: How much would you say that decisions in [country] politics are transparent, meaning that everyone can see how they were made?

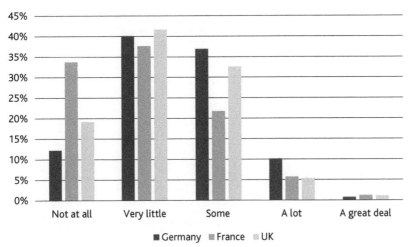

Germany France UK

Source: European Social Survey 2018.

cross-national analysis of the trust and transparency in the Netherlands and South Korea that 'national cultural values play a significant role in how people perceive and appreciate government transparency'. Our primary aim was to explore whether such an effect could also be found within states as much as between them, following the challenge to methodological nationalism presented by Jeffery and Wincott (2010) and in keeping with the tradition of territorial politics research. However, like many research projects we were constrained by the realities of our resources: for example, the project team was able to secure funding and carry out an original survey in France but were unable to replicate this in Germany and the UK. In France, the CEVIPOF Trust Barometer and YouGov survey carried out in our project illustrated that scale was a factor in public trust, for example, the latter finding that it was the municipality level (28%) which was most often seen as most representing the needs and concern of the population. However, notably, the level of government which followed the municipality level was the national (16%) level, followed by the regional level (14%), highlighting that although scale does appear to be a factor, it is frequently not a straightforward dynamic. Comparable data in Germany and the UK was patchy at best, but in the latter we seem to see the broad trend that the public generally perceived levels of government which are closer to them, whether it be at the local or regional level, to be more likely to have their interests at heart. The most consistent comparable data source is the Eurobarometer question on trust in regional and local authorities, which, although somewhat vague, provides a picture in stark contrast to the national-level data previously discussed (Figure 7.3).

Figure 7.3: Trust in regional and local public authorities: tend to trust

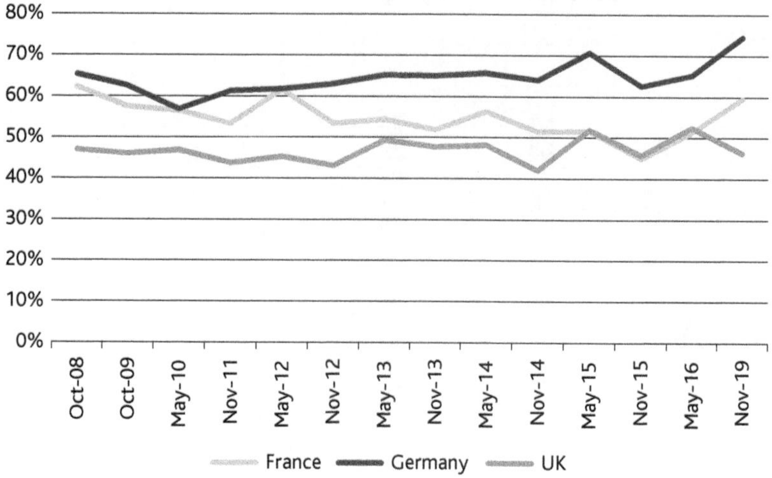

France ——— Germany ——— UK

Source: Eurobarometer 2008–19.

Table 7.2: Trust–transparency matrix

Trust	Transparency	
	High	Low
High	Synergy	Blind faith
Low	Negligible or counterproductive effects	Dual dysfunctionality

The data on public attitudes to transparency at the subnational level is almost entirely absent and therefore remains a significant gap in our knowledge.

In applying the trust–transparency matrix (Table 7.2) we can see a nuanced picture of the interplay between trust and transparency in all of our cases. In the UK, the analysis of 'thin' political trust at the national level suggests that the transparency measures adopted in the UK appear to have had a 'negligible or counterproductive effect' on public attitudes, and the precise role that transparency plays at the subnational level is unclear. Indeed, based on the qualitative fieldwork, the general perception was that there may actually be a reduced level of transparency at the devolved level in the North West and Wales, due to the lack of understanding of devolved arrangements and, particularly in the Welsh context, the absence of a robust media. In contrast, the general picture of trust–transparency in terms of 'thick' forms of trust embedded in civil society relations was much closer to 'synergy', with transparency being a key building block of both interpersonal and interorganisational trust. In Germany, the picture presented of both public attitudes to 'thin' political trust and 'thick' forms of trust in civil society relations provided a mixed picture. The emphasis placed on transparency through new public management reforms provides evidence of 'synergy', while there was also clear evidence of 'confidential trust', a variant of 'blind faith' where trust is maintained but full transparency is not required due to the need for confidentiality. However, there was also some evidence of 'dual dysfunctionality', particularly in Saxony-Anhalt, where anti-elite populist movements had become more significant. In France, the picture is also somewhat nuanced, although perhaps to a lesser extent than in Germany. While the overriding theme appears to be 'dual dysfunctionality' and high levels of mistrust, there was some evidence that reflected at least some movement towards other ideal types. For example, in terms of the relationships between individuals and organisations, both a degree of 'synergy' and 'confidential trust' were identified in the fieldwork. Therefore, even in the French case, transparency of the rules of the game was a key element for understanding functioning relationships and therefore building trust.

The analysis of the key factors which shaped processes of building and maintaining trust between civil society actors at the subnational level within the wider context of increasingly complex forms of multi-level governance identified a range of overarching themes within and between our cases. These themes highlighted the importance of Worthy and Grimmelikhuijsen's (2012) characterisation of external or macro influences, the wider political environment and internal or micro influences, the individual-level factors. In the UK, civil society actors were given a central role in both North West England and Wales, and there was a clear emphasis on partnership and collaboration between civil society actors themselves and with government institutions. To an extent this can be seen as an almost inevitable consequence of the impact of austerity measures, but this underestimates the long-term commitment to partnership-working and the shared commitment to delivering for their respective localities. In contrast, in the two German Länder considered in our research, the key factor shaping the trust–transparency nexus at the subnational level was the importance placed on the law and legal norms, and less emphasis was placed on partnership and collaboration. For example, transparency was not framed as a starting point for political accountability and a legal culture based on rules and legal norms. In France, the fieldwork emphasised the central role of public authorities and the historic scepticism regarding the potential role of civil society actors or associations. This highlights the importance of the wider political environment in terms of shaping the nature of the trust–transparency nexus at the subnational level, as Chapter 6 notes, the research team once encountered the perception that there is no such thing as civil society in France. While the fieldwork completed for this project suggests that such a claim is perhaps too bold, it does provide some indication of the core factors which have shaped variations across our three cases. However, interestingly, in explaining variation within these cases, there are some similarities across the six subnational localities.

The subnational fieldwork identified important themes in terms of the factors or influences which shaped differences between the subnational localities within the countries that were included in our study: France (Auvergne-Rhône-Alpes and Bretagne), Germany (Hesse and Saxony-Anhalt) and the UK (North West England and Wales). First, and perhaps the strongest similarity, was the importance of the historical setting in our subnational territories. In all three of our cases a comparison could be made between, on the one hand, territories or regions with a strong history of institutional continuity or close interaction between government and civil society actors and, on the other, territories or regions with a recent history and with variable levels of past cooperation at that scale. Bretagne, Wales and to a lesser extent Hesse were defined by a stronger sense of territorial identity and a much longer history of cooperation and partnership working which provided the foundations for trust. In contrast, to a greater or lesser extent this was either absent or in an earlier form in Auvergne-Rhône-Alpes, Saxony-Anhalt and North West England. The latter provides an interesting example where this trend can also be found in the subnational case study as the spatial scale for devolution lies beneath the regional level. On the one hand, in the Greater Manchester City Region the trust that underpins the evolving devolved arrangements and civil society relations has been built on several decades of partnership-working, whereas, on the other hand, the Liverpool City Region is at a much earlier stage of its devolution and partnership-working journey, and trust is therefore perhaps more fragile.

The second overarching theme that shaped variations within our three countries is somewhat related to the previous theme and concerns the impact of the restructuring of governance within our respective states. Broadly, in those territories which had been subject to recent processes of territorial restructuring or reorganisation, it was more likely that trust would face specific challenges related to spatial tensions. This theme was perhaps most marked in Auvergne-Rhône-Alpes, where a deficit of administrative transparency, relatively high levels of mistrust and political tensions were driven by the continued impact of the institutional merger of two existing regions, Auvergne and Rhône-Alpes. The impact of restructuring or reorganisation can also be found in North West England and to a lesser extent in Saxony-Anhalt. If we consider the North West as a whole, there is a clear sliding scale from the Greater Manchester City Region, which builds on pre-existing arrangements, through the Liverpool City Region, where tensions are more far more apparent, and finally to those parts of the region, such as the proposed Lancashire Combined Authority, where tensions have been a key factor in preventing the formalisation of governance arrangements. The case of Saxony-Anhalt is somewhat different, and this theme is illustrated over a much longer timespan, but its creation following German unification signifies weaker institutional continuity when compared with Hesse.

The third overarching theme highlighted by the fieldwork centred on the relative formality of arrangements that supported the building of trust within our subnational territories. This was perhaps most clearly exemplified in the UK case study, where in the Welsh case trust was most commonly perceived as being underpinned by the tight-knit interpersonal relations that characterised policy communities within a small country such as Wales. One stakeholder, for example, reflected that "in bigger ponds you would have that professional overlapping and shared history but you wouldn't necessarily have the personal stuff overlapping that as well" (Interview WAL04). In contrast, in North West England while interpersonal relations were important, there was much greater focus on creating formal agreements and compacts between organisations. On the one hand, these types of formal agreements were probably not as deep as the more personalised form of trust but, on the other, they are perhaps more resilient in terms of changes of personnel. Although the UK provided the starkest contrast around this theme within our fieldwork, these themes were also illustrated to some degree in our other cases. For example, Bretagne was closer to the Welsh model than Auvergne-Rhône-Alpes, and, as noted earlier, the German cases tended to be more reliant on formal legal agreements.

The final theme was highlighted most clearly in both the French and German case studies and centred on the impact of political conflict on trust at the subnational level. In both of the French subnational territories, the influence of both the far-right National Rally (Rassemblement national) and the 'gilets jaunes' (Yellow Vests) movement illustrated the pressures of political disaggregation and social disaffection that characterised other areas of France (Charmes, 2019; Tran, 2021). Similarly, the rise of Alternative für Deutschland in both Hesse and Saxony-Anhalt was a key contextual factor in terms of the shape of trust among political actors at the subnational level. In both German regions, the established parties combined to counter the threat of the AfD, whereas in Hesse this coalition was characterised as having a coherent progressive agenda, the Saxony-Anhalt coalition was portrayed as simply a defensive coalition. In contrast, this explicit political dimension was missing from the UK case studies. The populist agenda in the UK promulgated by the United Kingdom Independence Party (UKIP) and then the Brexit Party has failed to take a significant foothold in UK elections, particularly at the local and devolved level. Although the Additional Member System (AMS) used for devolved elections in Wales delivered seven seats for UKIP in 2016, there was no sense that this led to the type of impact highlighted in France and Germany.

Across our cases there was no uniform or clear role given to transparency by interviewees in building trust between civil society actors at the subnational level. Perhaps the strongest emphasis was identified by interviewees in North West England and Wales. For example, one interviewee reflected that transparency was a necessary ingredient for building trust, stating that "I don't think you can have trust until you've got transparency" (Interview WAL03). However, it is important to emphasise that transparency in this context was frequently articulated as an openness in terms of the 'rules of the game' and the interests of different actors. Therefore, a degree of transparency ensured that an actor was aware of the 'red lines' of other actors within policy communities. This form of transparency did not equate to 'full transparency' and, as noted above, a degree of confidentiality was often characterised as being essential for collaboration and decision-making. Indeed, as noted in Chapter 6, an interviewee in Bretagne characterised complete openness as "disruptive transparency" (Interview BRET15) and an interviewee in Auvergne-Rhône-Alpes agreed that "100% transparency serves no purpose and is counter-productive" (Interview AURA10). This sentiment was echoed in both the UK and German fieldwork, highlighting that more transparency did not necessarily generate more trust, and could prove counterproductive.

Conclusion

The project upon which this book draws was designed to examine questions of the interaction of trust and transparency, or the trust–transparency nexus, within civil society at the subnational level. The linking of trust and transparency was not new – indeed, a growing literature had emerged over the previous decade examining a variety of questions related to trust–transparency dynamics (Grimmelikhuijsen, 2012; Grimmelikhuijsen et al, 2013; Grimmelikhuijsen and Meijer, 2014; Porumbescu, 2015a; Douglas and Meijer, 2016; Piotrowski et al, 2017; Heald, 2018). The key problem was that these studies centred on the national level, replicating the methodological nationalism that characterises much social science analysis. We found this particularly problematic given that the existing literature emphasises that both trust and transparency are deeply embedded in the wider web of social, economic and political features of society (Newton, 2007; Grimmelikhuijsen et al, 2013). If context matters in terms of building and retaining trust, then there is scope that trust–transparency dynamics may differ as much within states as between them. The project was aimed at providing an empirical contribution to the literature by exploring these questions at the subnational level across three European states. In addition, in developing the trust–transparency matrix as a heuristic device to facilitate the systematic comparative analysis of qualitative fieldwork, we have hoped to contribute to the conceptual toolbox used to examine these questions.

As with any research, there were limitations to what we were able explore in the project, and areas that would benefit from further research. First, the project was designed to explore the trust–transparency nexus within the context of civil society and adopted the comparative case study approach with the aim to develop typological analysis via the trust–transparency matrix. In this respect, the project was not designed to provide a fine-grained measure of causality in terms of the interplay between trust and transparency as variables. However, we would argue that issues highlighted by our fieldwork indicate that there is fertile ground for these types of studies at the subnational level, either by utilising quasi-experimental or quantitative research methodologies. Second, the fieldwork completed across our three cases centred on qualitative fieldwork with civil society actors, but the survey of public attitudes in relation to trust and transparency in the French case highlighted that there is considerable scope to analyse the relationship between transparency and 'thin' forms of political trust at the subnational level. Indeed, the potential influence of key factors such as the existence of an effective territorial media suggests that there are important phenomena that need to be further explored. Finally, the range of cases explored in the project was inevitably limited by the size and scope of the research. In comparing six subnational territories across three European states we were able to confirm that the findings of Grimmelikhuijsen and colleagues (2013) in relation to cross-national differences could also be confirmed at the subnational level. However, one might expect differences at the subnational level to vary further in contexts where the role and status of civil society is quite different.

The COVID-19 pandemic, as noted at the start of this chapter, has renewed interest in trust in terms of both the role that it can play in facilitating an effective response to the pandemic, but also the impact that a government's response to the pandemic can have on the state of trust itself. At the time of writing, the focus of governments across the world has begun to shift from containment to the roll-out of vaccination programmes. Thus, questions around the role of trust in ensuring compliance with lockdown measures and other preventative interventions have been replaced by public debates around the safety of vaccines. Although the focus of the trust–transparency nexus raises pertinent questions for evaluating the response to the COVID-19 pandemic, the conceptual framework and fieldwork explored in this book were developed and carried out prior to the COVID-19 pandemic. They focus on more deep-rooted questions around the nature of trust among civil society actors, the rebuilding of trust in the context of complex forms of governance and the potential role that transparency could play in this process. However, the findings of this research clearly illustrate that if 'building back better' is to be anything more than well-meaning but essentially empty buzzwords, then we might expect trust and transparency, in terms of both civil society and the wider public, to play a pivotal role.

Appendix: qualitative fieldwork guide

The fieldwork was completed across our six sub-regional cases from 2016 to 2018, below is an anonymised outline organised via our country case studies.

UK: Wales and North West England

Interview code	Descriptor	Interview date
WAL01	Public Affairs/Think Tank stakeholder 1, Wales	08/08/2017
WAL02	Local government officer 1, Wales	09/08/2017
WAL03	Transport stakeholder, Wales	11/08/2017
WAL04	Education stakeholder 2, Wales	11/08/2017
WAL05	Public information stakeholder 1, Wales	15/08/2017
WAL06	Voluntary sector stakeholder 1, Wales	16/08/2017
WAL07	Environment stakeholder, Wales	23/08/2017
WAL08	Business stakeholder 1, Wales	29/08/2017
WAL09	Local government officer 2, Wales	30/08/2017
WAL10	Health stakeholder, Wales	31/08/2017
WAL11	Housing stakeholder 1, Wales	06/09/2017
WAL12	Voluntary sector stakeholder 2, Wales	07/09/2017
WAL13	Politician 1, Wales	12/09/2017
WAL14	Education stakeholder 1, Wales	13/09/2017
WAL15	Public information stakeholder 2, Wales	29/09/2017
WAL16	Business stakeholder 2, Wales	18/10/2017
WAL17	Media stakeholder, Wales	18/10/2017
WAL18	Trade union stakeholder, Wales	27/09/2017
WAL19	Housing stakeholder 2, Wales	31/10/2017
WAL20	Public Affairs/Think Tank stakeholder 2, Wales	21/11/2017
WAL21	Local government officer 3, Wales	22/11/2017
NW01	Voluntary sector stakeholder 1, North West	12/06/2018
NW02	Transport stakeholder 1, North West	12/06/2018
NW03	GMCR official 1, North West	11/06/2018
NW04	Local government politician 1, North West	13/06/2018
NW05	Health stakeholder 1, North West	18/06/2018
NW06	Voluntary sector stakeholder 2, North West	19/06/2018
NW07	Voluntary sector stakeholder 3, North West	12/07/2018
NW08	Local government politician 2, North West	12/07/2018

Interview code	Descriptor	Interview date
NW09	Trade union stakeholder 1, North West	13/07/2018
NW10	Voluntary sector stakeholder 4, North West	13/07/2018
NW11	Local government official 1, North West	23/07/2018
NW12	LCR official 1, North West	26/07/2018
NW13	Local government politician 3, North West	26/07/2018
NW14	GMCR official 2, North West	29/08/2018
NW15	LCR official 2, North West	30/08/2018
NW16	Local government politician 4, North West	03/09/2018
NW17	Education stakeholder 1, North West	03/09/2018
NW18	Local government politician 5, North West	10/09/2018

Germany: Hesse and Saxony-Anhalt

Interview code	Descriptor	Interview date
HE01	Media stakeholder 1, Hesse	20/02/2017
HE02	Former Landtag politician 1, Hesse	14/03/2017
HE03	Public information stakeholder 1, Hesse	06/02/2017
HE04	Education stakeholder 2, Hesse	21/02/2017
HE05	Faith groups stakeholder 1, Hesse	13/02/2017
HE06	Local government officer 1, Hesse	13/02/2017
HE07	Public information stakeholder 2, Hesse	08/02/2017
HE08	Public information stakeholder 3, Hesse	13/11/2017
HE09	Former Landtag politician 2, Hesse	22/03/2017
HE10	Former Landtag politician 3, Hesse	15/03/2017
SH01	Former Landtag politician 1, Saxony-Anhalt	16/11/2017
SH02	Former Landtag politician 2, Saxony-Anhalt	19/10/2017
SH03	Media stakeholder 1, Saxony-Anhalt	12/09/2017
SH04	Faith groups stakeholder 1, Saxony-Anhalt	13/09/2017
SH05	Faith groups stakeholder 2, Saxony-Anhalt	19/10/2017
SH06	Media stakeholder 2, Saxony-Anhalt	12/09/2017
SH07	Business stakeholder 1, Saxony-Anhalt	13/09/2017
SH08	Local government officer 1, Saxony-Anhalt	12/09/2017
SH09	Voluntary sector stakeholder 1, Saxony-Anhalt	19/10/2017

France: Auvergne-Rhône-Alpes and Bretagne

Interview code	Descriptor	Interview date
AURA01	Trade union stakeholder 1, Auvergne-Rhône-Alpes	02/11/2017
AURA02	Trade union stakeholder 2, Auvergne-Rhône-Alpes	15/03/2017
AURA03	Local (regional council) politician 1, Auvergne-Rhône-Alpes	07/03/2017
AURA04	Local (regional council) politician 2, Auvergne-Rhône-Alpes	28/02/2017
AURA05	Local (regional council) politician 3, Auvergne-Rhône-Alpes	02/03/2017
AURA06	Local (regional council) politician 5, Auvergne-Rhône-Alpes	17/03/2017
AURA07	Business stakeholder 1, Auvergne-Rhône-Alpes	11/05/2017
AURA08	Local government official 1, Auvergne-Rhône-Alpes	17/03/2017
AURA09	Business stakeholder 2, Auvergne-Rhône-Alpes	01/12/2016
AURA10	Voluntary sector stakeholder 1, Auvergne-Rhône-Alpes	30/09/2016
AURA11	Voluntary sector stakeholders 2, Auvergne-Rhône-Alpes	21/03/2017
AURA12	Local (regional council) politician 5, Auvergne-Rhône-Alpes	05/04/2017
AURA13	Housing stakeholder 1, Auvergne-Rhône-Alpes	01/11/2017
AURA14	Media stakeholder 1, Auvergne-Rhône-Alpes	01/11/2017
AURA15	Voluntary sector stakeholder 3, Auvergne-Rhône-Alpes	16/11/2017
AURA16	Local (regional council) politician 6, Auvergne-Rhône-Alpes	31/10/2017
AURA17	Mayor, medium-sized town, Auvergne-Rhône-Alpes	08/11/2017
AURA18	Local government official 2, Auvergne-Rhône-Alpes	03/03/2018
AURA19	National politician 1. Auvergne-Rhône-Alpes	04/04/2017
AURA20	Mayor, small commune, Auvergne-Rhône-Alpes	01/03/2018
AURA21	Voluntary sector stakeholder 4, Auvergne-Rhône-Alpes	02/03/2018
BRET01	Regional Social and Economic Committee, Bretagne	06/03/2017
BRET02	Official, City and Metropolis of Rennes 1, Bretagne	27/03/2017
BRET03	Business stakeholder 1, Bretagne	27/03/2017
BRET04	Official City and Metropolis of Rennes 2, Bretagne	28/03/2017
BRET05	Planning official, Bretagne Regional Council, Bretagne	29/03/2017
BRET06	President's Office, Bretagne Regional Council, Bretagne	29/03/2017
BRET07	Business stakeholder 2, Bretagne	05/04/2017
BRET08	Senior official, Bretagne Regional Council, Bretagne	05/04/2017
BRET09	Environmental stakeholder 1, Bretagne	06/04/2017
BRET10	Local politician (Rennes), Bretagne	11/04/2017
BRET11	Energy Association official, Bretagne	26/04/2017 02/05/2017
BRET12	Cultural Association official, Bretagne	26/04/2017

Interview code	Descriptor	Interview date
BRET13	Business stakeholder 3, Bretagne	28/04/2017
BRET14	Local politician (Mayor of Rennes), Bretagne	03/05/2017
BRET15	Regional politician, Bretagne	04/05/2017
BRET16	Mayor, small town, Bretagne	04/05/2017
BRET17	Brest city official, Bretagne	05/05/2017
BRET18	Mayor and regional politician, Bretagne	22/05/2017

References

Adcock, R. and Collier, D. (2001) 'Measurement Validity: A Shared Standard for Qualitative and Quantitative Research', *American Political Science Review*, 95(3): 529–46.

Adut, A. (2004) 'Scandal as Norm Entrepreneurship Strategy: Corruption and the French Investigating Magistrates', *Theory and Society*, 33(5): 529–78.

Agacinski, D. (2018) *Expertise et démocratie: Faire avec la defiance*, Paris: France Stratégie.

Algan, Y. and Cahuc, P. (2007) *La Société de défiance*, Paris: Editions ENS rue d'Ulm.

Algan, Y., Guriev, S., Papaioannou, E. and Passari, E. (2017) 'The European Trust Crisis and the Rise of Populism', *Brookings Papers on Economic Activity*, Washington, DC: Brookings Institution Press, pp 309–82.

Allen, N. and Birch, S. (2015) *Ethics and Integrity in British Politics: How Citizens Judge Their Politicians' Conduct and Why It Matters*, Cambridge: Cambridge University Press.

Alloa, E. (2018) 'Transparency: A Magic Concept of Modernity', in E. Alloa and D. Thomä (eds) *Transparency, Society and Subjectivity: Critical Perspectives*, Cham, Switzerland: Palgrave Macmillan, pp 21–55.

Alloa, E. and Thomä, D. (2018) *Transparency, Society and Subjectivity: Critical Perspectives*, Cham, Switzerland: Palgrave Macmillan.

Ambler, J. (1975) 'Trust in Political and Nonpolitical Authorities in France', *Comparative Politics*, 8(1): 31–58.

Anderson, R., Curtis, J. and Grabb, E. (2006) 'Trends in Civic Association Activity in Four Democracies: The Special Case of Women in the United States', *American Sociological Review*, 71(6): 376–400.

Andrews, W.G. and Hoffmann, S. (eds) (1981) *The Fifth Republic at Twenty*, New York: SUNY Press.

Ascher Barnstone, D. (2005) *The Transparent State: Architecture and Politics in Postwar Germany*, Abingdon: Routledge.

Avery, J.M. (2009) 'Political Mistrust among African Americans and Support for the Political System', *Political Research Quarterly*, 62(1): 132–45.

Awan-Scully, R. (2016) *2016 Welsh Election Study* [Online] Available from: (https://blogs.cardiff.ac.uk/electionsinwales/researchresources/ [Accessed 21 August 2020].

Ayres, S. and Stafford, I. (2009) 'Dealmaking in Whitehall: Competing and Complementary Motives behind the Review of Sub-National Economic Development and Regeneration', *International Journal of Public Sector Management*, 22(7): 605–22.

Ayres, S., Flinders, M. and Sandford, M. (2018) 'Territory, Power and Statecraft: Understanding English Devolution', *Regional Studies*, 52:6: 853–64.

Bachmann, R. (2001) 'Trust, Power and Control in Trans-Organizational Relations', *Organization Studies*, 22(2): 337–65.

Bachmann, R. and Inkpen, A.C. (2011) 'Understanding Institutional-Based Trust Building Processes in Inter-Organizational Relationships', *Organization Studies*, 32(2): 281–301.

Balme, R., Marie, J.-L. and Rozenberg, O. (2003) 'Les motifs de la confiance (et de la défiance) politique: Intérêt, connaissance et conviction dans les formes du raisonnement politique', *Revue internationale de politique compare*, 10(3): 433–61.

Barbalet, J. (2019) 'The Experience of Trust: Its Content and Basis', in M. Sasaki (ed) *Trust in Contemporary Society*, Leiden: Brill, pp 11–30.

Barthélemy, M. (2000) *Associations: Un nouvel âge de la participation?*, Paris: Presses de Sciences Po.

Bauer, P.C. and Freitag, M. (2017) 'Measuring Trust', in E.M. Uslaner (ed) *Oxford Handbook of Social and Political Trust*, Oxford: Oxford University Press, pp 15–36.

Baumgartner, F.R. (1998) 'The Nonprofit Sector in France', *French Politics and Society*, 16(1): 48–51.

Bavarez, N. (2003) *La France qui tombe*, Paris: Perrin.

Bedock C (2019) 'Enquêter in situ par questionnaire sur une mobilisation', *Revue française de science politique*, 69(5): 869–92.

Beel, D., Jones, M. and Jones, I.R. (2018) 'Regionalisation and Civil Society in a Time of Austerity: The Cases of Manchester and Sheffield', in C. Berry and A. Giovannini (eds) *Developing England's North*, Cham, Switzerland: Palgrave Macmillan, pp 241–60.

Behnke, N. and Benz, A. (2008) 'The Politics of Constitutional Change between Reform and Evolution', *Publius: The Journal of Federalism*, 39(2): 213–40.

Bennett, A. and George, A.L. (2005) *Case Studies and Theory Development in the Social Sciences*, Cambridge, MA: MIT Press.

Benz, A. (2007) 'Inter-Regional Competition in Cooperative Federalism: New Modes of Multilevel Governance in Germany', *Regional and Federal Studies*, 17(4): 421–36.

Benz, A. (2008) 'From Joint Decision Traps to Over-Regulated Federalism: Adverse Effects of a Successful Constitutional Reform', *German Politics*, 17(4): 440–56.

Benz, A. and Heinz, D. (2017) 'Managing the Economic Crisis in Germany: Building Multi-Level-Governance in Budget Policy', *Revue Internationale de Politique Comparée*, 23(3): 355–78.

Bezès, P. (2012) 'État, experts et savoirs néo-managériaux', *Actes de la recherche en sciences sociales*, 3: 16–37.

Birkenshaw, P.J. (2006) 'Freedom of Information and Openness: Fundamental Human Rights', *Administrative Law Review*, 58(1): 177–28.

Birkenshaw, P.J. and Varney, M. (2019) *Government and Information Rights: The Law Relating to Access, Disclosure and their Regulation* (5th edn), London: Bloomsbury Professional.

Bish, A. and Michie, S. (2010) 'Demographic and Attitudinal Determinants of Protective Behaviours during a Pandemic: A Review', *British Journal of Health Psychology*, 15: 797–824.

Blau, P.M. (1964) *Exchange and Power in Social Life*, New York: Wiley.

Blunkett, D., Flinders, M. and Prosser, B. (2016) 'Devolution, Evolution, Revolution … Democracy? What's Really Happening to English Local Governance?', *Political Quarterly*, 87(4): 553–64.

Borrás, S. (1993): ' "The Four Motors for Europe" and Its Promotion of R and D Linkages: Beyond Geographical Contiguity in Interregional Agreements?', *Regional Policy and Politics*, 3(3): 163–76.

Boserup, B., McKenney, M. and Elkbuli, A. (2020) 'Alarming Trends in US Domestic Violence during the COVID-19 Pandemic', *American Journal of Emergency Medicine*, 38: 2753–55.

Bourdieu, P. (1986) 'The Forms of Capital', in J.G. Richardson (ed) *Handbook of Theory and Research for the Sociology of Education*, Westport, CT: Greenwood, pp 241–58.

Bovens, M. and t'Hart, P. (2016) 'Revisiting the Study of Policy Failures', *Journal of European Public Policy*, 23(5): 653–66.

Bowles, N., Hamilton, J.T. and Levy, D.A.L. (eds) (2014) *Transparency in Politics and the Media: Accountability and Open Government*, Oxford: I.B. Tauris.

Boy, D. and Chiche, J. (2010) 'Confiances', in D. Boy, B. Cautrès and N. Sauger (eds) *Français des européens comme les autres*, Paris: Presses de Sciences Po, pp 45–71.

Bradford, B., Jackson, J. and Hough, M. (2018) 'Trust in Justice', in E.M. Uslaner (ed) *Oxford Handbook of Social and Political Trust*, Oxford: Oxford University Press, pp 633–53.

Braithwaite, V. and Levi, M. (eds) (1998) *Trust and Governance*, New York: Russell Sage Foundation.

Braun, D. and Trein, P. (2014) 'Federal Dynamics in Times of Economic and Financial Crisis', *European Journal of Political Research*, 53(4): 803–21.

Brenner, N. (2004) *New State Spaces: Urban Governance and the Rescaling of Statehood*, Oxford: Oxford University Press.

Brenner, N. (2009) 'Open Questions on State Rescaling', *Cambridge Journal of Regions, Economy and Society*, 2(1): 123–39.

Brettschneider, F. and Schuster, W. (2013) *Stuttgart 21: Ein Großprojekt zwischen Protest und Akzeptanz*, Wiesbaden: Springer.

Bristow, G., Entwistle, T., Jines, F. and Martin, S. (2009) 'New Spaces for Inclusion? Lessons from the "Three-Thirds" Partnerships in Wales', *International Journal of Urban and Regional Research*, 32(4): 903–21.

Cairney, P. and Wellstead, A. (2021) 'COVID-19: Effective Policymaking Depends on Trust in Experts, Politicians, and the Public', *Policy Design and Practice*, 4(1): 1–14.

Cambridge Dictionary (2018) *Cambridge Dictionary*, Cambridge: Cambridge University Press.

Carter, C. and Pasquier, R. (2010) 'The Europeanization of Regions as "Spaces for Politics": A Research Agenda', *Regional and Federal Studies*, 20(3): 295–314.

Cautrès, B. (2017) *Jusqu'ici tout va bien? La démocratie de la défiance en année électorale*, Paris: CEVIPOF.

Centre for Cities (2020) *City Region Research*, London: Centre for Cities.

CEVIPOF (2009) *La confiance dans tous ses états: les dimensions politique, économique, institutionnelle, sociétale et individuelle de la confiance*, Paris: CEVIPOF.

CEVIPOF (2014) 'Le baromètre de la confiance politique 5', *CEVIPOF*, [online] Available from: www.cevipof.com/fr/le-barometre-de-la-confiance-politique-du-cevipof/resultats-1/vague5/ [Accessed 24 July 2017].

CEVIPOF (2020) 'Le baromètre de la confiance politique 10', CEVIPOF, [online] Available from: www.sciencespo.fr/cevipof/sites/sciencespo.fr.cevipof/files/Round%2012%20-%20Barome%cc%80tre%20de%20la%20confiance%20en%20politique%20-%20vague12-1.pdf [Accessed 24 July 2017].

Chan, H.F., Supriyadi, M.W. and Torgler, B. (2018) 'Trust and Tax Morale', in E.M. Uslaner (ed) *Oxford Handbook of Social and Political Trust*, Oxford: Oxford University Press, pp 497–534.

Charmes, E. (2019) *La revanche des villages: Essai sur la France périurbaine*, Paris: Seuil.

Checkland, K., Segar, J., Voorhees, J. and Coleman, A. (2015) ' "Like a Circle in a Spiral, Like a Wheel within a Wheel": The Layers of Complexity and Challenge for Devolution of Health and Social Care in Greater Manchester', *Representation*, 51(4): 453–69.

Cheurfa, M. (2017) *Les exceptions à la confiance politique*, Paris: CEVIPOF.

Cheurfa, M. and Chanvri, F. (2019) *2009–2019: la crise de la confiance politique*, Paris: CEVIPOF.

Chevallier, J. (1988) 'Le discours de la qualité administrative', *Revue française d'Administration Publique*, 46: 121–43.

Christmann, P. and Taylor, G. (2002) 'Globalization and the Environment: Strategies for International Voluntary Environmental Initiatives', *Academy of Management Perspectives*, 16(3): 121–35.

Citrin, J. and Muste, C. (1999) 'Trust in Government', in J.P. Robinson, P.R. Shaver, and L. Wrightsman (eds) *Measures of Political Attitudes*, New York: Academic, pp 465–532.

Clark, A.K. (2014) 'Rethinking the Decline in Social Capital', *American Political Research*, 43(4): 569–601.

Clarke, J. and Newman, J. (2017) '"People in this country have had enough of experts": Brexit and the Paradoxes of Populism', *Critical Policy Studies*, 11(1): 101–16.

Clarke, J., Jennings, W., Moss, J. and Stoker, G. (2018) *The Good Politician: Folk Theories, Political Interaction, and the Rise of Anti-Politics*, Cambridge: Cambridge University Press.

Cole, A. (2002) 'A Strange Affair: The French Presidential and Parliamentary Elections of 2002', *Government and Opposition*, 37(3): 317–42.

Cole, A. (2008) *Governing and Governance in France*, Cambridge: Cambridge University Press.

Cole, A. (2017) *French Politics and Society* (3rd edn), London: Routledge.

Cole, A. (2019) *Emmanuel Macron and the Two Years That Changed France*, Manchester: Manchester University Press.

Cole, A. and Pasquier, R. (2015) 'The Breton Model between Convergence and Capacity', *Territory, Politics, Governance*, 3(1): 51–72.

Cole, A. and Stafford, I. (2015) *Devolution and Governance: Wales between Capacity and Constraint*, Basingstoke: Palgrave Macmillan.

Cole, A., Hargundéguy, J., Stafford, I., Pasquier, R. and De Visscher, C. (2015) 'States of Convergence in Territorial Governance', *Publius: The Journal of Federalism*, 45(2): 297–321.

Collier, D. (1993) 'The Comparative Method', in A.W. Finifter (ed) *Political Science: The State of the Discipline II*, Washington, DC: American Political Science Association, pp 105–19.

Collier, D., Brady, H.E. and Seawight, J. (2004) 'Sources of Leverage in Causal Inference: Toward an Alternative View of Methodology', in H.E. Brady and D. Collier (eds) *Rethinking Social Inquiry: Diverse Tools, Shared Standards*, Lanham, MD: Rowman and Littlefield, pp 229–66.

Colquitt, J.A., Lepine, J.A., Piccolo, R.F., Zapata, C.P. and Rich, B.L. (2012) 'Explaining the Justice–Performance Relationship: Trust as Exchange Deepener or Trust as Uncertainty Reducer?', *Journal of Applied Psychology*, 97(1): 1–15.

Commission on Public Service Governance Delivery (2014) *Full Report*, Cardiff: Welsh Government.

The Committee on Standards in Public Life (2013) *Survey of public attitudes towards conduct in public life 2012*, London: The Committee on Standards in Public Life.

Convention Citoyenne pour le Climat (2021) 'Rapport de la Convention Citoyenne pour le climat' Paris : Conseil eonomiqu, social et environmental. Available from: https://propositions.conventioncitoyennepourleclimat.fr/pdf/CCC-propositions-synthese.pdf [Accessed 31 October 2021].

Converse, P.E. and Dupeux, G. (1962) 'Politicization of the Electorate in France and the United States', *Public Opinion Quarterly*, 26(1): 1–23.

Copus, C., Roberts, M. and Wall, R. (2017) *Local Government in England: Centralisation, Autonomy and Control*, London: Palgrave Macmillan.

Corporate Europe Observatory and LobbyControl eV (2020) *Tainted Love: Corporate Lobbying and the Upcoming German EU Presidency*, Brussels and Cologne: Corporate Europe Observatory and LobbyControl eV.

Courtois, J. (ed) (1991) *Les associations: un monde inconnu*, Nanterre: Crédit coopératif.

Courty, J. and Gervais, J. (2016) *Le lobbying électoral: Groupes en campagne présidentielle 2012*, Villeneuve d'Ascq: Presses Universitaires du Septentrion.

Créhange, P. (2019) *Le mystérieux Club des trente, enquête sur le plus influent des lobbys Bretons*, Langrolay-sur-Rance: Du coin de la rue.

Crozier, M. (1963) *Le phénomène bureaucratique*, Paris: Seuil.

Crozier, M. (1970) *La société bloquée*, Paris: Seuil.

Cucciniello, M., Porumbescu, G.A. and Grimmelikhuijsen, S. (2017) '25 Years of Transparency Research: Evidence and Future Directions', *Public Administration Review*, 77(1): 32–44.

Cucciniello, M. and Nasi, G. (2014) 'Transparency for Trust in Government: How Effective is Formal Transparency?', *International Journal of Public Administration*, 37(13): 911–21.

Dalton, R.J. (2004) *Democratic Challenges, Democratic Choices: The Erosion of Political Support in Advanced Industrial Democracies*, Oxford: Oxford University Press.

Dalton, R.J. (2013) *Citizen Politics: Public Opinion and Political Parties in Advanced Industrial Democracies* (6th edn), Washington, DC: Congressional Quarterly Press.

Dalton, R.J. and Welzel, C. (2014) *The Civic Culture Transformed: From Allegiant to Assertive Citizens*, Cambridge: Cambridge University Press.

Damm, C., Prinos, I. and Sanderson, E. (2017) *Greater Manchester State of the Voluntary, Community and Social Enterprise Sector 2017: A Report on Social and Economic Impact*, Sheffield: Centre for Regional Economic and Social Research.

Davies, R. (1999) *Devolution – A Process Not an Event*, Cardiff: Institute of Welsh Affairs.

Davis, C.L. (1976) 'Social Mistrust as a Determinant of Political Cynicism in a Transitional Society: An Empirical Examination', *Journal of Developing Areas*, 11(1): 91–102.

De Coninck, I. and Förste, L. (2014) 'Transparency in Local Government: A Case Study of Transparency in Hamburg and Antwerp: Giving People What They Need?', *Practices of Transparency – Implementation and Challenges Volume 4*, Maastricht University: MaRBLe, pp 81–99.

de Fine Licht, J. (2011) 'Do We Really Want to Know? The Potentially Negative Effect of Transparency in Decision Making on Perceived Legitimacy', *Scandinavian Political Studies*, 34(3): 183–201.

de Fine Licht, J. (2014) 'Policy Area as a Potential Moderator of Transparency Effects: An Experiment', *Public Administration Review*, 74(3): 361–71.

de Fine Licht, J., Naurin, D., Esaiasson, P. and Gilljam, M. (2014) 'When Does Transparency Generate Legitimacy? Experimenting on a Context-Bound Relationship?', *Governance: An International Journal of Policy, Administration, and Institutions*, 27(1): 111–34.

Deas, I. (2014) 'The Search for Territorial Fixes in Subnational Governance: City-Regions and the Disputed Emergence of Post-Political Consensus in Manchester, England', *Urban Studies*, 51(11): 2285–314.

Defrasne, J. (1995) *La Vie associative en France*, Paris: PUF.

Denters, B. (2002) 'Size and Political Trust: Evidence from Denmark, the Netherlands, Norway, and the United Kingdom', *Environment and Planning C: Government and Policy*, 20(6): 793–812.

Department for Communities and Local Government (2015) *Local Government Transparency Code 2015*, London: Department for Communities and Local Government.

Desage, F. and Guéranger, D. (2011) *La politique confisquée: Sociologie des réformes et des institutions intercommunales*, Bellecombe-en-Bauges: Éditions du Croqua.

Detterbeck, K. (2010) 'Idee und Theorie des Föderalismus', in K. Detterbeck, W. Renzsch and S. Schieren (eds) *Föderalismus in Deutschland*, München: Oldenbourg Verlag, pp 31–51.

Deutsche Gesellschaft für Internationale Zusammenarbeit (2019) *Freedom of Information and Transparency in Germany*, Hamburg: Deutsche Gesellschaft für Internationale Zusammenarbeit.

Devine, D., Gaskell, J., Jennings, W. and Stoker, G. (2020) *Exploring Trust, Mistrust and Distrust*, Southampton: TrustGov Working Paper Series.

Devine, D., Gaskell, J., Jennings, W. and Stoker, G. (2021) 'Trust and the Coronavirus Pandemic: What Are the Consequences of and for Trust? An Early Review of the Literature', *Political Studies Review*, 19(2): 274-285.

Dinkel, R. (1977) 'Der Zusammenhang zwischen Bundestags und Landtagswahlergebnissen', *Politische Vierteljahresschrift* 18: 349–59.

Direction Générale des Collectivités Locales (2020) *Les Chiffres-clés des collectivités locales*, Paris: Interior Ministry.

Dogan, M. (ed) (2005) *Political Mistrust and the Discrediting of Politicians*, Boston, MA: Brill.

Dogan, M. and Pelassy, D. (1990) *How to Compare Nations: Strategies in Comparative Politics* (2nd edn), Chatham, NJ: Chatham House.

Douglas, S. and Meijer, A. (2016) 'Transparency and Public Value – Analyzing the Transparency Practices and Value Creation of Public Utilities', *International Journal of Public Administration*, 39(12): 940–51.

Drake, H. and Cole, A. (2021) 'Can the French Presidency Survive? Political Leadership in Crisis', in H. Drake, A. Cole, S. Meunier, S. and V. Tiberj (eds) *Developments in French Politics 6*, London: Macmillan, pp 19–35.

Earle, T. (2004) 'Thinking Aloud about Trust: A Protocol Analysis of Trust in Risk Management', *Risk Analysis*, 24(1): 169–83.

Earle, T. and Siegrist, M. (2008) 'Trust, Confidence and Cooperation Model: A Framework for Understanding the Relation between Trust and Risk Perception', *International Journal of Global Environmental Issues*, 8(1): 17–29.

Easton, D. (1965) *A Systems Analysis of Political Life*, New York: Wiley.

Edelenbos, J. and Eshuis, J. (2012) 'The Interplay between Trust and Control in Governance Processes: A Conceptual and Empirical Investigation', *Administration and Society*, 44(6): 647–74.

Edelenbos, J. and Klijn, E. (2007) 'Trust in Complex Decision-Making Networks: A Theoretical and Empirical Exploration', *Administration and Society*, 39(1): 25–50.

Edelman (2020) *Edelman Trust Barometer 2020*, New York: Edelman.

Edelman (2021) *Edelman Trust Barometer 2021*, New York: Edelman.

Elazar, D.J. (1987) *Exploring Federalism*, Tuscaloosa, AL: University of Alabama Press.

Enria, L., Waterlow, N., Trivedy Rogers, N., Brindle, H., Lai, S., Eggo, R.M., Lees, S. and Roberts, C.H. (2021) 'Trust and Transparency in Times of Crisis: Results from an Online Survey during the First Wave (April 2020) of the COVID-19 Epidemic in the UK', *PLOS ONE*, 16(2): 1–20.

Entwistle, T. (2006) 'The Distinctiveness of the Welsh Partnership Agenda', *International Journal of Public Sector Management*, 19(3): 228–37.

Entwistle, T., Downe, J., Guarneros-Meza, V. and Martin, S. (2014) 'The Multi-Level Governance of Wales: Layer Cake or Marble Cake?', *British Journal of Politics and International Relations*, 16(2): 310–25.

ESS Round 9: European Social Survey Round 9 Data (2018). Data file edition 3.1. NSD - Norwegian Centre for Research Data, Norway – Data Archive and distributor of ESS data for ESS ERIC. doi:10.21338/NSD-ESS9-2018

Etherington, D. and Jones, M. (2016) 'Re-Stating the Post-Political: Depoliticization, Social Inequalities, and City-Region Growth', *Environment and Planning A: Economy and Space*, 50(1): 51–72.

Etzioni, A. (2014) 'The Limits of Transparency', *Public Administration Review*, 74(6): 687–88.

European Social Survey Cumulative File, ESS 1-9 (2020). Data file edition 1.0. NSD - Norwegian Centre for Research Data, Norway - Data Archive and distributor of ESS data for ESS ERIC. doi:10.21338/ NSD-ESS-CUMULATIVE

European Union (2021) *Standard Eurobarometer* [Online] Available from: https://europa.eu/eurobarometer/surveys/browse/all/series/4961 [Accessed 12 December 2020].

Evans, G. (2020) 'Devolution in Wales: From Assembly to Parliament', *UK Constitutional Law Blog*, [online] 15 April, Available from: https://ukco nstitutionallaw.org/2020/04/15/gareth-evans-devolution-in-wales-from-assembly-to-parliament/ [Accessed 18 August 2020].

Fancourt, D., Steptoe, A. and Wright, L. (2020) 'The Cummings Effect: Politics, Trust, and Behaviours during the COVID-19 Pandemic' *The Lancet*, [online] 6 August, Available from: www.thelancet.com/action/ showPdf?pii=S0140-6736%2820%2931690-1 [Accessed 10 August 2020].

Fenster, M. (2017) *The Transparency Fix: Secrets, Leaks, and Uncontrollable Government Information*, Stanford, CA: Stanford University Press.

Fenwick, J. (2015) 'The Problem of Sub-National Governance in England', *Public Money and Management*, 35(1): 7–14.

Ferreira da Cruz, N., Tavares, A.F., Marques, R.C., Jorge, S. and de Sousa, L. (2016) 'Measuring Local Government Transparency', *Public Management Review*, 18(6): 866–93.

Fieldhouse, E., Green, J., Evans, G., Schmitt, H., van der Eijk, C., Mellon, J., Prosser, C. (2018). British Election Study, 2017: Face-to-Face Post-Election Survey [data collection]. http://doi.org/10.5255/UKDA-SN-8418-1

Fillieule, O. (1997) *Stratégies de la Rue: Les manifestations en France*, Paris: Presses de Sciences Po.

Fisher, J., van Heerde, J. and Tucker, A. (2010) 'Does On Trust Judgement Fit? Linking Theory and Empirics', *British Journal of Politics and International Relations*, 12(2): 161–88.

Fledderus, J. (2015) 'Building Trust through Public Service Co-Production', *International Journal of Public Sector Management*, 28(7): 550–65.

Fledderus, J., Brandsen, T. and Honingh, M. (2014) 'Restoring Trust through the Co-Production of Public Services: A Theoretical Elaboration', *Public Management Review*, 16(3): 424–43.

Fourastié, J. (1980) *Les Trente glorieuses ou la revolution invisible de 1946–1975*, Paris: Fayard.

Fraser, J. (1970) 'The Mistrustful-Efficacious Hypothesis and Political Participation', *Journal of Politics*, 32(2): 444–49.

Frears, J. (1988) 'The 1988 French Presidential Election', *Government and Opposition*, 23(3): 276–89.

Fuglsang, L. and Jagd, S. (2015) 'Making Sense of Institutional Trust in Organizations: Bridging Institutional Context and Trust', *Organization*, 22(1): 23–39.

Fukuyama, F. (1995) *Trust: Social Virtues and the Creation of Prosperity*, New York: Free Press.

Fukuyama, F. (1999) 'Social Capital and Civil Society', *International Monetary Fund*, [online] 1 October, Available from: www.imf.org/external/pubs/ft/seminar/1999/reforms/fukuyama.htm#6 [Accessed 27 March 2021].

Fung, A. Graham, M and Weil, D. (2007) *Full Disclosure: The Perils and Promise of Transparency*, Cambridge: Cambridge University Press

Gabel, M. (1998) 'Public Support for European Integration: An Empirical Test of Five Theories', *Journal of Politics*, 60(2): 333–54.

Gabriel, O.W. and Zmerli, S. (2006) 'Politisches Vertrauen: Deutschland in Europa', *Aus Politik und Zeitgeschichte*, 30–31: 8–15.

Gamson, W. (1968) *Power and Discontent*, Homewood, IL: Dorsey.

Garfinkel, H. (1967) *Studies in Ethnomethodology*, Englewood Cliffs, NJ: Prentice-Hall.

Gaskell, J., Stoker, G., Jennings, W. and Devine, D. (2020) 'Public Trust and COVID-19', *The UK in a Changing Europe blog*, [online] 24 July, Available from: https://ukandeu.ac.uk/public-trust-and-covid-19/ [Accessed 10 August 2020].

Geis, A. (2005) *Regieren mit Mediation: Das Beteiligungsverfahren zur zukünftigen Entwicklung des Frankfurter Flughafens*, Wiesbaden: VS Verlag für Sozialwissenschaften.

Gerring, J. (2007) *Case Study Research: Principles and Practices*, Cambridge: Cambridge University Press.

Geurkink, B., Zaslove, A., Sluiter, R. and Jacobs, K. (2020) 'Populist Attitudes, Political Trust, and External Political Efficacy: Old Wine in New Bottles?', *Political Studies*, 68(1): 247–67.

Giddens, A. (1984) *The Constitution of Society*, Berkeley, CA: University of California Press.

Giddens, A. (1990) *The Consequences of Modernity*, Stanford, CA: Stanford University Press.

GLES (2019). Rolling cross-section election campaign study with post-election panel wave, cumulation 2009–2017 (GLES). GESIS Data Archive, Cologne. ZA6834 Data file Version 1.0.0, https://doi.org/10.4232/1.13370

Grimmelikhuijsen, S. (2011) 'Being Transparent or Spinning the Message? An Experiment into the Effects of Varying Message Content on Trust in Government', *Information Polity*, 16(1): 35–50.

Grimmelikhuijsen, S. (2012) 'Linking Transparency, Knowledge and Citizen Trust in Government: An Experiment', *International Review of Administrative Sciences*, 78(1): 50–73.

Grimmelikhuijsen, S. and Klijn, A. (2015) 'The Effects of Judicial Transparency on Public Trust: Evidence from a Field Experiment', *Public Administration*, 93(4): 995–1011.

Grimmelikhuijsen, S. and Meijer, A.J. (2014) 'The Effects of Transparency on the Perceived Trustworthiness of a Government Organization: Evidence from an Online Experiment', *Journal of Public Administration Research and Theory*, 24(1): 137–57.

Grimmelikhuijsen, S. and Welch, E.W. (2012) 'Developing and Testing a Theoretical Framework for Computer-Mediated Transparency of Local Governments', *Public Administration Review*, 72(4): 562–71.

Grimmelikhuijsen, S., Porumbescu, G., Hong, B. and Im, T. (2013) 'The Effect of Transparency on Trust in Government: A Cross-National Comparative Experiment', *Public Administration Review*, 73(4): 575–86.

Grimmelikhuijsen, S., Weske, U., Bouwman, R. and Tummers, L. (2017) 'Public Sector Transparency', in O. James, S. Jilke and G. Van Ryzin (eds) *Experiments in Public Management Research. Challenges and Contributions*, Cambridge: Cambridge University Press, pp 291–312.

Grimmelikhuijsen, S., John, P., Meijer, A. and Worthy, B. (2019) 'Do Freedom of Information laws Increase the Transparency of Government? A Pre-registered Replication of a Field Experiment', *Journal of Behavioral Public Administration*, 2(1): 1–10.

Grossman, E. and Sauger, N. (2017) *Pourquoi détestons-nous autant nos politiques?*, Paris: Presses de Sciences-Po.

Group of States against Corruption (2020) *Evaluation Report: Germany*, Strasbourg: GRECO Secretariat Council of Europe.

Guilani, J-D. (1991) *Marchands d'influence: les lobbies en France*, Paris: Seuil.

Guilluy, C. (2010) *Fractures françaises*, Paris: François Bourin.

Gunlicks, A. (2007) 'German Federalism Reform: Part One', *German Law Journal*, 8(1): 111–31.

Hambleton, R. (2017) 'The Super-Centralisation of the English State – Why We Need to Move beyond the Devolution Deception', *Local Economy*, 32(1): 3–13.

Han, B. (2015) *The Transparency Society*, Stanford, CA: Stanford University Pres.

Hardin, R. (2002) *Trust and Trustworthiness*, New York: Russell Sage Foundation.

Hardin, R. (2006) *Trust*, Cambridge: Polity Press.

Hayward, J. (1973) *The One and Indivisible Republic*, London: Weidenfeld and Nicolson.

Heald, D. (2006) 'Varieties of Transparency', in C. Hood and D. Heald (eds) *Transparency: The Key to Better Governance?*, Oxford: Oxford University Press, pp 25–43.

Heald, D. (2018) 'Transparency-Generated Trust: The Problematic Theorization of Public Audit', *Financial Accountability and Management*, 34(4): 317–35.

Hibbing, J.R. and Theiss-Morse, E. (2001) 'Process Preferences and American Politics: What the People Want Government to Be', *American Political Science Review*, 95(1): 145–53.

HM Treasury (2014) 'Chancellor: "We Need a Northern Powerhouse"', *Gov.UK website*, [online] 23 June 2014, Available from: www.gov.uk/government/speeches/chancellor-we-need-a-northern-powerhouse [Accessed 18 August 2020].

Hodgson, L. (2004a) 'Manufactured Civil Society: Counting the Cost', *Critical Social Policy*, 24(2): 139–64.

Hodgson, L. (2004b) 'The National Assembly for Wales, Civil Society and Consultation', *Politics*, 24(2): 88–95.

Hoffmann, S. (1963) 'Paradoxes of the French Political Community', in S. Hoffman, C.P. Kindleberger, L. Wylie, J.R. Pitts, J. Duroselle and F. Goguel (eds) *In Search of France: The Economy, Society and Political System in the Twentieth Century*, Cambridge, MA: Harvard University Press, pp 1–117.

Hoffmann, S. (1994) 'Les français sont-ils gouvernables?', *Pouvoirs*, 68: 7–14.

Hollyer, J.R., Rosendorff, B.P. and Vreeland, J.R. (2014) 'Measuring Transparency', *Political Analysis*, 22(4): 413–34.

Holtkamp, L. (2008) 'Das Scheitern des Neuen Steuerungsmodell', *Der Modern Staat*, 2(08): 423–46.

Hood, C. (2001) 'Transparency', in P.B. Clarke and J. Foweraker (eds) *Encyclopedia of Democratic Thought*, London: Routledge, pp 700–04.

Hood, C. (2006) 'Transparency in Historical Perspective', in C. Hood and D. Heald (eds) *Transparency: The Key to Better Governance?*, Oxford: Oxford University Press, pp 3–23.

Hood, C. (2007) 'Public Service Management by Numbers: Why Does It Vary? Where Has It Come From? What Are the Gaps and the Puzzles?', *Public Money and Management*, 27(2): 95–102.

Hood, C. and Heald, D. (eds) (2006) *Transparency: The Key to Better Governance?*, Oxford: Oxford University Press.

Hooghe, L. (1996) 'Building a Europe with the Regions: The Changing Role of the European Commission', in L. Hooghe (ed) *Cohesion Policy and European Integration: Building Multi-Level Governance*, Oxford: Oxford University Press, pp 89–128.

Hooghe, L. and Marks, G. (2001) *Multi-Level Governance and European Integration*, Oxford: Rowman and Littlefield.

Hooghe, L. and Marks, G. (2003) 'Unraveling the Central State, but How? Types of Multi-level Governance', *American Political Science Review*, 97(2): 222–43.

Hooghe, L. and Marks, G. (2005) 'Contrasting Visions of Multi-Level Governance', in I. Bache and M. Flinders (eds) *Multi-Level Governance*, Oxford: Oxford University Press, pp 15–30.

Hooghe, M. and Zmerli, S. (2011) 'Introduction: The Context of Political Trust', in S. Zmerli and M. Hooghe (eds) *Political Trust: Why Context Matters*, Colchester: ECPR Press, pp 1–11.

Hooghe, L., Marks, G. and Schakel, A.H. (2010) *The Rise of Regional Authority: A Comparative Study of 42 Democracies*, London: Routledge.

Hooghe, L., Marks, G., Schakel, A.H., Chapman Osterkatz, S., Niedzwiecki, S. and Shair-Rosenfield, S. (2016) *Measuring Regional Authority: A Postfunctionalist Theory of Governance, vol 1*, Oxford: Oxford University Press.

Hooghe, L., Marks, G., Niedwiecki, S., Chapman-Osterkatz, S., Schakel, A.H. and Shair-Rosenfield, S. (2021) 'Regional Authority – RAI-MLG', Gary Marks website, University of North Carolina at Chapel Hill [online], Available from: https://garymarks.web.unc.edu/data/regional-authority [Accessed 24 February 2021].

Hosking, G. (2019) 'The Decline of Trust in Government', in M. Sasaki (ed) *Trust in Contemporary Society*, Leiden: Brill, pp 77–103.

Huxham, C. and Vangen, S. (2005) *Managing to Collaborate: The Theory and Practice of Collaborative Advantage*, London: Routledge.

Inside Housing (2017) 'A Stark Warning: The Shepherd's Bush Tower Block Fire', *Inside Housing*, [online] 11 May, Available from: www.insidehousing. co.uk/home/home/a-stark-warning-the-shepherds-bush-tower-block-fire-50566 [Accessed 28 May 2017].

Jeffery, C. (2007) 'The Unfinished Business of Devolution: Seven Open Questions', *Public Policy and Administration*, 22(1): 92–108.

Jeffery, C. (2009) 'Devolution in the United Kingdom: Problems of a Piecemeal Approach to Constitutional Change', *Publius: The Journal of Federalism*, 39(2): 289–313.

Jeffery, C. (2014) 'Introduction: Regional Public Attitudes beyond Methodological Nationalism', in A. Henderson, C. Jeffery and D. Wincott (eds) *Citizenship after the Nation State: Regionalism, Nationalism and Public Attitudes in Europe*, Basingstoke: Palgrave Macmillan, pp 1–30.

Jeffery, C. and Wincott, D. (2010) 'The Challenge of Territorial Politics: Beyond Methodological Nationalism', in C. Hay (ed) *New Directions in Political Science: Responding to the Challenges of an Interdependent World*, Basingstoke: Palgrave Macmillan, pp 167–88.

Jennings, J. (2000) 'Citizenship, Republicanism and Multiculturalism in Contemporary France', *British Journal of Political Science*, 30(4): 575–59.

Jennings, W. (2020) 'COVID-19 and the "Rally-around-the Flag" Effect', *UK in a Changing Europe*, [online] 30 March, Available from: https:// ukandeu.ac.uk/covid-19-and-the-rally-round-the-flag-effect/ [Accessed 20 August 2020].

Jennings, W. and Lodge, M. (2019) 'Brexit, the Tides and Canute: The Fracturing Politics of the British State', *Journal of European Public Policy*, 26(5): 772–89.

Jennings, W., Stoker, G. and Twyman, J. (2016) 'The Dimensions and Impact of Political Discontent in Britain', *Parliamentary Affairs*, 69(4): 876–900.

Jennings, W., Clarke, N., Moss, J.T. and Stoker, G. (2017) 'The Decline in Diffuse Support for National Politics: The Long View on Political Discontent in Britain', *Public Opinion Quarterly*, 81(3): 748–58.

Jennings, W., Stoker, G. and Norris, P. (2019) 'Is a Crisis of Trust Necessarily a Bad Thing?', *Political Quarterly Blog*, [online] 17 September, Available from: https://politicalquarterly.blog/2019/09/17/is-a-crisis-of-trust-s-a-bad-thing/ [Accessed 14 January 2020].

Jennings, W., Stoker, G., Gaskell, R. and Devine, D. (2020) 'Political Trust Realigned after the General Election', *The UK in a Changing Europe website*, [online] 9 March, Available from: https://ukandeu.ac.uk/political-trust-realigned-after-the-general-election/ [Accessed 10 August 2020].

Jessop, B., Brenner, N. and Jones, M. (2008) 'Theorizing Sociospatial Relations', *Environment and Planning D: Society and Space*, 26(3): 389–401.

Jobert, B. and Muller P. (1987) *L'Etat en Action*, Paris: Presses universitaires de France.

John, P. and Cole, A. (2000) *Local Governance in England and France*, London: Routledge.

Johnston, L. and Fenwick, J. (2020) 'Sub-National Governance in England – Institutions and Places', *Public Money and Management*, 41(1): 5–6.

Jones, G. and Meegan, R. (2015) *Measuring the Size and Scope of the Liverpool City Region Voluntary and Community Sector*, Liverpool: Liverpool John Moores University.

Kaase, M. (1999) 'Interpersonal Trust, Political Trust and Non-Institutionalised Political Participation in Western Europe', *West European Politics*, 22(3): 1–21.

Keating, M. (1998) *The New Regionalism in Western Europe: Territorial Restructuring and Political Change*, Northampton: Edward Elgar.

Keating, M. (2001) *Nations against the State: The New Politics of Nationalism in Quebec, Catalonia and Scotland*, Basingstoke: Palgrave Macmillan.

Keating, M. and Della Porta, D. (2010) 'In Defence of Pluralism in the Social Sciences', *European Political Science*, 9(1): 111–20.

Kenealy, D. (2016) 'A Tale of One City: The Devo Manc Deal and Its Implications for English Devolution', *Political Quarterly*, 87(4): 572–81.

Khodyakov, D. (2007) 'Trust as a Process: A Three-Dimensional Approach', *Sociology*, 41(1): 115–32.

Khosravi, M. (2020) 'Perceived Risk of COVID-19 Pandemic: The Role of Public Worry and Trust', *Electronic Journal of General Medicine*, 17(4): em203.

Kim, S. and Lee. J. (2012) 'E-Participation, Transparency, and Trust in Local Government', *Public Administration Review*, 72(6): 819–28.

Kipfer, S. (2019) 'What Colour is Your Vest? Reflections on the Yellow Vest Movement in France', *Studies in Political Economy: A Socialist Review*, 100(3): 209–31.

Klijn, E.H. and Koppenjan, J. (2016) *Governance Networks in the Public Sector*, London: Routledge.

Klijn, E.H., Edelenbos, J. and Steijn, B. (2010) 'Trust in Governance Networks: Its Impacts on Outcomes'. *Administration and Society*, 42(2): 193–221.

Kohler Koch, B. and Quittkat, C. (2013) *De-Mystification of Participatory Democracy: EU-Governance and Civil Society*, Oxford: Oxford University Press.

Kuenssberg, L. (2020) 'The Decade That Shattered Trust in Politics', BBC News, [online] 29 February, Available from: www.bbc.co.uk/news/uk-politics-51679944 [Accessed 10 August 2020].

Lafortune, G. and Ubaldi, B. (2018) *OECD 2017 OURdata Index: Methodology and results*, Paris: OECD Publishing.

Landman, T. (2000) *Issues and Methods in Comparative Politics: An Introduction*, London: Routledge.

Lane, C. (1998) 'Introduction: Theories and Issues in the Study of Trust', in C. Lane and R. Bachmann (eds) *Trust within and between Organisations: Conceptual Issues and Empirical Applications*, Oxford: Oxford University Press, pp 1–30.

Lane, C. and Bachmann, R. (eds) (1998) *Trust within and between Organisations: Conceptual Issues and Empirical Applications*, Oxford: Oxford University Press.

Lane, J. and Ersson, S. (1999) *Politics and Society in Western Europe*, London: Sage.

Lascoumes, P. and Le Gales, P. (2005) *Gouverner par les instruments*, Paris: Presses de Sciences Po.

Lascoumes, P. and Simard, L. (2011) 'L'action publique au prisme de ses instruments. Introduction', *Revue française de science politique*, 61(1): 5–22.

Leach, S., Stewart, J. and Jones, G. (2018) *Centralisation, Devolution and the Future of Local Government in England*, London: Routledge.

Lehnert, M., Linhart, E. and Shikano, S. (2008) 'Never Say Never Again: Legislative Failure in German Bicameralism', *German Politics*, 17(3): 367–80.

Lenard, P.T. (2005) 'The Decline of Trust, The Decline of Democracy?', *Critical Review of International Social and Political Philosophy*, 8(3): 363–78.

Levi, M. (1998) 'A State of Trust', in V. Braithwaite and M. Levi (eds) *Trust and Governance*, New York: Sage, pp 77–101.

Levi, M. and Stoker, L. (2000) 'Political Trust and Trustworthiness', *Annual Review of Political Science*, 3: 475–507.

Levy, J.D. (2001) 'Territorial Politics after Decentralisation', in A. Guyomarch, H. Machin, P.A. Hall and J. Hayward (eds) *Developments in French Politics 2*, Basingstoke: Palgrave, pp 92–136.

Lijphart, A. (1999) *Patterns of Democracy*, New Haven, CT: Yale University Press.

Loorbach, D. and Verbong, G. (2012) 'Conclusion: Is Governance of the Energy Transition a Reality, an Illusion or a Necessity?', in G. Verbong and D. Loorbach (eds) *Governing the Energy Transition: Reality, Illusion or Necessity?*, London: Routledge, pp 317–36.

Lucas, C. (2011) *Le lobby Breton*, Paris: Nouveau monde éditions.

Luhmann, N. (1979) *Trust and Power*, Cambridge: Polity Press.

Lyall, S., Wood, M. and Bailey, D. (2015) *Democracy: The Missing Link in the Devolution Debate*, London: New Economics Foundation.

Mabillard, V. and Pasquier, M. (2016) 'Transparency and Trust in Government (2007–2014): A Comparative Study', *NISPAcee Journal of Public Administration and Policy*, 9(2): 69–92.

MacLeod, G. and Jones, M. (2007) 'Territorial, Scalar, Networked, Connected: In What Sense a "Regional World"?', *Regional Studies* 41(9): 1177–91.

Marcou, G. (2011) 'Clause générale de compétence', in R. Pasquier, S. Guigner and A. Cole (eds) *Dictionnaire des politiques territoriales*, Paris: Presses de Sciences Po, pp 57–62.

Marks, G. (1992) 'Structural Policy in the European Community', in A. Sbragia (ed) *Europolitics: Institutions and Policy Making in the 'New' European Community*, Washington, DC: The Brookings Institution, pp 191–224.

Marks, G. (1993) 'Structural Policy and Multilevel Governance in the EC', in A. Cafruny and G. Rosenthal (eds) *The State of the European Community*, New York: Lynne Rienner, pp 391–410.

Marks, G., Hooghe, L. and Blank, K. (1996) 'European Integration from the 1980s: State-Centric v Multi-Level Governance', *Journal of Common Market Studies*, 34(3): 341–78.

Marsh, D. and Rhodes, R.A.W. (eds) (1992) *Policy Networks in British Government*, Oxford: Oxford University Press.

Martin, S., Downe, J., Grace, C. and Nutley, S. (2013) 'New Development: All Change? Performance Assessment Regimes in UK Local Government', *Public Money and Management*, 33(4): 277–80.

Mason, D., Hillenbrand, C. and Money, K. (2013) 'Are Informed Citizens More Trusting? Transparency of Performance Data and Trust towards a British Police Force', *Journal of Business Ethics*, 122(2): 321–41.

Mayer, N. and Perrineau, P. (1989) *Le Front National à découvert*, Paris: Presses de la Fondation nationale des sciences politiques.

Mayer, R.C., Davis, J.H. and Schoorman, F.D. (1995) 'An Integrative Model of Organizational Trust', *Academy of Management Review*, 20(3): 709–34.

McAngus, C., Huggins, C., Connolly, J. and van der Zwet, A. (2019) 'Brexit, Fisheries and Scottish Devolution: An Intergovernmental Disruption', *Political Quarterly*, 90(4): 802–07.

McConnell, A. (2010) 'Policy Success, Policy Failure and Grey Areas In-Between', *Journal of Public Policy*, 30(3): 345–62.

McEwan, N., Kenny, M., Sheldon, J. and Brown Swan, C. (2020) 'Intergovernmental Relations in the UK: Time for a Radical Overhaul?', *Political Quarterly*, 91(3): 632–40.

Meijer, A. (2009) 'Understanding Modern Transparency', *International Review of Administrative Sciences*, 75 (2): 255–69.

Meijer, A. (2013) 'Understanding the Complex Dynamics of Transparency', *Public Administration Review*, 73(3): 429–39.

Meijer, A., t'Hart, P. and Worthy, B. (2018) 'Assessing Government Transparency: An Interpretive Framework', *Administration and Society*, 50(4): 501–26.

Mendras, H. (1989) *La Séconde Révolution française*, Paris: Gallimard.

Mény, Y. (1986) 'La légitimation des groupes d'intérêt par l'administration française', *Revue française de l'administration publique*, 39: 99–110.

Möllering, G. and Sydow, J. (2019) 'Trust Trap? Self-Reinforcing Processes in the Constitution of Interorganizational Trust', in M. Sasaki (ed) (2019) *Trust in Contemporary Society*, Leiden, Netherlands: Brill, pp 141–60.

Morvan, F. (2017) *Bretagne, l'histoire confisquée*, Paris: Le Cherche Midi.

Moses, J. and Knutsen, T. (2012) *Ways of Knowing: Competing Methodologies in Social and Political Research*, Basingstoke: Palgrave.

Muller, P. (1984) *Le technocrate et le paysan*, Paris: Economie et humanisme.

Muno, W. (2009) 'Fallstudien und die vergleichende Methode', in S. Pickel, G. Pickel, H. Lauth and D. Jahn (eds) *Methoden der vergleichenden Politik- und Sozialwissenschaft*, Wiesbaden: NeueEntwicklungen und Anwendungen, pp 113–32.

Muñoz, J., Torcal, M. and Bonet, E. (2011) 'Institutional Trust and Multilevel Government in the European Union: Congruence or Compensation?', *European Union Politics*, 12(4): 551–74.

Mycock, A. (2016) 'The Politics of England', *Political Quarterly*, 87(4): 534–45.

National Assembly for Wales (2015) 'The Record of Proceedings 29/09/2015', National Assembly for Wales, [online] 29 September, Available from: https://business.senedd.wales/ieListDocuments.aspx?CId=153&MId=3431&Ver=4 [Accessed 21 August 2020].

National Assembly for Wales Culture, Welsh Language and Communications Committee (2018) *Read All About It: Inquiry into News Journalism in Wales*, Cardiff: National Assembly for Wales.

Newton, K. (2001) 'Trust, Social Capital, Civil Society, and Democracy', *International Political Science Review*, 22(2): 201–14.

Newton, K. (2007) 'Social and Political Trust', in R.J. Dalton and H. Klingemann (eds) *The Oxford Handbook of Political Behavior*, Oxford: Oxford University Press, pp 342–61.

Newton, K. (2020) 'Government Communications, Political Trust and Compliant Social Behaviour: The Politics of Covid-19 in Britain', *Political Quarterly*, 91(3): 502–13.

Nohlen, D. (1994) 'Vergleichende Methode', in J. Kriz, D, Nohlen and R.O. Schultze (eds) *Lexikon der Politik: Politikwissenschaftliche Methoden. Band 2*, München: C.H. Beck, pp 507–17.

Nooteboom, B. (1996) 'Trust, Opportunism and Governance: A Process and Control Model', *Organization Studies*, 17(6): 985–1010.

Nooteboom, B. (2002) *Trust: Forms, Foundations, Functions, Failures and Figures*, Cheltenham: Edward Elgar.

Norris, P., Jennings, W. and Stoker, G. (2019) 'In Praise of Scepticism: Trust but Verify', *TrustGov Working Paper*, [online] Available from: https://trustgov. net/working-papers#:~:text=In%20praise%20of%20scepticism%3A%20Tr ust%20but%20verify&text=We%20outline%20a%20new%20typol ogy,of%20expression%20in%20open%20societies [Accessed 14 January 2020].

O'Neill, O. (2002) *A Question of Trust*, Cambridge: Cambridge University Press.

OECD (2017) *Trust and Public Policy: How Better Governance Can Help Rebuild Public Trust*, Paris: OECD Publishing.

OECD (2020) *OECD Open, Useful and Re-usable Data (OURdata) Index: 2019*, Paris: OECD Publishing.

OECD (2021) *Open, Useful and Re-usable data (OURdata) Index: 2017 & 2019* [online] Available from: https://stats.oecd.org/ [Accessed on 12/12/2020].

Oliver, R.E. (2004) *What Is Transparency?*, New York: McGraw Hill Professional.

Owens, N. and Jones, I. (2019) *Public Understanding of Tax Devolution: Baseline Report*, Cardiff: Welsh Government.

Owens, N. and Jones, I. (2020) *Public Understanding of Tax Devolution: 2020 Update Report*, Cardiff: Welsh Government.

Page, E.C. (2012) *Policy without Politicians: Bureaucratic Influence in Comparative Perspective*, Oxford: Oxford University Press.

Park, H. and Blenkinsopp, J. (2011) 'The Roles of Transparency and Trust in the Relationship between Corruption and Citizen Satisfaction', *International Review of Administrative Sciences*, 77(2): 254–74.

Parker, G., Parker, R. and Towner, T.L. (2014) 'Rethinking the Meaning and Measurement of Political Trust', in C. Eder, I.C. Mochmann and M. Quandt (eds) *Political Trust and Disenchantment with Politics International Perspectives*, Leiden: Brill, pp 59–82.

Parrado, S., Van Ryzin, G.G., Bovaird, T. and Löffler, E. (2013) 'Correlates of Co-Production: Evidence from a Five-Nation Survey of Citizens', *International Public Management Journal*, 16(1): 86–112.

Pasquier, M. and Villeneuve, J. (2007) 'Organizational Barriers to Transparency: A Typology and Analysis of Organizational Behaviour Tending to Prevent or Restrict Access to Information', *International Review of Administrative Sciences*, 73(1): 147–62.

Pasquier, R. (2014) *Regional Governance and Power in France*, Basingstoke: Palgrave Macmillan.

Passey, A. and Tonkiss, F. (2000) 'Trust, Voluntary Association and Civil Society', in F. Tonkiss and A. Passey (eds) *Trust and Civil Society*, Basingstoke: Macmillan, pp 31–51.

Paton, D. (2013) 'Disaster Resilient Communities: Developing and Testing an All-Hazards Theory', *Journal of Integrated Disaster Risk Management*, 3(1): 1–17.

Pattie, C. and Johnson, C. (2012) 'The Electoral Impact of the UK 2009 MPs' Expenses Scandal', *Political Studies*, 60(4): 730–50.

Paxton, P. and Ressler, R.W. (2018) 'Trust and Participation in Associations', in E.M. Uslaner (ed) *The Oxford Handbook of Social and Political Trust*, Oxford: Oxford University Press, pp 149–72.

Pemberton, S. (2000) 'The 1996 Reorganization of Local Government in Wales: Issues, Process and Uneven Outcomes', *Contemporary Wales*, 12(5): 77–106.

Perlaviciute, G., Schuitema, G., Devine-Wright, P. and Ram, B. (2018) 'At the Heart of a Sustainable Energy Transition', *IEEE Power and Energy Magazine*, 16(1): 49–55.

Perona, M. and Senik, C. (2021) *Le Bien-être en France: Rapport 2020*, Paris: CEPREMAP.

Peters, B.G. (2013) *Strategies for Comparative Research in Political Science*, Basingstoke: Palgrave Macmillan.

Piatonni, S. (2010) *The Theory of Multi-level Governance: Conceptual, Empirical, and Normative Challenges*, Oxford: Oxford University Press.

Pike, A., Marlow, D., McCarthy, A., O'Brien, P. and Tomaney, J. (2015) 'Local Institutions and Local Economic Development: The Local Enterprise Partnerships in England, 2010–', *Cambridge Journal of Regions, Economy and Society*, 8(2): 185–204.

Piotrowski, S., Grimmelikhuijsen, S. and Deat, F. (2017) 'Numbers over Narratives? How Government Message Strategies Affect Citizens', Attitudes' *Public Performance and Management Review*, 42(5): 1005–28.

Porumbescu, G. (2015a) 'Linking Transparency to Trust in Government and Voice', *American Review of Public Administration*, 47(5): 520–37.

Porumbescu, G. (2015b) 'Does Transparency Improve Citizens' Perceptions of Government Performance? Evidence from Seoul, South Korea', *Administration and Society*, 49(3): 443–68.

Porumbescu, G., Belle, N., Cucciniello, M. and Nasi, G. (2017) 'Translating Policy Transparency into Policy Understanding and Policy Support: Evidence from a Survey Experiment', *Public Administration*, 95(4): 990–1008.

Pozen, D.E. and Schudson, M. (eds) (2018) *Troubling Transparency: The History and Future of Freedom of Information*, New York: Columbia University Press

Presse- und Informationsamt der Bundesregierung, Berlin (2021). Trust in state and society during the corona crisis (June/July 2020). GESIS Data Archive, Cologne. ZA7675 Data file Version 1.0.0, https://doi.org/10.4232/1.13654

Przeworski, A. and Teune, H. (1970) *The Logic of Comparative Social Inquiry*, New York: Wiley-Interscience.

Putnam, R.D. (1993) *Making Democracy Work: Civic Traditions in Modern Italy*, Princeton, NJ: Princeton University Press.

Putnam, R.D. (1995) 'Bowling Alone: America's Declining Social Capital', *Journal of Democracy*, 6(1): 65–78.

Putnam, R.D. (2000) *Bowling Alone: The Collapse and Revival of American Community*, New York: Simon and Schuster.

Ragin, C.C. (1987) *The Comparative Method: Moving Beyond Qualitative and Quantitative Strategies*, Berkeley: University of California Press.

Ragin, C.C. and Becker, H.S. (1992) *What Is a Case?: Exploring the Foundations of Social Inquiry*, Cambridge: Cambridge University Press.

Rahn, W.M. and Rudolph, T.J. (2005) 'A Tale of Political Trust in American Cities', *Public Opinion Quarterly*, 69(4): 530–60.

Raikes, L. (2020) *The Devolution Parliament: Devolving Power to England's Regions, Towns and Cities*, Manchester: IPPR North.

Randall, J. and Casebourne, J. (2016) *Making Devolution Deals Work*, London: Institute for Government.

Rawlings, R. (2017) *Brexit and the Territorial Constitution: Devolution, Re-Regulation and Intergovernmental Relations*, London: Constitution Society.

Reinl, A. and Schäfer, C. (2020) 'How the 2017 Federal Election in Germany Affected Satisfaction with Democracy among AfD Voters', *German Politics*.

République Française (2018) *For a Transparent and Collaborative Government: France National Action Plan 2018–2020*, Paris: République Française.

Riker, W.H. (1964) *Federalism: Origin, Operation, Significance*, Boston, MA: Little Brown.

Ring, P.S. and van de Ven, A.H. (1994) 'Developmental Processes of Cooperative Interorganizational Relationships', *Academy of Management Review*, 19(1): 90–118.

Robert, C. (2018) 'Les dispositifs de transparence entre instruments de gouvernement et 'machines à scandales': fabrique et mobilisations des formes de connaissance sur le lobbying européen', *Politique européenne*, 61(3): 174–210.

Rodríguez-Pose, A. and Gill, N. (2003) 'The Global Trend towards Devolution and Its Implications', *Environment and Planning C: Government and Policy*, 21(3): 333–51.

Rose, R. (1993) *Lesson-Drawing in Public Policy: A Guide to Learning across Time and Space*, Chatham, NJ: Chatham House.

Rose, R. and Wessels, B. (2019) 'Money, Sex and Broken Promises: Politicians' Bad Behaviour Reduces Trust', *Parliamentary Affairs*, 72(3): 481–500.

Rouban, L. (2016) 'Les seniors au centre de l'élection présidentielle 2017', *L'Enquête électorale française: comprendre 2017, Note #17/vague 3*, [online] 30 April, Available from: www.sciencespo.fr/cevipof/sites/sciencespo. fr.cevipof/files/NOTE17_VAGUE3_ENEF2017.pdf [Accessed 7 September 2019].

Rousseau, D.M., Sitkin, S.B., Burt, R.S. and Camerer, C. (1998) 'Not So Different after All: A Cross-Discipline View of Trust', *Academy of Management Review*, 23(3): 393–404.

Rumbul, R. (2016a) 'Critical Friend or Absent Partner? Institutional and Organisational Barriers to the Development of Regional Civil Society', *European Urban and Regional Studies*, 23(4): 848–61.

Rumbul, R. (2016b) 'The Trouble with Civil Society in Wales', *Agenda – Journal of the Institute of Welsh Affairs*, [online] 3 March, Available from: www. iwa.wales/agenda/2016/03/the-trouble-with-civil-society-in-wales/ [Accessed 10 September 2020].

Sainclivier, E. (2004) *Cri d'un Purotin pour une putain*, Paris: La Compagnie Littéraire.

Sandford, M. (2017) 'Signing Up to Devolution: The Prevalence of Contract over Governance in English Devolution Policy', *Regional and Federal Studies*, 27(1): 63–82.

Sandford, M. (2020a) 'Giving Power Away? The "De-Words" and the Downward Transfer of Power in Mid-2010s England', *Regional and Federal Studies*, 30(1): 25–46.

Sandford, M. (2020b) *Devolution to Local Government in England*, London: House of Commons Library.

Sartori, G. (1994) *Comparative Constitutional Engineering: An Inquiry into Structures, Incentives and Outcomes*, New York: New York University Press.

Schaal, G.D. (2004) *Vertraun, Verfassung und Demokratie: Über den Einfluss konstitutioneller Prozesse und Prozeduren auf die Genese von Vertrauensbeziehungen in modernen Demokratien*, Wiesbaden: VS Verlag für sozialwissenschaften.

Scharpf, F.W. (1988) 'The Joint-Decision Trap: Lessons from German Federalism and European Integration', *Public Administration*, 66 (3): 239–78.

Scharpf, F.W. (2005) *No Exit from the Joint Decision Trap? Can German Federalism Reform Itself?*, EUI-RSCAS Working Papers 24, Florence: European University Institute.

Schmidt, V.A. (2006) *Democracy in Europe: The EU and National Polities*, Oxford: Oxford University Press.

Schneider, H.P. (2013) *Der neue deutsche Bundesstaat: Bericht über die Umsetzung der Föderalismusreform I*, Baden-Baden: Nomos.

Schudson, M. (2015) *The Rise of the Right to Know: Politics and the Culture of Transparency, 1945–1975*, Cambridge, MA: Harvard University Press.

Schwadel, P. and Stout, M. (2012) 'Age, Period and Cohort Effects on Social Capital', *Social Forces*, 91(1): 233–52.

Seligman, A.B. (1997) *The Problem of Trust*, Princeton, NJ: Princeton University Press.

Senik, C. (2014) 'The French Unhappiness Puzzle: The Cultural Dimension of Happiness', *Journal of Economic Behaviour and Organisation*, 106: 379–401.

Seyd, B. (2016) 'How Should We Measure Political Trust?', *Paper for PSA Annual Conference, Brighton*, 21–23 March 2016, [online], Available from: www.psa.ac.uk/sites/default/files/conference/papers/2016/Paper. v2.pdf [Accessed 14 June 2017].

Shair-Rosenfield, S., Schakel, A.H., Niedzwiecki, A., Marks, G., Hooghe, L. and Chapman-Osterkatz, S. (2021) 'Language Difference and Regional Authority', *Regional and Federal Studies*, 31(1): 73–97.

Shutt, J. and Liddle, J. (2019) 'Are Combined Authorities in England Strategic and Fit for Purpose?', *Local Economy*, 34(2): 196–207.

Siegrist, M. and Zingg, A. (2013) 'The Role of Public Trust during Pandemics: Implications for Crisis Communication', *European Psychologist*, 19(1): 23–32.

Simmel, G. (1978) *The Philosophy of Money*, London: Routledge.

Sintomer, Y. and De Maillard, J. (2007) 'The Limits to Local Participation and Deliberation in the French "politique de la ville"', *European Journal of Political Research*, 46 (4), 503–29.

Smith, T.B. (2004) *France in Crisis: Welfare, Inequality and Globalisation since 1980*, New York: Cambridge University Press.

Stafford, I. (2011) 'Devolution in Wales and the 2011 Referendum: The Beginning of a New Era?', *Scottish Affairs*, 77(1): 28–55.

Steckel-Assouère, M. (2015) *Les finances publiques en schémas*, Paris: Ellipses.

Stecker, C. (2016) 'The Effects of Federalism Reform on the Legislative Process in Germany', *Regional and Federal Studies*, 26(5), 603–24.

Steffani, W. (ed) (1971) *Parlamentarismus ohne Transparenz*, Wiesbaden: VS Verlag für Sozialwissenschaften.

Steffani, W. (1997) *Gewaltenteilung und Parteien im Wandel*, Wiesbaden: VS Verlag für Sozialwissenschaften.

Stokes, D.E. (1962) 'Popular Evaluations of Government: An Empirical Assessment', in H. Cleveland and H.D. Lasswell (eds) *Ethics and Bigness: Scientific, Academic, Religious, Political, and Military*, New York: Harper and Brothers, pp 61–72.

Sullivan, H. and Skelcher, C. (2002) *Working across Boundaries: Collaboration in Public Services*, Basingstoke: Palgrave.

Svare, H., Haugen Gausdal, A. and Möllering, G. (2020) 'The Function of Ability, Benevolence, and Integrity-Based Trust in Innovation Networks', *Industry and Innovation*, 27(6): 585–604.

Swanson, G. (1971) 'Frameworks for Comparative Research: Structural Anthropology and the Theory of Action', in I. Vallier (ed) *Comparative Methods in Sociology: Essays on Trends and Applications*, Berkeley, CA: University of California Press, pp 141–202.

Swenden, W. (2006) *Federalism and Regionalism in Western Europe: A Comparative and Thematic Analysis*, Basingstoke: Palgrave Macmillan.

Sydow, J. (1998) 'Understanding the Constitution of Interorganisational Trust', in C. Lane and R. Bachmann (eds) *Trust within and between Organisations: Conceptual Issues and Empirical Applications*, Oxford: Oxford University Press, pp 31–63.

Sydow, J. (2006) 'How Can Systems Trust Systems? Structuration Perspective on Trust-Building in Inter-Organisational Relations', in R. Bachmann and A. Zaheer (eds) *Handbook of Trust Research*, Cheltenham: Edward Elgar, pp 377–92.

Sztompka, P. (2006) 'New Perspectives on Trust', *American Journal of Sociology*, 112(3): 905–19.

Tarrow. S. (1994) *Power in Movement: Social Movements and Contentious Politics*, Cambridge: Cambridge University Press.

Taylor, R. and Kelsey, T. (2016) *Transparency and the Open Society: Practical Lessons for Effective Policy*, Bristol: Policy Press.

Thomas, A. (1994) 'The Myth of Consensus: The Local Government Review in Wales', *Contemporary Wales*, 7: 47–60.

Tilly, C. (1986) *The Contentious French*, Cambridge, MA: Belknap Press of Harvard University Press.

Todd, E. (1995) 'Aux origines du malaise politique française: Les classes sociales et leur représentation', *Le Débat*, 1: 3–104.

Townsend, A. (2019) 'Combined Authorities for More Sub-Regions? Learning the Adverse Lessons from England beyond the Metropolitan Conurbations', *Local Economy*, 34(2): 123–38.

Tran, E. (2021) 'The Yellow Vests Movement: Causes, Consequences and Significance', in H. Drake, A. Cole, S. Meunier and V. Tiberi (eds) *Developments in French Politics 6*, Basingstoke: Palgrave, pp 179–98.

Transparency International (2017) *Open Data and the Fight against Corruption in France*, Berlin: Transparency International.

Transparency International (2020) *Corruption Perceptions Index 2020*, Berlin: Transparency International.

UN Secretary General (2018) 'Secretary-General's Address to the General Assembly', *UN Secretary-General*, [online] 25 September, Available from: www.un.org/sg/en/content/sg/statement/2018-09-25/secretary-generals-address-general-assembly-delivered-trilingual [Accessed 20 August 2020].

Uslaner, E.M. (2002) *The Moral Foundations of Trust*, Cambridge: Cambridge University Press.

van de Walle, S., van Roosbroek, S. and Bouckaert, G. (2008) 'Trust in the Public Sector: Is There Any Evidence for a Long-Term Decline?', *International Review of Administrative Sciences*, 74(1): 47–64.

van der Meer, T. (2010) 'In What We Trust? A Multi-Level Study into Trust in Parliament as an Evaluation of State Characteristics', *International Review of Administrative Sciences*, 76(3): 517–36.

van der Meer, T. and Dekker, P. (2011) 'Trustworthy States, Trusting Citizens? A Multilevel Study into Objective and Subjective Determinants of Political Trust', in S. Zmerli and M. Hooghe (eds) *Political Trust: Why Context Matters*, Colchester: ECPR, pp 95–116.

van der Meer, T. and Hakhverdian, A. (2017) 'Political Trust as the Evaluation of Process and Performance: A Cross-National Study of 42 European Countries', *Political Studies*, 65(1): 81–102.

van der Meer, T. and Zmerli, S. (2017) 'The Deeply Rooted Concern with Political Trust', in S. Zmerli and T. van der Meer (eds) *Handbook on Political Trust*, Cheltenham: Edward Elgar, pp 1–15.

van der Weerd, W., Timmermans, D.R.M., Beujean, D.J.M.A., Oudhoff, J. and van Steenbergen, J.E. (2011) 'Monitoring the Level of Government Trust, Risk Perception and Intention of the General Public to Adopt Protective Measures during the Influenza A (H1N1) Pandemic in the Netherlands', *BMC Public Health*, 11: 575.

van Deth, J., Maraffi, M., Newton, K, and Whiteley P. (eds) (1991) *Social Capital and European Democracy*, London: Routledge.

Vanneste, B.S. (2014) 'From Interpersonal to Interorganisational Trust: The Role of Indirect Reciprocity', *Journal of Trust Research*, 6(1): 7–36.

Vanneste, B.S., Puranam, P., and Kretschmer, T. (2014) 'Trust over Time in Exchange Relationships: Meta-Analysis and Theory', *Strategic Management Journal*, 35(12): 1891–902.

Vavakova, B. and Wolfe, D.A. (1999) 'Regional Innovation Policy: Rhône-Alpes and Ontario', *Regional and Federal Studies*, 9(3): 107–29.

Vignaud, L. (2021) 'If the French Distrust Vaccines, It's Because They Distrust Their Politicians', *The Guardian*, [online] 15 February, Available from: www.theguardian.com/commentisfree/2021/feb/15/french-distrust-vaccines-politicians [Accessed 20 February 2021].

Völkl, K. (2016) 'Länder Elections in German Federalism: Does Federal or Land-Level Influence Predominate?', *German Politics*, 25(2): 243–64.

Wales Governance Centre and the Constitution Unit (2016) *Challenge and Opportunity: The Draft Wales Bill 2015*, Cardiff: The Wales Governance Centre.

Wall, R. and Bessa-Vilela, N. (2016) 'Deal or No Deal: English Devolution, a Top-Down Approach', *Lex Localis: Journal of Local Self-Government*, 14(3): 655–70.

Walshe, K., Coleman, A., McDonald, R., Lorne, C. and Munford, L. (2016) 'Health and Social Care Devolution: The Greater Manchester Experiment', *British Medical Journal*, 352:i1495. doi:10.1136/bmj.i1495.

Ward, K., Deas, I., Haughton, G., and Hincks, S. (2015) 'Placing Greater Manchester', *Representation*, 51(4): 417–24.

Warren, M.E. (ed) (1999a) *Democracy and Trust*, Cambridge: Cambridge University Press.

Warren, M.E. (1999b) 'Democratic Theory and Trust', in M.E. Warren (ed) *Democracy and Trust*, Cambridge: Cambridge University Press, pp 310–45.

Warren, M.E. (1999c) 'Conclusion', in M.E. Warren (ed) *Democracy and Trust*, Cambridge: Cambridge University Press, pp 346–60.

Weisskircher, M. (2020) 'The Strength of Far-Right AfD in Eastern Germany: The East–West Divide and the Multiple Causes behind "Populism"', *Political Quarterly*, 91(3): 614–22.

Welsh Government (2021) *National Survey for Wales* [online] Available from: https://gov.wales/national-survey-wales [Accessed 26 September 2020].

Weyand, S. (1996) 'Inter-Regional Associations and the European Integration Process', *Regional and Federal Studies*, 6(2): 166–82.

Whiteley, P., Clarke, H.D., Sanders, D. and Stewart, M. (2016) 'Why Do Voters Lose Trust in Governments? Public Perceptions of Government Honesty and Trustworthiness in Britain 2000–2013', *British Journal of Politics and International Relations* 18(1): 234–54.

Williams, P. (2012) *Collaboration in Public Policy and Practice: Perspectives on Boundary Spanners*, Bristol: Policy Press.

Williams, P.M. (1964) *Crisis and Compromise: Politics in the Fourth Republic*, London: Longman.

References

Woelfert, F.S. and Kunst, J.R. (2020) 'How Political and Social Trust Can Impact Social Distancing Practices during COVID-19 in Unexpected Ways', *Frontiers in Psychology*, 11: 572966.

Wollebæk, D., Lundåsen, S.W. and Trägårdh, L. (2012) 'Three Forms of Interpersonal Trust: Evidence from Swedish Municipalities', *Scandinavian Political Studies*, 35(4): 319–46.

World Justice Project (2015) WJP Open Government Index 2015 [online] Available from: https://worldjusticeproject.org/our-work/wjp-rule-law-index/wjp-open-government-index-2015 [Accessed 12 December 2020].

World Justice Project (2020) 'WJP Open Government Index', *WJP Website*, [online], Available from: http://worldjusticeproject.org/opengov/ [Accessed 8 August 2020].

Worthy, B. (2010) 'More Open but Not More Trusted? The Effect of the Freedom of Information Act 2000 on the United Kingdom Central Government', *Governance: An International Journal of Policy, Administration, and Institutions*, 23(4): 561–82.

Worthy, B. (2013) '"Some Are More Open than Others": Comparing the Impact of the Freedom of Information Act 2000 on Local and Central Government in the UK', *Journal of Comparative Policy Analysis: Research and Practice*, 15(5): 395–414.

Worthy, B. and Grimmelikhuijsen, S. (2012) 'How Political Culture and Institutions Shape Transparency and Trust in the UK and the Netherlands', *Paper presented at the Transatlantic Conference on Transparency Research*, 7–9 June 2012, Utrecht: Utrecht University.

Worthy, B. and Hazell, R. (2017) 'Disruptive, Dynamic and Democratic? Ten Years of FOI in the UK', *Parliamentary Affairs*, 70(1): 22–42.

Worthy, B., John, P. and Vannoni, M. (2017) 'Transparency at the Parish Pump: A Field Experiment to Measure the Effectiveness of Freedom of Information Requests in England', *Journal of Public Administration Research And Theory*, 27(3): 485–500.

Wright, V. (1989) *The Government and Politics of France* (3rd edn), London: Unwin.

Wyn Jones, R. and Scully. R. (2012) *Wales Says Yes: Devolution and the 2011 Welsh Referendum*, Cardiff: University of Wales.

Yorkshire Post (2019) 'One Yorkshire Deal Rejected by Government as James Brokenshire Claims Plan Does Not Meet "Devolution Criteria"', *Yorkshire Post*, [online] 12 February, Available from: www.yorkshirepost.co.uk/news/politics/one-yorkshire-deal-rejected-government-james-brokenshire-claims-plan-does-not-meet-devolution-criteria-70499 [Accessed 20 August 2020].

Zaheer, A., McEvily, B. and Perrone, V. (1998) 'Does Trust Matter? Exploring the Effects of Interorganizational and Interpersonal Trust on Performance', *Organization Science*, 9(2): 141–59.

183

Zand, D.E. (1972) 'Trust and Problem Solving', *Administrative Science Quarterly*, 17(2): 229–39.

Zeh, W. (1989) 'Das Ausschußsystem im Bundestag', in H. Schneider and W. Zeh (eds) *Parlamentsrecht und Parlamentspraxis in der Bundesrepublik Deutschland*, Berlin: De Gruyter, pp 1087–102.

Ziller, C. and Schübel, T. (2015) ' "The Pure People" versus "the Corrupt Elite"? Political Corruption, Political Trust and the Success of Radical Right Parties in Europe', *Journal of Elections, Public Opinion and Parties*, 25(3): 368–86.

Zmerli, S. and Hooghe, M. (2011) (eds) *Political Trust: Why Context Matters*, Colchester: ECPR.

Zmerli, S. and Newton, K. (2011) 'Winners, Losers and Three Types of Trust', in S. Zmerli and M. Hooghe (eds) *Political Trust: Why Context Matters*, Colchester: ECPR, pp 67–94.

Zucker, L.G. (1986) 'Production of Trust: Institutional Sources of Economic Structure, 1840–1920', *Research in Organizational Behavior*, 8: 53–111.

Index

References to figures appear in *italic* type;
those in **bold** type refer to tables.

Index